The Science and Politics of Race in Mexico and the United States, 1910–1950

The Science and Politics of Race in Mexico and the United States, 1910–1950

Karin Alejandra Rosemblatt

The University of North Carolina Press *Chapel Hill*

© 2018 Karin Alejandra Rosemblatt
All rights reserved
Set in Espinosa Nova and Alegreya Sans by codeMantra
Manufactured in the United States of America

The University of North Carolina Press has been a member of the
Green Press Initiative since 2003.

Cover illustration: Oscar S. Frías and Universidad Nacional Autónoma
de México, Instituto de Investigaciones Sociales. Mapa etnográfico de la
República mexicana / [México, D.F.] UNAM: Instituto de Investigaciones
Sociales, 1940.

Library of Congress Cataloging-in-Publication Data
Names: Rosemblatt, Karin Alejandra, author.
Title: The science and politics of race in Mexico and the United States,
 1910–1950 / Karin Alejandra Rosemblatt.
Description: Chapel Hill : The University of North Carolina Press, [2018] |
 Includes bibliographical references and index.
Identifiers: LCCN 2017033407 | ISBN 9781469636399 (cloth : alk. paper) |
 ISBN 9781469636405 (pbk : alk. paper) | ISBN 9781469636412 (ebook)
Subjects: LCSH: Science—Social aspects—Mexico. | Science—Social
 aspects—United States. | Race—Social aspects—Mexico. | Race—
 Social aspects—United States. | Minorities—Government policy—
 Mexico. | Minorities—Government policy—United States. | Policy
 scientists—Mexico. | Policy scientists—United States. | Social
 sciences—Philosophy—History—20th century.
Classification: LCC Q175.52.M6 R67 2018 | DDC 306.4/50970904—dc23
LC record available at https://lccn.loc.gov/2017033407

Para Héctor (For Hector)

Contents

Figures

Acknowledgments

This started out as a different book, one about the genesis of Oscar Lewis's culture of poverty formulation. Along the way, I decided I needed to understand the Mexican and U.S. contexts for Lewis's work, and I got waylaid. On this tortuous journey, I had a lot of help.

The institutions that supported me are not immaterial. I began this book at the glorious Radcliffe Institute for Advanced Study, where I was able to think and read and talk about race. Any measure of creativity in this book owes quite a bit to the staff and colleagues at Radcliffe. A National Science Foundation Scholar Award under Award Number 0959921 helped me advance my writing. The University of Maryland, College Park, provided much-needed additional leave.

Many colleagues have read and commented on parts of this work and have generously provided wise counsel. Robyn Muncy helped with bibliography on U.S. history, and Gladys McCormick was my indispensable guide to the historiography of Mexico. Thanks go to Julie Greene, Chantel Rodríguez, and Colleen Woods for helping me sharpen my arguments regarding the immigration and foreign policies of the United States. James Maffie helped me understand some finer points of epistemology, and Erika Milam and Alexandra Minna Stern helped me situate myself within the history of science and medicine. Alex not only shared copies of documents she had collected in Mexico but also carted them in a duffel bag from Ann Arbor to New York City. Leandro Benmergui, Shane Dillingham, Eileen Findlay, and Paula Halperin gave incisive feedback on a sprawling chapter on the Indian New Deal. Leandro also helped me research that chapter and did a lot of menial work as my research assistant. His "No te preocupes" were like miracles. Sarah Chambers read the introduction, and colleagues in the Washington Seminar on the History of Latin America debated parts of this book and helped me understand how it mattered. The two readers for UNC Press, Alexander Dawson and Peter Wade, knew what I was trying to do in this book and helped me do it. Their own work on race and indigeneity provided the foundations for my own. I could have cited each of them on almost every page of this book.

David Sartorius, who read this entire book at an early stage, deserves a major thank you for being the kind of person who I could call on when I needed some help in a hurry. Along with sharp observations on this project, he has been an all-around good colleague and terrific preparer of scrumptious meals, dessert included. Alejandro Cañeque and Daryle Williams rounded out the Maryland Latin Americanist Dream Team. Other colleagues at Maryland and across the Americas helped me move this book, and my career, forward. Mary Kay Vaughan has been an advocate for forever. She has provided a model of how to produce engaged scholarship and live an engaged life. Her work and advice on Mexico has been with me at every turn. Barbara Weinstein gave me a lot of sage counsel and wrote a lot of letters of recommendation. Claudio Barrientos, Ray Craib, Liz Hutchison, Thomas Miller Klubock, Margaret Power, Joel Stillerman, Heidi Tinsman, and Ericka Verba are such outstanding interlocutors that they may still get me back into the Chileanist camp. Daniela Spenser gave me a place to land in Mexico City and provided insights onto Mexican politics. I am indebted to Nancy Appelbaum for teaching me about race, about how to reason carefully, and about how to navigate petty academic politics. The graduate students I have had the pleasure of working with have been integral to the development of the ideas in this book. They are all good friends and great historians, too. Here's a shout-out to Ted Cohen, Sabrina González, Reid Gustafson, Diego Hurtado, Lisa Jarvinen, Shawn Moura, Fred Opie, Shari Orisich, Daniel Richter, Brandi Townsend, Joshua Walker, and Sarah Walsh.

I had a lot of help in crafting this book. Help with archival research and footnotes came from a set of accomplished historians and professionals who took time out from their own exciting projects: Minerva Colín, Halina Gutiérrez, Miguel Ángel Ibaceta General, Eben Levey, Nicole Mottier, Sarah Osten, Adolfo Polo y la Borda Ramos, Sandra Shaker, and Jesse Zarley. Amy Brown, Blenda Femenías, and Carole Sargeant helped keep me on track. Blenda's timely, relevant comments are the product of a longtime collaboration for which I am appreciative. Brian Crawford of the University of Maryland cheerfully scanned images for this book. At UNC Press, Jessica Newman, Jay Mazzocchi, and Becki Reibman moved things along graciously. I was lucky to have copyeditor Laura Dooley on my team. Elaine Maisner was simply great—wise without being stuffy, a patient advocate, an astute reader.

I appreciate my many witty and fascinating friends from inside and outside academia. Thanks go to Linda Alcoff; Eugenia Breiva; Christine

Clamp; Laurence Fabre and Michel Welmond; Steven Fretwell; Don, Caitlin, and Megan Gianniny; Saverio Giovacchini and Ingalisa Schrobsdorff; Beth and Kim Griffith; Peter Huitzacua; Norman Kutcher and Richard Wallach; Edgardo Menvielle and Marcos Dávalos; Jacqueline Messing; Kent, Kent, and Linden Taylor; and Susan Traverso.

The family never stopped asking when I would be done with this book, and for the most part they seemed certain I would finish even when I was not so sure. For that confidence, I am grateful to the siblings and siblings-in-law: Ivan Rosemblatt, Mariana Rosemblatt, Isabel Rosemblatt, Martín Rosemblatt, Brian Beutler, Lisa Beutler, Kelley Dillon, Jones Parker, and Carlos Ulisse. Natalia Meta has cheerfully put up with me on sometimes long stays in Chile. The Parada Valderrama branch of the family—Albertina, Jorge, Mirtha, Viviana, Camilo, and Pato—welcomed me even after I had taken their son, brother, and uncle to distant lands. Ernesto Parada and Joaquín Parada took me for what I was; no more, no less. Gracias. To my parents, Luz Klecky and Mario Rosemblatt, I am indebted for any and all of my accomplishments. They have believed in me and given me the freedom to pursue a life on my own terms. Each in their own way is a lot of fun to be with! Every time I wrote the words "cosmopolitan" or "intellectual" in this book, I thought of Héctor Parada. Whatever this book may contribute to a better future, it is miniscule in comparison to the perceptiveness, tolerance, empathy, and understanding Héctor gives every day. I look forward to continuing to benefit from his keen sensitivity and expansive intellect.

The Science and Politics of Race
in Mexico and the United States,
1910–1950

Introduction

Liberalism, Race, Nation, Modernity

I stayed in Tepoztlan but a short time in the spring of 1930. Some months later there came into my hands a book by Mr. Robert Redfield, an American ethnologist from the University of Chicago, who had remained there nearly a year, studying every phase of the town's life. With this invaluable document, I was able to check my own impressions, and still better, to draw evidence for a more serious study in comparative civilizations. Robert Redfield's *Tepoztlan*, laid upon Robert and Helen Lynd's *Middletown*, provides as exciting a series of parallel columns as any sociologist could wish. One can compare item by item the work habits, play habits, religious habits; the food, houses, clothing, education, social organization of two communities, one north, the other south of the Rio Grande, but a whole world apart. The one is still following the leisurely pattern of the handicraft age, with many cultural traditions from the greatest indigenous civilization which the Western Hemisphere produced; the other is firmly locked into the culture of the machine age, deriving most of its traditions and mores from the Eastern Hemisphere. The machine has entered Tepoztlan, as we have seen, but it is as yet the shyest of visitors. If it and its products were barred tomorrow, the white pyjamas of the men would have to give way to native cloth woven from a local tree fibre (the old looms still survive). Otherwise the village life would proceed largely unimpaired.

—Stuart Chase, *Mexico: A Study of Two Americas* (1931)

In 1930, Stuart Chase, a Harvard- and MIT-trained economist, vacationed in Mexico with author Marian Tyler, his wife. He had just published two books condemning the ill effects of industrial capitalism, and like many intellectuals of his generation, he found in Mexico a preindustrial idyll. Chase and Tyler soon returned to Mexico, spending a total of five months there, mostly outside the capital. Back in the United States, they wrote a book that compared Tepoztlán, Cuernavaca, to Muncie, Indiana, the presumably typical U.S. town that sociologists Helen and Robert Lynd had described in *Middletown* (1929). Soon after Chase completed this book on Mexico, he published *A New Deal*, a book credited with inspiring Franklin D. Roosevelt's program and popularizing—if not inventing—the very term "New Deal."[1]

Tepoztlán was a mere fifty miles from Mexico City as the crow flies. But it was accessible only by train and foot, and for Chase, it was distant from the disruptive industrial machine age afflicting the United States. In making this assessment, Chase drew from the work of Robert Redfield, a University of Chicago Ph.D. student who had done research in Tepoztlán in 1926–27 and later took a position in the university's sociology and anthropology department. Redfield employed an evolutionary paradigm that characterized Tepoztlán as a "folk" culture halfway between tradition and modernity. Chase built from Redfield's framework to argue that the simpler and more primitive Tepoztlán provided a "dramatic contrast" to industrial, urban, middle-class U.S. culture. "The gospel of Middletown is work," Chase wrote, "and the gospel of Tepoztlan is play." Middletown was "practical," Tepoztlán "mystical." But Tepoztlán's excess of fiestas and virgins was not all bad. Middletown was losing its individuality as it adopted mass industrial culture. Tepoztlán was less efficient, but unlike Middletown, it was not "a cog in the wheel, but an economically independent community."[2]

Racial differences were at the heart of Chase's "dramatic contrast." Ninety-nine percent of Middletowners were of "European or African stock," Chase noted. Tepoztlán was ninety-nine percent "Indian." Yet Chase's ideas about race also challenged the notion that the United States provided a standard against which to measure Mexico. "In race as well as in culture," Chase wrote, "Tepoztlan is almost pure American, while the northern community, in the state called Indiana, is an omelette of English, French, Poles, Italians, Czechs, Russians, Negroes, Germans, Irish, and heaven and the Bureau of the Census know how many other nationalities." If, as many of Chase's contemporaries believed, nations derived their strength from shared cultural traditions as well as economic prosperity, the "omelette" nation represented by Middletown could hardly constitute a standard against which to measure other countries. In fact, Chase inverted prevailing views of the United States and Mexico by suggesting that Middle America was not homogeneous and white but *mestizo* (mixed), while Tepoztlán was "pure American." Tepoztlán represented an American ideal to which the United States might aspire. There were, after all, no Indians in "Indiana." At the same time, because "America" also meant the United States, Chase's use of the term "American" for a continent populated by Native peoples implied that the United States might be subsumed within a broader "American" norm represented by Tepoztlán. Perhaps, then, Chase's "dramatic contrast" was not so terribly dramatic after all. Still, Chase continued to signal differences: "Tepoztlan is far more American than Middletown when all is said and done, but it is alien to everything we regard as typically 'American.'" Readers of Chase's book might easily infer that what was truly "American" was hard to pin down.[3]

CHASE AND REDFIELD were not alone in drawing distinctions between the United States and Mexico. Other U.S. scholars who lived in and studied Mexico made similarly stark comparisons. So did Mexicans. Although these Mexican and U.S. assertions of difference grew out of real historic and contemporary divergences between the two countries, they hid from view the variety of peoples within each country; the transnational connections that bound Mexico and the United States; and the parallels between the two nations, including shared colonial pasts and, by the 1920s, substantial new immigrant populations. This book lifts the smokescreen of comparison to reveal the connections, resemblances, and shared histories that Chase and others perceived, albeit at times only faintly. It thereby calls into question entrenched national narratives and the ideas about race that grounded those narratives.

The book focuses on anthropologists, sociologists, biologists, physicians, psychologists, economists, geologists, and agronomists who were involved in transnational exchanges and who worked with state officials to understand how to manage racial differences within and across nations. They include Redfield, one of the first U.S. scholars to conduct ethnographic fieldwork in Mexico; Franz Boas, a key figure in U.S. anthropology with ties to Mexico; Manuel Gamio, a student and collaborator of Boas's who is considered Mexico's first Ph.D. anthropologist; John Collier, U.S. commissioner of Indian affairs from 1933 to 1945; and anthropologist Laura Thompson, one of Collier's closest collaborators. Despite unequal access to resources and academic prestige, these figures collaborated across borders in the period that began with the Mexican Revolution (1910–17) and ended with the reorganization of the global order following World War II. During this period, universities grew, new academic disciplines emerged, and intellectuals north and south of the Rio Grande consolidated their influence within national policy circles.[4] Pan-American social reform networks took shape, and Mexican and U.S. scholars and policymakers exchanged viewpoints in conferences and journals and through fieldwork and other forms of travel. They forged transnational disciplines, institutions, and networks in which they discussed Native peoples and other ethnic "minorities." In so doing, they refashioned race as a scientific category that enabled cross-border discussions.

Mexican and U.S. scholars understood their own countries and their countries' places in the world in terms of models of modernity that ranked nation-states according to racial criteria. But this book does not simply repeat the oft-told story of how the United States and the West cemented their superiority by fashioning themselves as the epitome of modern, homogeneous nationhood.[5] Instead, it shines a spotlight on the contradictions and ambiguities that made it difficult for scientists involved in transnational debates regarding race, nation, and modernity to place clearly their nations, and each other, on an evolutionary scale. As Chase's playful jibes show, stark comparisons did not always hold. The polysemy of geographic and racial terms, and of the practices they described, allowed for at least the partial subversion of racial hierarchies among and within nations. Mexican experts sought to assimilate Native peoples into a modern, Euro-Mexican nation that could compete with the United States. Yet they also sought to make indigenous heritage compatible with a modernity not necessarily based on Euro-U.S. models. Many U.S. intellectuals took their own Anglo-U.S. origins as normative and sought to modernize not just less-developed countries like Mexico but also U.S. immigrant, Afro-descendant, and Native peoples. Other academics criticized these approaches. Given the association of indigeneity, and non-Euro-American peoples generally, with recalcitrant backwardness and divisive heterogeneity, intellectuals who tried to craft a united, modern nation that harbored diverse lifeways ultimately came up short. Still, the creative thinking that came out of their interactions with the people they studied and with their colleagues at home and abroad generated conceptual resources—and cautions—that help us today to rethink the conundrums of modernity.

The Mexicans studied in this book often diverged from their U.S. counterparts in the specific attributes they deemed compatible with modernity. Still, scholars north and south of the Rio Grande viewed modernity as comprising a cluster of cultural, economic, political, psychic, bodily, and technological characteristics. Racial concepts emerged from these discourses of liberal modernity and could blend, chameleonlike, with them.[6] Political and academic authorities suggested that proper citizens ought to consume in certain ways, engage in particular forms of commerce, use specific tools, work efficiently and by the clock, and dress and eat in specified ways—all for the good of the nation. They envisioned an ideal modern citizen who had a strong and able body, believed in stipulated forms of the supernatural, prevented illnesses with vaccination and not divination, spoke and read and wrote the national language, attended school regularly, and engaged in peaceful and civilized political discourse.[7]

Science and rationality were absolutely central to the modern national communities and national economies these experts envisioned. Science and rationality were the basis of economic progress and democratic dialogue. And they were intimately bound up in ideas regarding race. The generalizing, consensus-building attributes of science echoed the attributes of a liberalism premised on the notion that all humans were innately equal and shared a set of ostensibly universal characteristics. Proponents of liberalism relegated differences to a private sphere presumably divorced from politics, and they therefore grappled with whether and how to use state policies to attend to differences. The supposed public sameness of citizens enjoying formal equality made it harder to see and therefore to address inequalities. It could lead policymakers to insist on race-blind policies or integration. But private behaviors inevitably intruded on the public sphere, and what was presumed to be universal was often aligned with modern Euro-American ideals.[8]

Along with the dilemmas of liberal modernity, U.S. and Mexican experts shared a ubiquitous, but polysemous, racial lexicon. Past studies of the African diaspora, along with some newer studies of immigration, have shown how experts applied that racial lexicon across borders.[9] Yet early twentieth-century transnational debates regarding race encompassed not just immigrants, blacks, and whites but also Native peoples, a fact that scholars are only beginning to acknowledge.[10] This book uses a transnational lens to examine policies toward Native peoples across borders.[11] Thinking and practices regarding indigeneity, I show, shaped racial ideologies more broadly, an insight that dovetails with a critical indigenous studies that is trying to move beyond more essentialist formulations of indigeneity and to bring the study of Native peoples into more robust dialogue with other currents of scholarship.[12]

The transnational networks I analyze in this book moved among discussions of African and European descendants, immigrants, and Native peoples. Participants used the term "race" to refer to distinctions among groups that they characterized based on biological and/or hereditary criteria (and they characterized heredity as social, biological, or a combination of the two). They used "race" to refer to skin color or other bodily characteristics, visible or invisible, though many recognized that the body itself was shaped by factors that were not inherited or intrinsic, such as diet, health care, or time spent in the sun. Especially in the first decades of the twentieth century, contemporaries almost always saw social, economic, and cultural factors as contributing to racial distinctions. In the aftermath of Nazi racism and World War II, some in the human sciences began to define race as strictly biological but wholly separate from culture and therefore inconsequential. But this view was not widely accepted before 1945, and even afterward it never fully took hold. People continued to see nations and regions as having racial characteristics and to refer to peoples of indigenous, immigrant, Asian, and African descent as making up races even as they also referred to them as cultures, ethnicities, or social classes. Stuart Chase switched easily from talking about "race and culture" to talking about "stock" and "nationalities." In many cases, and in Mexico especially, race was not the most salient category for scholars or policymakers.[13] The term might pop up unexpectedly—unconsciously even—in a text that elsewhere denied the existence of race and avoided the term. Most Mexicans and a good many U.S. scholars preferred to talk about education, evolution, or health, about Otomí, Hopi, Tarahumara, or Navajo. Despite, or maybe because of, the ubiquity of race concepts, policymaking and social scientific knowledge regarding race were full of gaps, incongruities, disagreements, contradictions, and aporias—all of which, paradoxically, facilitated conversation across as well as within borders.

THIS BOOK DEMONSTRATES that Mexico and the United States navigated many of the same global currents and traveled toward the same shoreline but crafted paddles of differing materials and landed on different piers. Mexican and U.S. scholars might have chosen to speak about the common waters. More often, they focused on the different piers. Scholars from the United States largely ignored their country's immigrant, Native, and Afro-descendant populations so as to constitute a white, Anglo-European national image. They claimed that the Mexican people were degenerating due to racial mixing, even as Mexicans denounced U.S. intolerance and bigotry. The United States had decimated its Native peoples, Mexican intellectuals pointed out, and housed the remaining indigenous groups on reservations, a form of segregation that the Mexicans viewed as akin to Jim Crow. Policies in the United States stressed difference over equality in part by using biological markers to define who belonged to a given ethnic group or geopolitical entity, Mexicans said. In contrast, Mexican policymakers made a conscious decision, based in part on long-standing allegiances to liberal notions of formal equality, to equate the rural poor and indigenous people. Mexico had long attempted to integrate Native peoples into the nation as citizens, and postrevolutionary Mexican rural policies addressed poor indigenous *and* mestizo peasants equally, subsuming race and ethnicity to class.

This book shows the many commonalities between U.S. and Mexican scholars and their mutual influence while analyzing why they presented their views as being so different. Experts in both countries drew stark contrasts that promoted exceptionalist nationalisms and papered over connections, including wide-ranging conversations regarding race that provided ample space for exchange among scholars, policymakers, and broader publics. Mexican and U.S. exceptionalism occluded similarities that made Mexico and the United States comparable, including the settlement of both nations by Europeans who enriched themselves at the expense of imported African slaves, Native peoples, and immigrant workers.[14] Indeed, some U.S. intellectuals viewed Mexico as a natural laboratory that might help them sort out the perhaps salutary effects of the social and biological mixing taking place in their own country. Some Mexicans viewed U.S. recognition of Native sovereignty as a precedent on which to build.

That U.S. politicians and policymakers applied lessons learned at home to foreign nations is well documented. Third World scholars have long denounced this U.S. intellectual imperialism. But there has been little recognition of how U.S. intellectuals and politicians drew on the ideas of Mexicans and about Mexico to understand a variety of U.S. domestic racial "minorities." When U.S. scholars studying Latin America first began to institutionalize their presence within the academy, at the dawn of U.S. Latin American studies, their work was intimately connected to interest in U.S. ethnic minority groups.[15] Mexico was not just the Other that defined the uniqueness of the United States. It was also a source of data and knowledge that could be applied at home. Knowledge traveled from South to North as well as from North to South.

Mexican experts for their part vied for authority at home and beyond by engaging in global conversations and billing themselves as participants in modern scientific debate. They gained authority abroad by insisting that they spoke not just for Mexico's dispossessed but also for a dispossessed Mexico that they contrasted to the Anglo-U.S. West. In so doing, they often conflated themselves and Mexico's disenfranchised, although neither Mexican science nor the Mexican state could truly speak for Mexico's Native peoples or its impoverished rural peasants and workers. Mexican nationalism downplayed the way that postrevolutionary governments, and the experts who supported them, reproduced political hierarchies.[16]

Although this book highlights connections and similarities across borders, it does not discount the strength of the nation-states that so firmly shaped research agendas or the often distinct nationalisms that emerged from transnational conversations. Yet it attempts to show how national narratives were constructed. In so doing, it builds on scholarship that has shown how comparisons have helped to create and cement differences, especially national differences, and to elevate the importance of the specific categories compared. Essentialized and often rigid views of race have been especially important in shaping notions of national character. Latin Americans have long countered the accusation that Latin America was less civilized and more economically backward than the United States by asserting that Latin America was more racially democratic. In turn, U.S. policymakers and public opinion have taken pride in the United States as the land of economic opportunity, social mobility, and the American Dream.[17] Rather than taking sides in the often strident debates about racial democracy and economic development, I unearth the circulation of ideas and people across borders that undergirded those debates. I thereby cut against the grain of a long tradition of ranking nations based on the extent of their economic or racial democracy.[18]

My approach builds on Ann Stoler's insight that comparison and hierarchy may rest on notions of commensurability, or shared frameworks for measurement.[19] The act of comparing, I suggest, may lead to the assertion of similarity or to projections from one context to another. It may lead to empathy. And lack of comparison may lead to strident assertions of singularity and hierarchy.[20] To understand how a range of comparisons worked in practice, we need contextual, historical analyses that track the transit and translation of ideas and their relation to the exercise of power. Ironically, given how experts and politician mobilized race to create national mythologies, ideas regarding race were in fact quite fluid and consequently able to function in and across nations and localities. Academics translated racial concepts, and indeed what race itself meant, to fit local and national needs.

CONTACT BETWEEN U.S. and Mexican scholars was neither fully reciprocal nor based on equality. Scholars from the United States studied Mexico as a way of grappling with their nation's own domestic minorities and with the foreign populations the United States confronted globally. Mexicans for their part lived in, and knew a good deal about, their neighbor to the north but did not usually conduct fieldwork in the United States or write books about it. Mexicans were crucial interlocutors and gatekeepers for U.S. scholars who did fieldwork and sought to generate knowledge that was global in scope. Yet those U.S. scholars rarely acknowledged their foreign interlocutors. As a result, even U.S. academics' most earnest efforts to create a truly global science based on transnational collaboration ended up affirming the West as the locus of both science and the modernity that science epitomized.

In a pivotal essay exploring how liberal discourses of nationhood and citizenship have defined a purportedly universal experience based on Western norms, historian Dipesh Chakrabarty has shown that those discourses have relegated non-Western experiences to the category of the particular. Non-Western peoples, he notes, have been forced to engage in a dialogue with the epistemological project of liberal modernity, which has operated with at least the partial consent of its postcolonial subjects. One way to undo this epistemological bind, Chakrabarty suggests, is by "provincializing" the West. This is not, he insists, a call for pluralism, the recognition of difference, or a total rejection of Western rationality. Cultural pluralism—the recognition of the differences among bounded units often geographically defined—can, and perhaps almost always does, work to reassert ethnic forms of hierarchy, even when celebrating rather than merely tolerating or naming difference. Still, provincializing Europe does require an understanding how "Europe" or the West has been constituted as the object of theoretical knowledge and positioned other histories as fleshing out the European "theoretical skeleton."[21]

This book examines a variety of ways in which intellectuals North and South sought to reconcile universal theories and particular cases. Mexican intellectuals envisioned a potential North-South solidarity based on a shared humanity and a shared rationality, a universalism not based solely on Western norms, and a Mexican modernity that was also, in part, indigenous. They believed that they could do real science in Mexico. But as Mexico's cosmopolitan social scientists delved into differences, I suggest, they at times realized the impossibility of a truly universal modernity and found themselves unable to generalize based on the study of their country and its presumably backward and heterogeneous peoples. The global democratic solidarity they imagined ultimately broke down. Those Mexicans who recognized the intransigence of difference and the obstacles to a truly cosmopolitan modernity perhaps took a step toward "provincializing" Euro-U.S. modernity, and the manifestations of that Western modernity in the provinces of the West. They embraced particularity rather than seeing it as failure.

Where Chakrabarty highlights the universal pretensions of the West, historians of science have traditionally been less concerned with the geopolitics of knowledge. They have focused rather on how scientists affirm their authority by mobilizing detachment and positivism and a "view from nowhere." Scientists' claim to have an omniscient view has allowed scientific concepts and procedures to travel with ease but has obscured the inevitably grounded nature of scientific procedures. Historians of science have shown how scientific claims of an objective "view from nowhere" obfuscate scientific practice. These historians have foregrounded the contexts in which scientists have worked or, in some versions, the networks through which scientific knowledges have emerged. In so doing, they have implicitly, and in some cases explicitly, begun to provincialize Western science.[22]

Recent histories of science have stressed the contingencies that shape scientists' relation to state projects and other powerful actors. Fieldwork and laboratories at times promoted empathy, flexibility, or observation rather than detached manipulation, thereby augmenting the effects of the people, places, or things studied. Fieldworkers often found themselves in conditions where their expertise counted for little, or they were swayed by what they saw and whom they met.[23] My account takes note of the sometimes contingent encounters that shaped the trajectories of individual scholars. I also insist on the epistemological effects of those individuals' place within power-laden global and national networks.

In a study of the United Nations Educational, Scientific and Cultural Organization (UNESCO), historian Perrin Selcer focuses on how science mediated relations between the West and the non-West in the decade following World War II. Selcer construes intellectual collaboration across borders as a conversation among scholars, policymakers, and broader publics aimed at building a democratic consensus. Drawing inspiration from pragmatist philosophical frameworks, he argues that UNESCO social scientists saw universally accepted truths and shared categories as contingent and that they advocated a democracy that could accommodate differences. Rather than an objective, positivist view from nowhere, they mobilized a "view from everywhere" in which "truth emerged from the process of international collaboration." Though hampered by the lack of equality among nations, UNESCO intellectuals sought to avoid the imperial imposition of normative truths based on the experiences of the West and instead tried to distill universal truths from diverse national experiences.[24]

To this view, Chakrabarty and other postcolonial scholars, including those who use postcolonial approaches to science studies, counterpose a "politics of despair" that continually makes visible the way that the institutional sites of knowledge production and the very epistemologies of history and modernity make dialogue among equals illusory.[25] Just as liberal politicians failed to recognize that their ideals of citizenship were based not on universal human qualities but on the particular experiences of white male propertied citizens, scientific efforts to forge consensus have overlooked existing hierarchies. Scholars of those efforts may, like Selcer, confuse aspiration and reality.

Still, Selcer and others correctly recognize that certain social scientific practices, and fieldwork experiences especially, changed the people who engaged in them and offered small spaces for remaking prevailing norms. My book takes seriously the efforts of researchers who believed that their work was furthering democracy even when that work did not always lead to larger changes. It also takes seriously the unrecognized hierarchies, indeed the violence, that made experts' views and actions quixotic *and* indispensable—quixotic because those views and actions could not escape prevailing paradigms and practices, and indispensable because they constituted ethical responses to perceived injustices and attempts to forge partial consensuses. Contemporaries themselves deliberated what it meant to serve the state or other political projects and how researchers' relationships to state projects affected their ability to generate truths. Historians of science should likewise attend to the scope and limits of the processes of translation they study.[26]

THIS BOOK GROUNDS its discussion of science by focusing on the writings and trajectories of a few key scholars and policymakers. Manuel Gamio is a central character here. A prolific author and an important player in Mexico's early postrevolutionary efforts to address the problems of Native peoples, Gamio traveled to the United States in 1909–12 to study at Columbia University. He then became an active participant in Pan-American intellectual circuits. Returning to the United States in 1925, he began research on Mexican migration to the United States the following year. Through these trips and his presence in international conferences and forums, Gamio established himself as a crucial interlocutor for the many U.S. scholars who read his work in English and counted on his contacts when conducting research in Mexico. He also conveyed foreign social science to Mexico. In 1917, he founded the first state agency devoted to addressing the plight of Native peoples. He served briefly as assistant secretary of education in 1924–25.[27]

In the 1930s, Gamio was partially eclipsed by other state-sponsored intellectuals who figured more prominently within national politics, notably Moisés Sáenz, an acolyte of John Dewey and collaborator of Commissioner of Indian Affairs John Collier. Sáenz held key posts in the Secretaría de Educación Pública (SEP, Department of Education) after Gamio resigned his position there. Historian Luis Chávez Orozco, ethnographer Miguel Othón de Mendizábal, educator Carlos Basauri, and lawyer and sociologist Lucio Mendieta y Núñez also undertook important studies on Native peoples and held important academic and government positions. After 1941, when Sáenz died unexpectedly, Gamio, who had been cycling through a series of relatively minor bureaucratic posts, reemerged on the national scene, taking Sáenz's place at the helm of the Inter-American Indigenous Institute (IAII, Instituto Indigenista Interamericano). From that position, Gamio cemented his influence at home and abroad, remaining head of the IAII until his death in 1960.[28]

Gamio's importance is reflected in his greater archival presence. Other Mexican *indigenista* intellectuals—champions of their nation's indigenous heritage who sought to uplift contemporary Native peoples—left smaller archival footprints. By contrast, Commissioner of Indian Affairs John Collier has a massive presence in the archives. Collier habitually fired off at least a handful of letters a day and published numerous reflections on his career, providing considerable insight into not just his own work but also that of his closest interlocutors, including anthropologist Laura Thompson, who worked with Collier on a number of projects, including projects related to Mexico. Collier's writings also provide insight into his contacts with, and borrowing from, Mexico and other foreign nations and empires. Collier was candid about his use of knowledge from abroad. Other U.S. intellectuals were less forthright, although the writings of Franz Boas, who mentored Gamio, and of Robert Redfield provide additional insights into U.S. scholarly contact with Gamio and with Mexico more generally. Other U.S. scholars tended to downplay the vital contacts that shaped their fieldwork and knowledge, portraying foreign places as providing data that they would organize. My research shows how their travels abroad and their reading of foreign authors shaped their ideas, procedures, and results.

My focus on individuals who left longer archival trails should not be read as implying that they singularly shaped knowledge projects or policies. Far from it. Gamio's and Collier's methods, insights, and frameworks, which no doubt reflected their idiosyncratic life histories and the circuits in which they traveled, also synthesized and displayed broader national and disciplinary trends. Throughout this book, I document how their individual trajectories were necessarily constrained by the networks and the institutional contexts in which they worked and lived, including their intimate connections to the states that shaped the problematics of the human sciences in general.

Anthropologists' day-to-day experiences in villages, as well as universities and other academic settings, mattered, too. The human sciences were arenas of face-to-face contact in which racial hierarchies were enacted and reframed, and scholars who traveled to often-distant field sites saw themselves as displaying the very modernity they championed: rational, secular, tolerant, democratic, and open to change.[29] Their often rarified techniques for collecting data—tests and surveys, timed puzzles, and storytelling exercises—reinforced differences between themselves and the peoples they studied. Fieldworkers themselves often recognized their techniques as vehicles of acculturation, change brought about by the meeting of distinct cultures. Mexican photographer Agustín Maya and U.S. ethnomusicologist Henrietta Yurchenco carted a massive wax-cylinder recording machine through Cora and Huichol land and to the Seri village of Desemboque in 1944. The machine surely made a statement, as the researchers no doubt imagined it would.[30]

Fieldwork was a two-way street. Researchers learned from the people they ostensibly served. To undermine hierarchy, investigators could choose open-ended questions or actively seek empathy and rapport. Deploying what they sometimes termed "action research," they enlisted state-employed teachers and doctors who had detailed knowledge of localities. In certain cases, they made Native informants into researchers themselves. But as direct or indirect agents of the states they served, researchers could administer or withhold incentives and intervene in local, regional, and national configurations of power. If fieldwork was a two-way street, the road was on a steep incline, making travel in one direction more strenuous than in the other. Certain individuals had stronger legs, but that was only one factor shaping encounters in the field.

THIS BOOK IS DIVIDED into two loosely chronological parts, each containing separate chapters on Mexico and the United States. Each part begins with a brief introduction that sets up a dialogue between the U.S. and Mexican cases. Part I opens with the Mexican Revolution and covers World War I and its immediate aftermath. Part II focuses primarily on the period following the rise to power of Presidents Franklin D. Roosevelt (1933–45) and Lázaro Cárdenas (1934–40).

In Chapter 1, Mexicans' scientific explorations of race are placed in the context of their involvement with U.S. and European racial sciences. Gamio built creatively from prevailing Mexican and foreign intellectual currents, but he suffered the condescension of his U.S. counterparts and had difficulty defining the parameters of a modernity that could accommodate Mexico's large Native population. Chapter 2 explores U.S. debates during a time of massive migration and intense debate regarding population movements. As experts debated Americanization, studies of Mexico and Latin America proliferated. They were part of a comparative project aimed at understanding the ostensibly backward peoples within the United States and the biological and cultural processes of contact and mixing through which they might be assimilated into prevailing Euro-U.S. lifeways. Franz Boas and his students faced off against those who sought to whiten and purify the nation. Repudiating determinist paradigms, they still underscored the importance of biological differences and inheritance.

Part II surveys John Collier's Indian New Deal and Mexican policies toward Native peoples as both governments turned leftward following the Great Depression. Chapter 3 examines the U.S. Indian Service (IS), the federal agency charged with administering government services on Native reservations, as it abandoned assimilationist strategies and hired anthropologists to develop more culturally appropriate policies. Collier, the IS head who spearheaded these innovations, claimed inspiration from indirect forms of colonial rule, including Spanish rule over New Spain, and he took postrevolutionary Mexico as a model for the scientific democratic governance of cultural and racial difference. During and after World War II, Collier applied the lessons he had learned in Mexico and from Mexicans to the IS-run Japanese American internment camp at Poston, Arizona. Along with Laura Thompson and other allies, he subsequently extended those lessons to U.S. dependencies abroad and "minorities" at home.[31]

In the 1930s and 1940s, Mexicans eschewed grand theories and approached modernization within a framework that was resolutely local and empirical. Mexican experts increasingly placed economics—rather than ethnicity, culture, or race—at the center of national policies. However, they took a localized, particularistic, ethnographic approach to economics. Somewhat paradoxically, their local and empirical approach deployed globalizing evolutionary paradigms. Chapter 4 examines the complex ways indigenistas reconciled their belief in universal progress and science with their attention to particularity by using strategies of compilation, categorization, and statistical aggregation.

The concluding chapter comes back to the questions of difference and modern liberal democracy. Economic and numerical criteria provided a way for Mexican scholars to create a presumably scientific yet flexible definition of race and indigeneity that subsumed particularity. Many U.S. scholars thought that the Mexicans were confused or misguided; others took the point and ran with it. More broadly, Mexicans' attention to particularity and their attempts to reconcile indigeneity with modernity and liberalism were a creative effort to generate new forms of governance and new policies. However, its architects shared problematic assumptions about progress and evolution that hampered the antiracist potential of their endeavors.

Overall, this book looks at experts who sought to forge united national polities based on notions of equality and equivalency among citizens in societies crossed by ethnic and racial differences. Liberal paradigms based on the notion that all humans and all citizens were equal and equivalent spurred epistemologies and forms of social engineering based on the creation of generalizable knowledge. Scholars struggled, often with great creativity, often unsuccessfully, to create impartial forms of government while recognizing differences. Their efforts generated a number of methods and techniques, including collection and aggregation, statistics and ethnography. They subsumed differences into global theories of evolution or cultural diffusion. But they could apply those global theories only loosely and partially.

Past accounts of these efforts have, quite rightly, stressed the implicit and explicit racism of experts and of the national projects they helped forge. My book moves beyond this approach to reveal their struggle to revamp liberal polities. Many forces hampered their efforts, including their inability to push past reigning Eurocentric, evolutionary paradigms. Recognition of those contrary forces should not stop us from acknowledging how experts articulated the limitations—indeed the insistent failures—of assimilationism. They learned those lessons, at home and abroad, as they came into contact with the Native, immigrant, and Afro-descendant peoples they studied. At the same time, their efforts were conditioned powerfully by national states and by the transnational scientific milieus in which they participated. Those milieus propped up notions of a normative Western modernity, but they also spawned disruptive knowledge that questioned a univocal liberal modernity.

Part I Science and Nation in an Age of Evolution and Eugenics, 1910–1934

The Mexican Revolution and World War I decisively reshaped ideas about race and its relation to national well-being in Mexico and the United States. After the death and destruction wrought by the revolution, Mexicans prioritized national unity and economic reconstruction in their efforts to rebuild the country. In the United States, the events of World War I and the continued influx of immigrants prompted experts and politicians to reconsider how best to preserve the nation's demographic vigor. For intellectuals in both countries, the rise of Mendelian theories of biological inheritance demanded a renewed attention to the mechanisms and direction of evolutionary changes. Experts worldwide debated a variety of evolutionary and eugenic theories as they sought solutions to pressing social conflicts.

In the second decade of the twentieth century, scholars and government officials moved haltingly away from orthodox political and economic liberalism. In the late nineteenth and early twentieth centuries, Mexican and U.S. political elites and intellectuals had invoked liberal discourses of individual rights to justify assimilationist measures toward Native peoples as well as immigrants. If Native peoples and immigrants were to be proper citizens, politicians had argued, they needed to assimilate to Euro-U.S. culture and obey the same laws as other citizens. This mind-set began to change, however, after the Great War, as intellectuals increasingly criticized homogenizing forms of mass culture and mass politics. Subsequently, the Great Depression kindled romantic critiques of industrialization. These global events led scholars to look for ways of integrating cultural differences within their nations and eventually prompted governments to turn away from assimilationist policies.[1] A broad cluster of parallel U.S. and Mexican policies decisively halted the aggressive, often violent efforts to assimilate Native peoples and immigrants. Those pluralist policies would coexist with forms of liberal antiracism that stressed formal equality within the nation and with the democratizing forms of state intervention that sprang up in the aftermath of the Depression and led governments to devise broad-based social policies applicable to national majorities.

In Mexico, some intellectuals had already begun to question assimilationist liberal policies toward the end of Porfirio Díaz's despotic government (1876–1911, known as the *Porfiriato*). Yet it was the revolution, which swept away the old order and much of the country's infrastructure, that cleared a path for more rapid reform. Villages emptied when residents fled invading forces were rebuilt after the fighting ended, and the capital city swelled with migrants from the countryside. These conditions facilitated social, institutional, and intellectual experimentation. The progressive constitution of 1917 nationalized the subsoil and enshrined Native peoples' right to own land collectively. Mexicans began to build a new, secular nation that was, as Mary Kay Vaughan has described it, "brown."[2]

Postrevolutionary governments responded to rural social mobilization by improving the distribution of land and social conditions in the countryside. In contrast to the rest of Latin America and the United States, where the reforms of the 1920s through 1940s largely overlooked agricultural workers and small-scale farmers, Mexico's earliest social and labor legislation targeted rural areas. Postrevolutionary leaders extended schooling and health care to previously ignored villages, and moved quickly to address the pressing issue of access to land, especially in southern Mexico. At the same time, the revolution transformed the balance of local and regional political power, a matter that was for many Mexicans as important as the redistribution of land.[3]

The revolution was more rural and mestizo than indigenous. Some Native villagers mobilized during the revolutionary fighting, but the revolution remained distant in many more remote and less accessible communities.[4] Postrevolutionary reforms nonetheless encompassed Native peoples along with mestizo campesinos. Like Latin American elites elsewhere, Mexico's new leaders revamped the rhetoric of *mestizaje* (racial mixing) and combined it with *indigenismo*. They exalted the mixed Spanish and Indian heritage of their nation, sought to uplift contemporary Native peoples, and protected certain aspects of Native lifeways.[5]

In the United States, World War I retarded reforms and spawned coercive Americanization campaigns. Prior Progressive efforts to Americanize immigrants by teaching them English and hygienic, efficient modern habits gave way to government persecution of German Americans and Reds, deemed un-American or criminal or both, as in the case of Nicola Sacco and Bartolomeo Vanzetti. With even greater intensity at the close of the war, elites worked to stanch the flow of immigrants and isolate newcomers that they deemed deviant. The racism of ordinary citizens grew more virulent as well. The Ku Klux Klan rode high in the Midwest and South, persecuting immigrants along with blacks, and Madison Grant touted the virtues of the "Nordic race" in his best-selling 1916 book *The Passing of the Great Race*. Race riots shook East Saint Louis, Chicago, and other cities in 1917 and 1919. Debates regarding immigration restriction, which had begun in the nineteenth century with the exclusion of Chinese immigrants, took center stage in late 1910s and early 1920s. Congress passed the Johnson-Reed Act (1924), which barred even broader swaths of Asians and definitively and severely curtailed immigration from Southern and Eastern Europe.[6] Wartime nationalism affected U.S. academic institutions as well. At Columbia University, psychologist James McKeen Cattell was fired from his position for his opposition to U.S. involvement in the war. Franz Boas, who strenuously opposed McKeen Cattell's removal, was subsequently censured by the American Anthropological Association (AAA), which branded him unpatriotic for denouncing four U.S. anthropologists whom he believed had spied for the federal government in Central America.[7]

As Mexican, and eventually U.S., scholars and policymakers pushed back against certain aspects of liberalism, they began to scrutinize the conditions faced by Native peoples specifically. In both Mexico and the United States, governments had responded to the rapid growth of capitalist and market agriculture, mining, and railways by sanctioning public and private encroachment on Native lands. In the United States, the policy of allotment, begun with the Dawes Act of 1887, had divided Native peoples' communally owned lands among reservation residents and thereby laid the groundwork for the sale of those lands to white settlers. In Mexico, disentailment, legislated in 1857, had enabled the breakup of community lands and led to the parceling of property, its distribution to individuals, and eventually its sale to or usurpation by non-Natives. Individual ownership of private property, U.S. and Mexican officials believed, would school Native peoples in the autonomy needed for the adequate exercise of citizenship. Native peoples should not have special protections, many argued, and in the United States, "termination," or the devolution to the states of federal responsibilities for Native peoples, was debated repeatedly by Congress in the 1920s and 1930s. Advocates of termination argued against the paternalistic protection of Native peoples. In the process they also questioned the status of Native groups as nations that had secured collective treaty rights from the federal government.[8]

Mexico had never had a centralized federal agency akin to the U.S. Indian Service, or IS, which oversaw schooling, health care, land sales and leases, and courts on Native lands, and Mexicans generally were proud that Native peoples were subject to the same laws and forms of government as non-Natives. Yet Mexico's postrevolutionary land legislation sanctioned the *ejido*, a form of communal land tenure that postrevolutionary intellectuals touted as building on traditional forms of Native landholding. Because ejido lands were collectively owned and could not be sold, the creation of ejidos would ensure that Native and non-Native peoples held on to land.[9] More generally, postrevolutionary elites scrutinized assimilationist viewpoints and harsh policies of integration, and mestizaje began to mean more than whitening or evolutionary uplift toward a Euro-U.S. norm.[10]

In the United States, too, the state's relationship to Native peoples began to change. In the 1920s, a pro-Indian lobby made up of Native and white organizations emerged, and Congress granted Native peoples citizenship in 1924 (though states with large Native populations such as Arizona and New Mexico denied voting rights to Native peoples until 1948). The secretary of the interior responded to social mobilizations around Native peoples by commissioning a report on Indian administration. The 1928 study, *The Problem of Indian Administration,* produced by the Brookings Institution and Lewis Meriam, condemned the subdivision of Native lands under the allotment system and called for an end to the suppression of Native rituals and dances. The Meriam Report, as it became known, also argued for the dismantling of boarding schools that ripped Native children from their homes, taught them to speak only English, and aimed to assimilate them to a presumably superior "American" culture. In 1933, President Roosevelt appointed John Collier, who had been an influential member of the Anglo-U.S. pro-Indian lobby, to lead the Indian Service. Commissioner Collier's Indian New Deal implemented many of the Meriam Report's recommendations.[11]

More generally, in both Mexico and the United States, by 1930, melting pot was giving way to mosaic as people searched for ways of integrating difference without annihilating it. Yet officials continued to exhort Native peoples to learn the national languages, wash their hands, and forego superstition. Assimilationist measures aimed at making Native peoples—along with immigrants—part of the national mainstream vied with more pluralist policies. The shift toward pluralism that had begun in the wake of World War I and accelerated after the 1929 stock market crash did not completely erase prior perspectives; formulations that overlapped and borrowed from one another also interacted with social movements and state policies in often haphazard ways.

AS POLITICIANS DEBATED whether all citizens were actually or potentially the same and whether and how laws and policies should be adapted to address cultural and racial differences, scholars staged related debates regarding evolution. Would peoples of different cultures and races diverge or converge, and if so, how? Academics tried to pinpoint the mechanisms of evolutionary change. What role did natural environments play? What about geographical isolation and movement? Intermarriage? Would mixture have beneficial effects or lead to degeneration, and how might social environments, including reproductive choices, shape the mental and physical characteristics of peoples? Were social or natural environments more important?[12]

Overall, early twentieth-century biologists, sociologists, anthropologists, and political economists who studied racial differences debated whether universal laws of nature existed and, if so, how they operated across diverse times and places. Despite important differences, thinkers combined elements of distinct theories in myriad ways and changed their views over time. Some intellectuals saw presumably backward peoples as being on a lower rung of a universal evolutionary ladder. For instance, Robert Redfield, who had motivated Stuart Chase's comparison of Tepoztlán and Middletown, ranked the barrios of Tepoztlán according to their level of civilization. The Santo Domingo barrio, he wrote, was civilized and patriotic, in contrast to both the "primitive" and enclosed Catholic barrio of Santa Cruz and the barrio of San Pedro, which was made up of "poor, illiterate people who preserve to a marked extent [an] ancient mentality and resent the presence of outsiders in their midst, etc." Yet according to Redfield, modernity would inevitably spread to the more traditional places with "the diffusion of tools and rational techniques." In later work on four villages in Yucatán, Redfield and his Mexican coauthor Alfonso Villa Rojas projected a similar gradient of civilization onto space.[13]

In contradistinction to Redfield, other intellectuals, including many Mexicans, adopted an evolutionary perspective that saw distinct peoples as climbing different ladders—but climbing nonetheless. Evolution, many Mexicans believed, proceeded upward, but because it also reflected adaptation to environments that were diverse, it might not be, as researchers put it, "unilateral." Perhaps evolution was more like a branching tree than a ladder.[14] Still other intellectuals followed Boas in eschewing teleologies altogether in favor of a historical analysis that made space for contingency. And a good many social scientists therefore recognized, tolerated, and even at times appreciated differences that might otherwise be cataloged as evidence of backwardness.

Mexico's postrevolutionary intellectuals had been educated by a generation of Porfirian thinkers steeped in Lamarckian and Social Darwinist theories of evolution. According to neo-Lamarckian theories that were popular in both the United States and Mexico in the nineteenth century, social and biological factors interacted to shape evolution, and characteristics acquired during an individual's lifetime could be passed on to successive generations. Social conditions were important mechanisms of transformation that could be etched onto the body and then passed down from parent to child. Habitual actions, along with mental habits that developed in response to environmental pressures, could therefore affect physical and mental evolution.[15]

The neo-Lamarckian focus on social factors did not necessarily make intellectuals less teleological or more likely to promote reforms aimed at mitigating inequality and difference. In the United States, early neo-Lamarckians characterized human actions as reflecting the desires of a Divine Creator, reinscribing evolution within a deterministic teleology. Divinely sanctioned human actions would produce an orderly and ascendant evolution. Neo-Lamarckians also argued that environments simply stimulated the transformation of traits that then became hereditary. And their accounts of social and biological evolution fused with Malthusian theories that emphasized competition for scarce resources. From this point of view, competition was supposedly an innate drive and improvement was therefore inevitable. Natural selection would favor the better adapted, and more efficient, members of a species, and social reforms that prompted the survival of the less fit were therefore ill-advised.[16] These views were uniquely suited to a laissez-faire capitalist social order.

Unlike U.S. Social Darwinists, the Comtian positivists of the Porfiriato tended to characterize their country as underpopulated and rich in natural resources and therefore to reject Malthusian arguments. The postrevolutionary generation extended this anti-Malthusianism. They spurned the laissez-faire view that the less fit should be allowed to die out, which they associated with the competitive capitalism of the Porfiriato, and stressed the importance of education. Education would guide the less fit toward behaviors that would improve their chances of survival—a position many prerevolutionary intellectuals had in fact embraced. Education and public health measures, not competition, would make Mexicans more efficient and more modern.[17]

The role of natural environments was also a foremost consideration for postrevolutionary intellectuals. Mexico harbored Native peoples who since pre-Columbian times had lived in and adapted to distinct ecologies, migrating from place to place and sometimes settling in isolated regions. As a result of this combination of isolation and movement, new civilizations or ethnic groups had come into being; existing groups stopped evolving or died out; and peoples developed upward but also outward, away from one another. Mexicans' attention to the specificity of local environments thus pointed to a universal upward movement while stressing diversity. At the same time, twentieth-century Mexicans saw the natural environment as shaped by culture and vice versa. Government action could and should affect the land itself as well as people's adaptation to it. Irrigation, new seed varieties, and new agricultural techniques would help rural people eat better and become stronger across generations.[18] These Mexican views of evolution were compatible with neo-Lamarckian and Darwinian teleologies.

In contrast to Mexicans, U.S. intellectuals of the post–World War I era took inspiration from newly rediscovered Mendelian laws and the new theories of biological inheritance pioneered by Germany's August Weismann, who posited the existence of germ cells that alone influenced inheritance. This approach foregrounded inherent, immutable biology and posited the biological development of organisms as innate, or orthogenetic—a determinist view of biology and one that downplayed the effects of natural and social environments on organisms. Weismann specifically sought to refute neo-Lamarckianism, which consequently lost ground in the United States in the 1910s and 1920s.[19]

Yet even as the rediscovery of Mendelian laws prompted greater consideration of biological inheritance, scientists could not yet pinpoint the precise mechanisms of transmission from one generation to the next, and some scholars combined the insights of Mendelianism with prevailing neo-Lamarckian explanations. Since U.S. scientists could not in any definitive way know the effects of environments or fully understand the outcomes of the biological mixing of previously separate populations, they began looking to Mexico and the rest of Latin America as laboratories that might help them discover the precise mechanisms of evolution in mixed populations. The ultimate goal was to shape suitable state policies. Should governments pass laws that authorized the sterilization of the "feebleminded" or build schools? Should they seek to change diets or exclude immigrants considered to be weak or potentially infirm?[20]

The advance in the United States of a more hereditarian view of biology, though admittedly uneven, led to the reordering of disciplines and their relative influence. As physical anthropologists focused more and more on the transmission of hereditary biological traits, cultural anthropologists responded by distancing themselves from biology and physical anthropology, a move that brought them closer to the strands of neo-Larmarckianism prevailing in Mexico.[21] At the same time, Mexicans shared elements of the historical and diffusionist approaches that were pioneered and employed by Franz Boas and the students he trained at Columbia University, including Manuel Gamio. It was a viewpoint particularly appropriate to an age in which isolated, bounded cultures seemed to be vanishing as migration and travel accelerated. In the 1930s, as U.S. and Mexican cultural anthropologists inspired by Boas began to abandon unilineal and teleological views of culture, anthropological theories of "acculturation" took their place. Acculturation was compatible with a diffusionism that tracked the historical spread of traits across space. Though it encompassed assimilation (the incorporation of the cultural attributes of one more powerful group by another weaker group), acculturation referred to a broader spectrum of interactions.[22] Cultural contact could involve individuals as well as groups of differing sizes, and the degree to which discrepancies of power were at stake varied. Acculturation encompassed immigration, travel, exogamous marriage, conquest, and trade. But because social scientists were interested in the relation of Native and Afro-descended groups to national majorities, they often used the term "acculturation" rather than "assimilation" when referring to national norms associated with modernity and whiteness, a kind of unilineal cultural evolutionism.

As more and more anthropologists went into the field during these years, they scrutinized these cultural evolutionist viewpoints. Indeed, globalizing theories and the search for laws themselves came into question for these social scientists. Among the groups they studied, neither contact with "more advanced" Native civilizations nor internal development seemed to generate linear progress among peoples, much less a process that replicated itself. How could one apprehend, much less rank, Native peoples who adopted Western medicine but still visited the traditional healer or irrigated their fields and prayed to the rain deities? What effect did selling wool to a trader or rugs to a tourist have on the internal organization of families and communities? What about wage work in mines or coffee plantations or logging camps or factories? What effect did migration to the city have? Would plows or new seed varieties or the introduction of fruit trees inevitably spur other changes? Perhaps characteristics, habits, and practices did not all move in harmony. Which were most important in shaping change? How to know? Indigenistas would come to see that whether a Yucatecan spoke Maya might not matter, and especially after World War I and the Great Depression, some politicians and intellectuals manifested a marked ambivalence toward certain aspects of modernity. Chase praised Tepoztecos' mental balance, and José Vasconcelos, who served as minister of education from 1921 to 1924, lauded Mexicans' spirituality and derided North Americans' crass materialism. Anthropologist Manuel Gamio asked whether Native forms of collective decision making and landholding could be made compatible with modern liberal ideals of democracy and private property. In the United States, anthropologist Melville J. Herskovits set out to prove that African Americans were, like immigrant groups (and his own family), melding racially and culturally into the American ideal. He ended up documenting the survival of cultures and biologies originating in Africa and becoming an expert on the peoples of the African continent.[23] Perhaps in some way, then, old-stock American racial and cultural characters did not have the homogenizing, assimilating force some thought they had. Perhaps they would not inevitably impose themselves, or perhaps only some of them would prevail.[24]

AS SCIENTIFIC INTERACTIONS among Latin America, the United States, and Europe intensified at the close of World War I, transatlantic scientific and policymaking networks that had been silent reestablished themselves. Eugenic circles concerned with how to improve national populations and, less often, humanity were among the more active.[25] The war had spurred concerns about national strength and its relation to population movements, prompting intellectual and political elites around the globe to worry about the quantity as well as the quality of their populations. The emerging field of population studies, which was closely linked to the eugenics movement, tracked differential birth and death rates among different races and ethnicities to determine how demographic changes altered the racial composition and vigor of nations.[26] Health professionals worried about infant mortality and child health. Feminist and child welfare advocates focused on hygiene and puericulture, the science of child rearing.[27] Eugenicists, who took part in all these overlapping networks, focused on how biological and social inheritances and immigration shaped the health and vigor of populations. They took special interest in the study of isolated groups, asking whether and under what conditions separation and inbreeding or contact and mixing led to degeneration or regeneration. The answers to these questions shaped distinct population policies. Some countries adopted and enforced immigration restrictions designed to improve the quality and unity of national populations. Others adopted pronatalist measures to increase the population overall or to allow the allegedly superior segments of the population to multiply. Still others sanctioned sterilization or advocated birth control measures for the poor and unfit.

Neither eugenics nor population studies spoke in one voice. Especially in the United States, many scientists preferred a more hard-line approach that marshaled Mendelian ideas about inheritance, viewed biological heredity as immutable, favored sterilization and selective eugenics, and sought to regulate biological reproduction through coercive means. They advocated for racial purity and for restrictions on immigration based on the view that certain races were either unassimilable or degraded the national stock. Yet the resurgent eugenic and racial concerns of the interwar period cannot be reduced to Nazi or hard-line U.S. eugenics. A good many eugenicists focused instead on improving hygiene and social environments, and some were openly antiracist.[28]

In general, Mexicans and other Latin Americans active in eugenic-inspired reform efforts sought to counter racial poisons such as alcohol, drugs, and venereal diseases that would lead to sickness and racial degeneration. Neo-Lamarckian eugenic circles promoted public health measures such as vaccination and the provision of running water that could curb morbidity and mortality, improve the demographic profile of their nations, and increase citizens' ability to work. Reformers were especially concerned with the condition of children, who functioned as a synecdoche for the nation. Drawing from the recapitulationist view that the ontogenetic development of children repeated phylogenetic evolutionary changes, they believed that the proper development of children echoed national development on a smaller scale; the degeneration of the race would manifest as sickly children. For all these reasons, schooling and hygiene became linchpins of social reform. Without sanitary school buildings and health education, the national race would not grow or develop.

Scientists thus had differing viewpoints on heredity. But all worked together within institutions devoted to eugenics, population studies, and child welfare. For instance, the Italian statistician Corrado Gini collaborated with Benito Mussolini, but as chair of the Commission on Vital Statistics of the Primitive Races of the International Union for the Scientific Investigation of Population Problems (IUSIPP), he served with the antiracist Franz Boas. Likewise, in 1926, Boas served on the Committee on the Negro of the National Research Council (NRC) with Charles Davenport, one of the most influential U.S. supporters of selective eugenics and sterilization. Davenport and Boas disagreed on both the nature of racial distinctions and the role government should play in shaping national populations. But Boas consistently sought to contest racism using many of the same scientific paradigms and methods as Davenport. Both men circulated within the same scientific milieus.[29]

The ecumenical nature of eugenic, population, and child welfare institutions notwithstanding, by the 1930s they were openly divided by invented geographies. Perhaps the most important schism pitted "Latin" eugenicists, led by Gini, against Anglo-U.S. and German eugenicists. The issue of sterilization, which the Catholic Church strenuously opposed, prompted especially impassioned debate among eugenicists and demographers. Equally important, the Latin eugenics movement rejected the neo-Malthusianism prevalent within Anglo-American eugenics, facilitating the adhesion of Mexican and Latin American intellectuals. In contrast to the more racist currents within the United States, Mexicans and other Latin Americans showed little concern with the allegedly excessive fertility of the poor, uncivilized, darker, or less fit. Latin American nations were underpopulated, they argued, and their well-being would be nourished by health measures, education, and hygiene, and by introducing diversity through immigration. Although Mexican and Latin American governments restricted immigration by groups deemed disease-prone or unfit for hard labor, especially Chinese immigrants, Latin American scholars and medical professionals tended not to support such restrictions or popular anti-immigrant sentiment. Latin eugenicists rejected the restrictions on immigration that U.S. participants pushed in Pan-American forums.[30]

Gini and his Mexican collaborators differentiated themselves by stressing the value of mixing through intermarriage and cultural contact. In their view, migrations and race mixture were dynamic forces that introduced variation and innovation into populations. They resisted the view, popular in the United States, that race crossing led to degeneration. These differences eventually split the global forums devoted to population studies and eugenics. The IUSIPP divided almost immediately after its founding, when British and U.S. members refused to attend a 1931 congress in Rome and held a separate conference in London. Not long after, Gini abandoned the International Federation of Eugenics Organizations (IFEO) and launched a rival Latin Eugenics Federation, which met in Buenos Aires in 1934 in conjunction with the Second Pan-American Congress on Eugenics and Homiculture and in Mexico City in 1935 in conjunction with the Seventh Pan-American Child Congress.[31]

Neither the Anglo-U.S. nor the Latin eugenics circles were internally united, however. Most Mexican eugenicists stressed environmental factors, but some supported eugenic sterilization, which was legalized in the state of Veracruz in 1932 (although no forced sterilizations seem to have taken place).[32] In the United States, a good number of social scientists faced off against the determinist biological thinking of hard-line eugenicists. These conflicting viewpoints were openly expressed in U.S. discussions of immigration.[33] The NRC, an organization focused on marshaling the natural sciences to assist the U.S. government, organized a committee on immigration that included social scientists. But that committee struggled to combine the natural and social sciences effectively, and within a couple of years the recently formed Social Science Research Council (SSRC, an institution devoted to setting broad social science agendas) took up the questions regarding labor markets and employment that the NRC, with its emphasis on biology, had been unable to address. When Anglo-U.S. scientists involved with population issues distanced themselves from Gini and Mussolini shortly after the creation of the IUSIPP, the NRC and SSRC argued that eugenics was overly politicized and was failing to take a detached scientific stance. They subsequently withdrew funding from the IUSIPP.[34]

In Mexico, some reformers who embraced Latin eugenics differentiated themselves from U.S. and Northern European eugenicists. Others sought to mold perspectives from abroad to Mexican intellectual traditions and national realities or to combine domestic and foreign perspectives. Still others embraced tenets of more hard-line U.S. eugenics. These impulses echoed those of indigenistas—eugenic and indigenista circles had overlapping but distinct memberships—as they sought membership in an international scientific fraternity while adapting ideas regarding modernity and liberal universalism to Mexican realities. The two chapters that follow chart ideas about North-South differences, and the U.S. and Mexican exceptionalisms, that resulted. They also reveal a good many similarities as well as shared vocabularies.

1

Mexican Indigenismo and the International Fraternity of Science

In 1924, Mexico's assistant secretary of education, Manuel Gamio, delivered a talk defending inter-American cooperation at the Carnegie Institution of Washington. Greater international understanding, he asserted, would come about only if people acquired deeper knowledge of foreign nations. The goal of that collaboration should be human improvement and not money making.

> In my humble opinion, it is a lack of mutual acquaintance which accounts for the fact that thus far international and Pan American diplomacy have not yielded more fruitful and positive results along political and scientific lines. I refer to human rather than to geographic, commercial, or industrial relationships. The fact that a hundred American merchants know that Mexico furnishes a good market for locomotives, automobiles, and plows seems to me to be of less importance than would be a knowledge, on the part of 10 of these men, of the lives of the buyers of these things, their good and bad qualities, how they think, and some of their deepest longings and aspirations. When this comes to pass those 10 merchants will not only sell as much or more merchandise than the others, but they will be bound to their customers by spiritual ties which develop social solidarity and, in the end, international fraternity.[1]

Gamio believed that science would provide a neutral ground on which South-North and North-South exchanges could take place. Research teams that were international would produce investigations that were unbiased and untainted by "individual habits" or "alien . . . grammatical habits." Mexican and U.S. researchers would, as scientists, share methods and goals, and Gamio welcomed colleagues from the North to his country, praising the interdisciplinary team, which the Carnegie Institution had assembled to explore Yucatán, for having brought together Mexican and U.S. investigators. Wishing to extend this model, on his 1924 trip to the United States, Gamio sought to set up a series of coordinated studies converging "toward specific goals . . . [and to be] carried out in Mexico and the United States." If U.S. researchers could work in Mexico, then Mexicans could work in the United States. The magazine *Mexican American* suggested that Gamio replicate his study of Teotihuacán in the U.S. South.[2]

Beginning in 1926, Gamio would work with U.S. colleagues on a study of Mexican immigrants to the United States funded jointly by the Social Science Research Council and the Mexican government. But beyond that one study, the cross-national research of the United States he advocated did not materialize. Perhaps one reason was that Gamio's U.S. interlocutors did not consider him or his Mexican colleagues their equals. In 1931, Alfred Kidder, head of the Carnegie Institution's Division of Historical Research, gave "a cold-blooded estimate" of a plan for cross-border collaboration that Gamio had developed: "I do not regard Dr. Gamio as a first-class archaeologist. But he is probably better than any other native Mexican; and in this particular sort of investigation, which probably would not involve complicated stratigraphic observations, he would presumably do the work satisfactorily. The archaeology of the Valley of Mexico, however, does not form part of our Central problem. . . . On purely scientific grounds, it would accordingly not seem to me desirable to back Dr. Gamio." Kidder added that although Gamio was not at the moment influential in Mexico (Gamio having resigned his position as assistant secretary of education after accusing his boss of corruption), he might be in the future. It would therefore "be most desirable to retain his good will."[3] In public, Kidder and his colleagues were, like Gamio himself, more diplomatic, and their decorum supported a fair amount of goodwill between U.S. and Mexican investigators. Especially when their self-interests coincided, friendly cooperation took hold. But the belief that U.S. science was superior—indeed that science was primarily a product of the United States and the West—and consequently that U.S. scientists had the right to determine which problems were "central," undercut the possibility of more horizontal relationships based on a shared allegiance to rationality. Over the years, Gamio would reiterate his message regarding fraternal international collaboration. He garnered meager results, and eventually he soured on the project.

Mexican intellectuals articulated a science attuned to differences within and across borders. They worked within a transnational milieu shaped by projects of liberal nation-building that took the experiences of Europe and the United States as sitting at the apex of universal evolutionary processes. How, then, did the collaboration between U.S. and Mexican intellectuals shape the knowledge Mexicans produced about their country? Gamio, like other Mexican policymakers, sought to develop an applied anthropology that could unite the Mexican nation in the wake of its divisive revolutionary war.

To do so, he drew selectively from the cultural relativism of Boas, seeking to identify, preserve, and combine only those aspects of indigeneity and of Mexicanness he deemed positive. He also drew from an evolutionary faith in science, which he characterized as universal and global and therefore as the basis for both national unity and international scientific fraternity. Gamio was perhaps more adamant about the importance of science than other Mexican intellectuals. He had, after all, published a treatise on physics. But he was also a writer of fiction, and he grappled with what it meant to remain wedded to a presumably neutral secular rationalism while developing sympathy toward his fellow Mexicans.[4] Along with other Mexican indigenistas, he responded to this challenge by developing a plan for a hybrid nation that was modern but also grounded in indigenous traditions. His plan was inevitably full of inconsistencies. Amid more assimilationist, Westernizing views of modernization, he struggled to keep the plan alive.

Throughout the 1910s, 1920s, and 1930s, in print and at Pan-American conferences, Mexican and U.S. scholars engaged in extended conversation regarding the difficulties each country faced in managing difference. Despite extensive contacts and similar difficulties managing heterogeneous populations, they stressed differences in their Native policies and in their approaches to eugenics. In fact, Mexican scholars portrayed the U.S. housing of Native peoples on reservations as segregation, a mirror image of a Mexican indigenismo that sought incorporation or integration. And although some Mexicans endorsed hard-line eugenics as practiced in the United States, they were more likely to contest Anglo-U.S. and German racial doctrines aimed at excluding or containing unwanted peoples, and most adhered to a "Latin" eugenics movement that stressed nurture over nature.

National and Global Roots of State-Sponsored Professional Anthropology in Mexico

Even before Mexico's independence from Spain, the proud and civilized Aztecs had been emblems of Mexican national identity. Mexico's amateur archaeologists, abetted and assisted by their foreign counterparts, had long scoured the countryside for valuable Native antiquities that could provide clues regarding the Aztec and Mexican pasts.[5] As foreign investment poured into Mexico during the later years of the Porfiriato, the flow of foreign explorers searching for pyramids, statues, and other artifacts quickened. The Díaz government responded to foreigners' pillaging by affirming the nation's ownership of antiquities, and in 1885 it created an Inspección de

Monumentos Arqueológicos (Archaeological Monuments Inspectorate) to police archaeological activity.[6] The postrevolutionary leaders who replaced Díaz sought even tighter control over foreign archaeologists. Beginning in 1926, they prosecuted Edward Thompson, the U.S. consul in Mérida, who during the Porfiriato had shipped valuable Maya artifacts from the sacred *cenote* (well) on the Chichén Itzá hacienda to the Peabody Museum at Harvard University.[7] It was in this context, as Mexico asserted its ownership over the nation's archaeological treasures, that Mexican anthropology began to professionalize. Gamio was among the handful of students who attended Mexico's first course in ethnology, organized in 1906 by the Museo Nacional de Arqueología, Historia, y Etnología (National Museum of Archaeology, History, and Ethnology). His teachers there reflected the amateur nature of the profession in Mexico and indeed around the world. A motley crew of doctors, architects, engineers, and lawyers taught Gamio and his classmates physical anthropology, ethnology, archaeology, and linguistics (in this case, the study of Nahuatl), combining natural history with anthropology.[8]

Shortly after Gamio began his studies at the museum, Zelia Nuttall—a U.S. scholar living in Mexico City who had been appointed honorary professor at the museum—recommended Gamio to Franz Boas. While working at the American Museum of Natural History in New York, Boas had planned an expedition to the Huichol of north-central Mexico with his German friend and colleague Eduard Seler. When Boas left the museum in 1906 to take a faculty post at Columbia, they shelved the expedition. Boas nevertheless continued to plan for work in Mexico, and he wrote to Nuttall in the hopes of recruiting a Mexican who could help him. The immigrant Boas was committed to international scientific collaboration and, like Gamio, desired a cosmopolitan science. He lobbied the president of the Carnegie Institution of Washington for funding by arguing that although the "nearness" of North America made it important to U.S. scholars, work in Africa, South America, and Australia was "from an abstract scientific point of view . . . no less important." For Boas, the Americas in general and Mexico specifically provided an excellent context in which to study the global issues of acculturation that preoccupied him. By the time he wrote to Nuttall, he was already developing the idea of an international school of Americanist anthropology in Mexico, modeled after the Archaeological Institute of America's Schools of Classical Studies in Rome and Athens. The school would train anthropologists from around the world. Migration and cultural contact would be its central topics, conquest and immigration its subtexts.[9]

In November 1909, Gamio boarded a boat in Veracruz, en route to New York City and graduate study at Columbia.[10] The following September, with Díaz still in office, Boas attended the International Congress of Americanists in Mexico City—scheduled to coincide with Mexico's centennial celebrations—and finalized his plans for an International School of Archaeology and Ethnology. Participants in the Americanists' congress traveled to Teotihuacán, where the Pyramid of the Sun had been excavated for the festivities. There they ate what one participant called an "elaborate dinner" in the grotto near the pyramid.[11] According to an apocryphal story, the inspector of monuments responsible for excavating Teotihuacán had champagne carried to the top of the pyramid for his guests' breakfast.[12] Mexico displayed its archaeological acumen and refinement to the world. Later that year, Boas visited Mexico again to deliver an inaugural course at the Escuela de Altos Estudios (School of Advanced Studies) within the newly formed Universidad Nacional (National University). Boas's lectures addressed the question of race, an issue of Pan-American—indeed global—interest, and he focused in part on the use of statistics to catalog the physical characteristics of populations. The lectures were published in 1911 as *The Mind of Primitive Man*.[13]

The following year, Boas returned to Mexico to celebrate the opening of the International School. Díaz graced the inaugural ceremonies.[14] The leadership and financing of the school were to be international. The governments of Mexico, Germany, and France contributed funds along with Columbia University, Harvard University, the University of Pennsylvania, and the Hispanic Society of America. Seler became the school's first director. He would be followed by Boas, George Engerrand of the University of Texas, Alfred Tozzer of Harvard University, and Gamio. The school's main intellectual problem, according to Boas, was to identify the "succession of civilizations in the Valley of Mexico." Students and faculty did linguistic studies and collected folklore along with carrying out archaeological work—all aimed at tracking the historical diffusion of cultures. The school functioned for only four years before the tumult of revolutionary fighting and the U.S. invasion of Veracruz in 1914 forced it to close.[15]

Ethnographic Relativism and Evolution

Franz Boas advocated a historical method that tracked the internal development of dynamic cultures and their appropriation of cultural elements obtained through contact with other cultures. He criticized orthogenetic evolutionary models that posited the sources of change as internal to individuals and societies. In his view, not all cultures followed the same intrinsic evolutionary trajectory. Orthogenetic evolutionary models were inadequate because they both denied external influences and characterized development as a movement "towards our own modern civilization." Boas also criticized aspects of diffusionism, saying that it portrayed cultures as internally static and cultural change as ensuing only from external events. "We rather see that each cultural group has its own unique history," Boas explained, "dependent partly upon the peculiar inner development of the social group, and partly upon the foreign influences to which it has been subjected."[16]

Recent analyses of Gamio's thinking have suggested that he was an evolutionist who adhered incompletely if at all to Boasian relativism.[17] There is no doubt that Gamio, who began his anthropological training in Mexico during the Porfiriato, absorbed elements of the Spencerian evolutionism that had been so pronounced among Porfirian intellectuals. But especially in his early writings, Gamio evinced a cultural, religious, political, and linguistic relativism that borrowed not just from Boas but also from Mexican sources. Indeed, Mexican intellectuals had long recognized that "Mexico" was a place where cultures, from precolonial times forward, had mixed, clashed, and declined. For instance, the well-known Porfirian intellectual Justo Sierra had argued that society was a "living being" that grew, developed, and underwent transformations. Those transformations depended, he said, on "the internal energy with which the social organism reacts to external elements, assimilating them and utilizing them in the course of its growth." Equating society with a biological organism, Sierra, like Boas, viewed evolution as reflecting the interplay between external environments and the internal constitution of society. Because societies, like children, began from different starting points and had different histories, their evolution would be different as well. As minister of education under Díaz, Sierra was responsible for promoting the creation of Mexico's National University as well as the first anthropology course at the Museo Nacional, which Gamio attended, and Boas's International School.[18]

In addition, the notion that there was a singular evolutionary trajectory and that Euro-U.S. society stood at its apex had also been challenged by a new generation of Mexican intellectuals in the closing years of the Porfiriato. The influential intellectual Andrés Molina Enríquez pointed out the detrimental effects of Mexico's nineteenth-century liberal land laws, which had disentailed community lands and undermined Native communities' land base. Molina Enríquez argued that in treating all Mexicans as if they were the same, those laws had deepened inequality. It would therefore be wise to set aside liberal ideas regarding private property and amend the laws, once again allowing collective ownership of Native lands.[19] Intellectuals grouped in the association known as Ateneo de la Juventud (Atheneum of Youth) praised Mexican particularities and censured the Westernizing perspective of Porfirian elites. New prescriptions regarding Mexico's indigenous, campesino, and working-class citizens followed—prescriptions that adapted universal liberal ideals to Mexican realities.

During the revolutionary fighting, Gamio, who was working in the Inspección de Monumentos Arqueológicos, tried to make that agency into an institution that could provide ethnological data of contemporary relevance. He took inspiration from the intellectual and social ferment around him and his friend Molina Enríquez, who had argued in a 1910 paper on ethnology as a science of government that effective government might best proceed on the basis of scientific knowledge of the peoples to be governed. In a presentation to the Second Pan-American Scientific Congress in Washington, D.C., Gamio told the assembled scientists: "It is axiomatic that anthropology in its broadest, real sense, should be the basic knowledge necessary for the exercise of good government, because it is through anthropology that we come to know the population that is the raw material with which we govern and for whom we govern."[20] Policies developed and applied without regard to differences would be ineffective, and Gamio praised the Spanish colonizers for basing government on ethnographic knowledge. Ethnographic research, Gamio added, would allow state officials to adapt landholding regimes to the disparate realities of Native peoples. Fustigating the kneejerk liberalism of postindependence Mexican governments, he offered in its place a Mexican precedent: the colonial Spanish Laws of the Indies, which had not only preserved pre-Hispanic landholding traditions but also protected indigenous people from being enslaved like Africans. In stressing the pluralism of the colonial project, however, Gamio failed to comment on the inequality this colonial legislation furthered or to note Spain's assimilationist insistence that Native peoples adopt the Catholic faith.[21]

In 1917, Gamio was finally able to further his plans for ethnographically grounded policies when he convinced the secretary of agriculture and development to create the Dirección de Estudios Arqueológicos y

Etnográficos (Department of Archaeological and Ethnographic Studies, later renamed the Dirección de Antropología), tasked with collecting ethnographic data. Gamio became its first head. Boldly, Gamio peddled his model abroad. The United States and the rest of Latin America, he suggested, should adopt an ethnographic approach based on Mexico's model.[22]

Gamio believed that political institutions as well as education and landholding should be adapted to the particularities of Native peoples. He proposed that indigenous communities be allowed to choose their representatives to Congress in the manner they saw fit, even using "seemingly primitive" and "patriarchal" community assemblies. This procedure would ensure that legislation was not "unilateral and therefore inadequate for the proper government of all the social groups that make up the Nation." Here, Gamio took inspiration from the colonial legal codes of England and France as well as Spain. The United States, he further noted, set up reservations, a form of communal landholding. Latin America's democratic constitutions, he believed, could do even better in adapting their liberal political institutions to the peoples they governed. Those constitutions could not merely copy the U.S. and European ones but should rely on deep knowledge of national populations. Lucio Mendieta y Núñez, a lawyer and legal scholar who worked closely with Gamio in the department, made a similar argument in an address to the Third Pan-American Scientific Congress in 1924. Because the "indigenous classes" of Latin America were "culturally unequal" to Latin American populations of European extraction, he suggested, a system of equality before the law might harm Native peoples. Latin American nations should therefore create laws "adapted" to their indigenous peoples' "evolutionary stage," even if the acceptance of Native peoples' rudimentary habits and customary laws contradicted "abstract juridical concepts."[23] If evolution was the goal, universal laws could not at present work.

It could not have been easy for indigenistas to arrive at an ethnographic pluralism that challenged liberal precepts regarding equality before the law and regarding individual property and voting rights. To reconcile pluralism with liberalism, they asserted that the proposed special legal provisions for Native peoples would be temporary measures and later abandoned, after Native peoples had further evolved. Ethnographic and legal pluralism thus combined with evolutionary teleologies premised on the notion that Native peoples could and should move toward at least some of the behaviors that Mexico's Westernized middle classes had already adopted. "Anthropology," Gamio averred, "provides the means of characterizing the abstract and physical characteristics of men and of people and to deduce the most appropriate means of facilitating their normal evolutionary development."[24] Mendieta y Núñez likewise invoked evolutionary stages.

But even as Gamio and other indigenistas employed evolutionary perspectives, they showed ambivalence about traveling along an evolutionary path on which Native Mexicans and Mexico as a whole never seemed to be able to catch up. Mendieta y Núñez, in a footnote to his 1924 paper for the Pan-American Scientific Congress, qualified his assertion that Native peoples were at a lower evolutionary stage, saying that it applied only to "indigenous groups in a savage state." In his view, other Native groups had been, or even were, more evolved. Clearly the Aztecs had been an advanced civilization. Elsewhere in the text Mendieta y Núñez lamented that the Spanish had imposed their will without regard to what was good in Native society and that the Spanish conquest had "stopped the juridical evolution of indigenous peoples."[25] This was the dark side of Spanish colonialism that the colonial friars had opposed and that Mexican postrevolutionary nationalism would reverse. Implicit in this formulation was the view that evolution did not necessarily proceed along a singular, predetermined path. Pre-Columbian society had been evolving in its own ways, and Spain had truncated that evolution. A more autochthonous evolution might be taken up again.

Because indigenistas could not completely jettison the ideals of liberal democracy that posited formal equality before the law and market mechanisms of equivalency and interchangeability, they could not fully develop a theory of how differences might be integrated into the nation or how Mexican nationalism would differ from nationalism in the North. Even as postrevolutionary indigenistas made concerted efforts to weave difference into a liberal political order, their pluralist policies were nascent at best, and intellectuals often characterized them as temporary stopgap measures—way-stations on the road to a nation of citizens who were culturally as well as politically interchangeable, as in France and England.

Forging Mexico

Gamio anticipated Mendieta y Núñez's negative evaluation of Spanish rule in his 1916 opus *Forjando patria*, which characterized Spanish colonialism as violent, abrupt, and based on ignorance when it strayed from its respect for difference. Evolution, Gamio argued in that book, could either be "artificial" and forced or "spontaneous," "natural," and harmonious.[26]

If Spain had not overpowered the ancient Mexicans, Gamio suggested, Mexico would have advanced on a natural evolutionary path not unlike that followed by the Chinese and Japanese empires. Spain, in eschewing the advice of its missionaries, had instantiated an artificial evolution that led to ethnic violence and later spawned civil wars. As a result Mexico was now more like the former Southern African republics or Europe's African colonies, places where the Europeans violently "suffocated" and "extinguished" manifestations of indigenous life, generating conflicts and revolutions rather than spontaneous, peaceful evolution.[27]

Forjando patria used the metaphor of Latin America as a forge. Gamio was drawing, perhaps, on the "melting pot" metaphor popularized by Israel Zangwill in a play that debuted in 1908, the year Gamio arrived in the United States. Rather than look for U.S. examples, Gamio looked to the rest of Latin America. Its pre-Columbian empires, he wrote, had first sought "to mix and confuse peoples, to consummate a miraculous alloy." This was a natural evolutionary mixture, but its mold was broken by Spain, which used the iron of the Latin race but discarded the indigenous bronze as slag. Spain unilaterally substituted the European for the Native rather than fusing them harmoniously. The next attempt to forge unity came with the forceful hammer of the Latin American independence heroes, which caused Latin America to splinter. The postindependence leaders built iron statues—the new nation-states—atop bronze bases, but they were balanced precariously, and they fell. Now, Mexico's revolution would don the apron and take up the hammer so that from "the marvelous anvil" there would surge forth "the new fatherland of iron and bronze melded together."[28]

Using the forge metaphor, Gamio portrayed evolution as deliberate, creative, and based on knowledge rather than violent, competitive, aggressive, or random—characteristics more acceptable within a laissez-faire Social Darwinist framework. Gamio, perhaps discouraged by the war in Europe as well as by Latin America's copious civil wars and the Mexican Revolution itself, sought to overcome distinctions that in his view divided and weakened the nation. The reference to the Southern African republics, which had become independent of Britain only to suffer internal conflicts and again become its colonies, was in this regard telling. It was not only formal colonial rule that caused conflict; the ethnic divisions that characterized heterogeneous nation-states could also cause strife, and Gamio suggested that the divisions created by Spanish colonialism "became deeper during contemporary times, because Independence—we must admit this without hypocrisy or reservations—was carried out by groups that were European in their inclinations and origins." A divided, weak Mexican nation would be vulnerable to aggression from the North. Mexico had, after all, lost Texas to the United States. Overall, comparing Mexico to a variety of other nations and empires, Gamio concluded that contemporary Mexico was deficient. The presumed cultural unity of a republican France or an imperial Japan was, for Gamio, superior to the violence of a postcolonial Southern Africa plagued by ethnic divisions, which also fed rivalries between nations. Gamio was ambivalent not just about the effects of colonialism but also about a nationalism that imposed European culture unilaterally.[29]

Gamio desired a harmonious melding of peoples but was uncertain about what the process might look like. Different interactions would lead to different kinds of mixing: one culture might substitute for another, elements of diverse cultures might coexist, elements of one culture might blend with another, or the content of one culture might be poured into a new mold. Using a keyword that would become central in the indigenista lexicon, he argued that "incorporating" the Indian did not mean "Europeanizing" him in one swipe. Incorporation would happen gradually and with some reciprocal admixture. "Let us 'Indianize' ourselves a bit to present to him our civilization already diluted with his own, which will make our civilization less exotic, cruel, bitter, and incomprehensible," Gamio wrote. Indianization, he quickly added, should not go too far.[30] But it was in the service of that Indianization—and of the creation of a national history that recognized Mexico's roots in pre-Hispanic civilizations—that indigenistas studied the indigenous past.

As an example of a harmonious fusion not imposed by force, Gamio pointed to the "advanced and happy racial fusion" of Yucatán, where Native and Spanish "races" mixed "more harmoniously and profusely than in any other region of the Republic."[31] In the cities, everyone spoke Spanish; in the countryside, everyone spoke Maya. As a result, all Yucatecans understood each other. Things were less happy in Morelos, where the "the continuous and intimate coexistence with whites" had led pure indigenous and mixed peoples to become incorporated into white society without assimilating white cultural manifestations. This led to "a mixture that was at times an *evolutionary fusion* but at other times resulted in an *artificial, hybrid, noxious juxtaposition. The first happened* when, using the wise intuition that spontaneous evolution brings with it, they gradually adopted new cultural manifestations that were appropriate given their nature and necessities or when they transformed their original civilization, pouring it into new molds. *The second has happened*—as early as the 16th century and up to today—every time the leadership of the white race and invading culture attempted to impose with one swift blow new government, new habits, new language, new necessities . . . new life force!"[32] Spanish and creole had lived side by side with Native peoples, but they had not been drawn together.

In Quintana Roo, where geographical distance had limited Maya contact with Mexico's mestizo or white culture, postrevolutionary governments had rightly respected the Maya's request "to live their own lives in the districts that legitimately belong to them." Gamio nonetheless wondered whether it was "right to abandon those *criaturas* [babes or creatures] to a way of life that, although no doubt their own and legitimate, has helped retard the ethnic, cultural, and linguistic fusion of the population." It was reasonable, he concluded, to ask them to contribute materially and culturally to the nation. Still, the Maya should be allowed to keep their lands and left alone—for now. The intervention that would eventually be necessary should be peaceful, and "the agreement arrived at should benefit both parts proportionately and not just benefit the elements of the white race, as has happened up until now."[33]

Gamio downplayed the history of dispossession and imposition that made Native peoples resent first Spanish colonial and then national-era Euro-Mexican rule.[34] He did recognize the effects of white racism, violence, and exploitation during colonial and national governments, but he believed that they could and should be wiped away easily: "If the overwhelming weight of the historical antecedents disappears, as it will when the Indian no longer remembers the three centuries of colonial humiliation and the hundred years of humiliation of the 'independentists' that circle around him; if people stop thinking, as they do now, that he is zoologically inferior to the white; if they improve his diet, clothing, education, recreation, the Indian will embrace contemporary culture just the same as the individual of any other race."[35]

Moisés Sáenz, who as assistant secretary of education became perhaps the most important indigenista policymaker when Gamio left Mexico for the United States in 1925, voiced a similar view. Mexico, Sáenz argued, needed to "incorporate the Indian into civilization." Later refining his formula to stress nation-building over universal civilization, he argued for incorporating the Indian into "the Mexican family," then settled on the need to "*integrate* the Indian," by which he meant bringing mestizo

Mexican ways of living and thinking to Native peoples, who would then transform them into a revamped Mexican national ethos. Because whites were a minority in Mexico and because the nation's white civilization was already a bit "brown," Sáenz suggested, a uniquely Mexican civilization would emerge once the postrevolutionary state made it possible for Native peoples to experience and transform white-mestizo civilization. "If we elaborate a Mexican culture that is loyal to the native wellspring and enriched by a white stream," he wrote, "we could produce a miracle in our land, an indolatino pattern of civilization that may serve as a norm for Latin America." Incorporation, Sáenz nonetheless had to admit, would in the end whittle away those characteristics that distinguished Native peoples.[36]

In 1936, Sáenz proposed a new agency devoted specifically to assisting Native peoples. Because he recognized that Native issues had their own specificity, Sáenz accepted the need for a separate organization devoted to Native affairs. He nonetheless continued to associate segregation with proponents of "Nordic" superiority and to insist that the Mexican constitution did not admit exceptions. The rights enshrined therein applied to all, as did the agrarian laws. For that reason, Native peoples would ultimately have to learn to speak Spanish and participate in national markets. As Native values and lifeways became integrated into a mestizo Mexicanness, so would the forms of distinction that made an Indian Indian. Sentimental efforts to promote indigenous lifeways were unhelpful. "The Indian qua Indian, has no future in Mexico," he asserted. Was this a new conquest, he asked? Well, yes, it was, but a conquest aimed at giving life, not taking it away.[37]

Linking this civilizing force to a Euro-U.S. culture that might need to be counterbalanced, Sáenz suggested that every effort to homogenize or civilize lessened the particular cultures that defined localities, regions, and nations, and would likely lead to the dehumanization that characterized the machine age. "To civilize ... means to generalize, to lose something of one's own, or to limit it in order to adjust ourselves to the universal. And how can we educators proceed so that we are able to spread schooling without sacrificing the essence of our race, our genius and our culture? . . . How can we make sure that clichéd formulas do not impose themselves? How can we, to the contrary, maintain our singularity and eventually create, if possible, a plurality of cultures that can understand each other and are totally integrated?"[38]

Sáenz had to admit that homogenization was in some ways inevitable. To unite Mexico, mestizos, whites, and Native peoples would have to comingle biologically, culturally, politically, and spiritually. This should be, as Gamio suggested, a peaceful and harmonious blending: "Let us not violate; let us cloak ourselves in humility," Sáenz wrote. "Let us be amenable to compromise, remembering that the Mexican ideal and the Mexican norm are in the process of formation." Indigenistas, he claimed, should express "the yearnings of those people who have lived in Mexico without being heard, people whom we now wish to make our own, not through a violating conquest but through an integrating deed that will establish a common ideal expressed in terms of particular desires." Using the term *violar* (to violate) as opposed to *violencia* (violence), Sáenz implicitly distinguished the harmonization he sought from a gendered and sexualized conquest.[39] It would presumably be more like a marriage of equals. Yet his very invocation of sexual violence underscored the possibility of hierarchies both gendered and racial.

Evolution and Science

Gamio's confidence in postrevolutionary leaders' ability to promote a harmonious national fusion stemmed from his faith in science and knowledge as tools of peaceful evolution. Science, he wrote, produced "better practical results, contributing with greater efficiency to the production of material and intellectual well-being, the principal goal [*tendencia*] of all human activity."[40] Unlike other cultural forces that might lead to improvement or decline, science followed an ascendant trajectory, based on truly novel discoveries. "Notwithstanding sophistic affirmations that apply the fatalistic '*nihil novum sub sole*' to science," Gamio explained, "in practice no one has been able to demonstrate the existence in historical times of the new conclusions of physics, chemistry, mechanics, cosmography."[41] Native peoples would readily accept scientific advances, Gamio believed, because science was the true ground of universality and unity, and this viewpoint tended to blunt Gamio's tolerance of difference. Still, Gamio did not see evolution as necessarily internal to a given society, predetermined, or singular.

Gamio further argued that science would bind Mexicans of all stripes and unite Mexico with the rest of the world. When Gamio served as head of the Inspección de Monumentos Arqueológicos in 1915–16, he told the Second Pan-American Scientific Congress that collaboration between foreigners and Mexicans was "indispensable" to a well-rounded scientific process. Although new Mexican legislation would safeguard his country's archaeological patrimony, the country would maintain a "liberal" attitude toward foreign researchers.[42] Universally valid science, Gamio implied, had to be based on collaboration across borders. Scientists were, "because of their communion of ideas, a universal fraternity," he reiterated in *Forjando patria*. In a 1923 essay in which he declared himself an "internationalist," Gamio further claimed that Mexican intellectuals were similar to their French, English, German, and American counterparts "of advanced ideals." Engaging in the "continual exchange of ideas with foreign institutions and intellectuals," the Mexicans swam in "the newest currents of thinking that are leading the way in the advanced countries." Gamio added, however, that "as compatriots of our brothers, ten million beings who struggle in an indigenous civilization that is several centuries behind, we think in a different way, as nationalists. We get rid of our modernist yearnings, which seek only that which is on the highest level of progress. We descend toward those Mexican pariahs. We live their lives and penetrate their souls, so as to understand the right methods of helping them to slowly but effectively reincorporate themselves."[43]

Once Mexico's Native peoples had been uplifted, Mexico might become part of the international federation to which Gamio aspired. Until then, to participate in such a federation would be to submit foolishly to control by the members from the more advanced nations.[44] Gamio thus saw science as the most desirable feature of Western modernity and U.S. and European scientific superiority as justifying, in part, their global dominance. Indigenistas' embrace of science justified, moreover, their dominance at home—as long as they did not act violently or divisively. Gamio accepted a measure of modernity that placed all Mexicans and especially Native peoples in an inferior position, even if only temporarily; science would unite the nation and improve and evolve its citizens.

Over time and perhaps as a result of his greater contact with the United States, Gamio became more aware of the danger of associating science with the West. When Gamio published a revised version of his 1923 essay in 1934, he characterized the "newest currents of thought" not as coming from the "advanced countries" but as simply "contemporary." "Foreign institutions and intellectuals" became "Mexican and foreign institutions and intellectuals," and he got rid of references to French, English, German, and American intellectuals. He now maintained that foreign ideals would be transmitted and translated by Mexicans.[45]

Gamio harbored no illusions about being able to prove that Mexico was civilized within the parameters set by the Northern Atlantic nations.

When he argued, as he often did, in favor of "contemporary" civilization, he did not mean a white European civilization. In his view, Mexico's "contemporary civilization" would not be a perfect copy of Northern examples, and this was perfectly fine since evolution was not in his view "unilateral." Native Mexican lifeways were not just part of a glorious truncated past. Some of those traditions might provide resources for the future. Mexico could reach back to its ancient Aztec and Maya civilizations for advanced artistic achievements, and some Native healing traditions might prove as useful as Western medicine. Native peoples were better adapted, physically and culturally, to Mexico's diverse geography and climate. "Tradition," Gamio wrote, "would miraculously transform itself in a thousand ways while maintaining its unity and typicality." It would become more modern but remain Mexican. From this perspective, Mexico's middle class could be the genesis of Mexican cultural unity, but it would need to reject "exotic" European culture and embrace indigenous cultural manifestations. Gamio harshly castigated renegade members of the middle class who embraced European culture, branding them "pedants and imbeciles." By contrast, the middle class's embrace of Native ways was understandable, given that the Mexican "physico-biological-social environment"—the crucible of Mexico—had shaped the bodies and minds of middle-class Mexicans.[46] In contrast to those who viewed the United States as the land of the new, where old ways were cast aside and self-creation prevailed, Gamio invoked history, looking at the past for clues about how to build a better future. It was the place—Mexico—the forge, perhaps, that most mattered. Its history needed to be learned and taught. Unlike a United States that some perceived as an empty land, a frontier to be civilized, Mexico had always been the crucible of civilizations.[47]

In sum, Gamio and other indigenistas responded to Mexico's problematic relation to modernity by positing evolution itself as multiple rather than universal. This formulation held out the hope that Mexico could be modern without simply following a preordained path based on Euro-U.S. trajectories. Gamio and his colleagues nonetheless accepted the notion that Mexico was, at least for now, backward. Science would help Mexico evolve on its own terms, but evolve it must. To address specific practical needs based on different societies' distinct evolutionary paths, Gamio argued that Western science needed to be adapted. Mexican indigenistas would become part of a universal scientific fraternity by articulating a science that was *national*. Mexican scientific endeavors should "rest on general precepts [*bases*] that are universally applicable, but we must adapt them to the particular social, biological, ethnic, etc., etc., conditions that characterize our population." The stepping stones to the airplane, automobile, and astral orbits—he added—were not just Icarus and the philosopher's stone but also the Egyptian pulley and the Aztec calendar. Gamio foresaw a distant future of greater national and even global homogeneity, a precondition for peaceful coexistence, but there was also ample room for different starting points and even divergence.[48]

Another, related response to Eurocentric formulations of progress—one that would become even more prevalent in the 1930s and 1940s—was to break modernity into its constituent parts and to recognize that not all parts moved in unison. Although the capacity of science to create a better life gave it precedence, Gamio wrote, science was only one part of Western culture: "It seems opportune to reflect on whether the most cultured people possesses the greatest morality, the best aesthetic criteria, the greatest scientific knowledge, the highest intellectualism, is in sum at once rich and powerful. I must confess at the outset that such a people with such superior talent harmoniously put together would be the most cultured. But where is it? A human group showing that precious integration has never existed." In Egypt and Rome, material wealth and an artistic renaissance had been accompanied by moral laxity. Moreover, peoples advanced by fits and start. Witness the carnage in Europe! "Before," he wrote, "men busted the crania of their enemies to expel them from their caverns and take them over. Today they use poison gases, products of a marvelous chemistry, to wring from them territory and commerce—a question of methods."[49] This response made room for the uneven nature of historical developments. But it also promoted intellectuals as the ultimate arbiters. Scientists would determine which aspects of an already existing modernity should be adopted and which rejected or transformed.

Mexican Integration and U.S. Segregation

When the Mexican Congress established the Secretaría de Educación Pública in 1921, it hoped to spread schooling throughout the country, especially to rural and indigenous areas, and to secure federal control over instruction. Schools were not just to teach the basics of reading and arithmetic but also to function as social centers that provided all community members with tools for improving their insertion into the national economy and learning the national language—in short, for becoming Mexican. The SEP soon became the principal locus for policymaking toward indigenous communities, especially after Gamio's Dirección de Estudios Arqueológicos y Etnográficos shuttered in 1924.

The first secretary of the SEP was José Vasconcelos (1921–24), a noted intellectual and staunch assimilationist who believed that Mexico's indigenous people should meld into a mestizo nation. In contrast to Gamio and Sáenz, Vasconcelos felt that policies toward Native peoples should not depart from policies toward rural people in general. Thus when Congress mandated the establishment of the Departamento de Cultura y Educación Indígena (Department of Indigenous Culture and Education) within the SEP in 1922, Vasconcelos opposed it, arguing that a separate system of schools for indigenous people was tantamount to segregation. Vasconcelos eventually gave in to the demand for distinct forms of schooling for Native youth, but he did so, he said, only because it might prepare them for later entry to regular schools. José Manuel Puig Casauranc, who replaced Vasconcelos as secretary of education (1924–28), held similar views and approved of the new Casa del Estudiante Indígena (Indigenous Students' Home), a boarding school in Mexico City, only because its charges were to attend the same schools as the city's nonindigenous children. Rafael Ramírez, who served for a time as head of the Departamento de Cultura y Educación Indígena and was a key figure in educational circles throughout the 1920s, argued similarly. Although Ramírez recognized that rural education could not be a carbon copy of urban education, he argued that both pursued similar goals, and he strenuously advocated the teaching of Spanish as a key tool of assimilation.[50]

The views of Vasconcelos, Puig Casauranc, and their deputies did not go unchallenged. Congress had, after all, mandated the creation of the Departamento de Cultura y Educación Indígena, and Gamio stressed the need for policies adapted to the realities of Mexico's regions and grounded in knowledge of ethnic and racial differences. Embodying these divergent impulses were the SEP's rural education projects, especially its cultural missions, which were tasked with training teachers who would extend schooling to previously ignored rural pockets of the nation. The missions reached back to the colonial era for models and were styled after those of the Franciscan and Dominican friars who studied, befriended, and evangelized the pre-Columbian people that inhabited the territory of Mexico. The SEP produced a series of pamphlets detailing the lives of these friars and commissioned portraits of them to hang in the SEP offices. As the notion of secular evangelization implied, the missions aimed to assimilate Native peoples. Yet in an effort to soften that assimilationist push and the liberal emphasis on the sameness of citizens, SEP officials also stressed that the friars were ethnographers. Sáenz noted that the postrevolutionary state, "inflamed by a revolutionary fervor . . . a fiery ministry," was made up of men who acted like "priests, ministers, and prophets," with all the good and bad that preaching implied. No one said much about the violence that had cleared the way for the colonial era missions.[51]

Gamio, too, foregrounded the friars' ethnography and veneration of difference. In a 1925 lecture he gave in the United States while serving as assistant secretary of education, he explained that anthropological research had been going on in Mexico for four hundred years: "Sahagún, Landa, Durán and other colonial chroniclers," he said of the friars, "set forth in their works the direct observations they made of the racial characteristics of the conquered indigenous people."[52]

As SEP teachers effected a new conquest of unknown territories and spread into the far corners of the country, they too filled out questionnaires detailing what they saw. The SEP's Departamento de Cultura y Educación Indígena planned to gather statistics on Mexico's indigenous races and languages, and it programmed a meeting of SEP missionaries to "adapt systems and methods of teaching" to different local conditions. The department's director toured indigenous regions to better understand the problems at hand, and he recruited speakers of Native languages as schoolteachers. At times, proposals favored a fairly radical pluralism, with SEP officials proposing that instruction take place in Native languages even at the university level. A 1923 SEP bulletin argued that the Departamento de Cultura y Educación Indígena should become an autonomous institution, one that would presumably tailor its policies to the specific populations it served.[53]

Vasconcelos, by contrast, embodied an assimilationist impulse that he justified by equating pluralism with segregation and exclusion. The SEP secretary had spent significant time in the United States, and he often invoked harmful U.S. policies as counterexamples. Speaking in 1922 to an audience in Washington, D.C., for instance, Vasconcelos told the "numerous partisans of creating special schools for Indians" that he had always been against creating U.S.-type reservations that "divided the population by caste and skin color." Mexico sought to "totally assimilate the Indian into our nationality," he asserted, not to "shunt him aside." Citing the friars of the colonial era, he characterized Mexico as "adapting the Indian to European civilization," creating a new race and a new country without isolating or killing as the United States had.[54]

Vasconcelos was an idealist who contrasted the pernicious materialism of U.S. society to the spirituality of Mexicans and other Latin Americans who were part of a providential "cosmic race." According to his historical account of the European conquest of the Americas, Spain had colonized through persuasion—the missionary ideal—rather than violence, whereas English settlers, in conquering a harsh geography and climate, had become stronger, setting the stage for their heirs' global ascendance. Yet he predicted that the power of the U.S. inheritors of English civilization would eventually decline, and in its place, a Latin American cosmic race would combine the material successes of "white" civilization with the artistic and spiritual merits of Latin America to create a worldwide racial fusion. Thus Vasconcelos, like Gamio, favored international as well as national unity. But he forcefully used the negative example of U.S. racial segregation, exclusion, and capitalist competition to argue for Mexico's trajectory of racial amalgamation as a positive example for other nations and indeed the world. Where Gamio fluctuated between seeing Mexico as similar to the United States in that it followed scientific advances but different in that it would build from distinct foundations, Vasconcelos stressed the differences. He contrasted a mestizo Mexico grounded in Spanish culture, which incorporated difference through its expansive spirit, to an exclusionary, segregationist United States.[55]

En route to the cosmic race, according to Vasconcelos, Spanish culture would modernize and Hispanicize the Indian: "The Indian has no door to the future that does not follow the path cleared by Latin civilization." But although the characteristics of whites might predominate in the cosmic race, this could come about only through "free choice according to taste and not as the result of violence or economic pressure."[56] Whites would also have to make difficult choices, setting aside their pride and finding redemption by embracing the soul of other "castes" and "varieties of the species."[57] Vasconcelos thus refuted Anglo-U.S. eugenic arguments that characterized variety and the mixing of different "castes" as leading to degeneration. And he repudiated U.S. desires for racial purity as well as the violence and segregation of the United States. At the same time, Vasconcelos showed disdain for blacks and believed that the distance between whites and blacks was greater than the distance between whites and Indians. That Indians could act as a bridge linking whites and blacks was one advantage Mexico had over the United States.[58]

Sáenz, who had studied education in the United States in 1921–22, also compared Mexico with the United States to underscore Mexican tolerance and liberal inclusion. It was in part, he said, the threat of Mexico's neighbor to the North, which claimed for itself a universal culture, that made Mexican national unity so urgent. "The eternal measuring of our people with the set square made by Nordic peoples exposes us to the disappointment of an apparent failure and downgrades Mexico to the role of second fiddle in an orchestra of Whites," he wrote.[59] Mexico needed to sketch its own, original "national physiognomy" internally, but also "face to face with other peoples."[60] As it had for Vasconcelos, the contrast with North America allowed Sáenz to underscore the uniqueness of Mexico's path. The United States homogenized not just its population and culture but also, through its "mechanical civilization," the land itself: "Because of their cowardice or pragmatism, those people reject variation; they prefer to govern themselves with rules that can be applied easily and assuredly. The most stubborn minority groups—the blacks and the Indians—do not pose an ethnic problem for the prevailing pragmatic philosophy because the Americans have excluded both of them from the spiritual community, locking the former up in 'reservations' and ignoring the latter. If they share their national life with the rest . . . they do so by employing a general model and a conventional law."[61] Intellectual generalizations went hand in hand with racial assimilation.

Other Mexicans shared Sáenz's misgivings regarding the repeated use of Anglo-American eugenics to disparage Mexicans. Vasconcelos clearly aimed to refute the racism of those like the eugenicist Madison Grant, who touted the supremacy of the "Nordic race": "It is not by suppressing differences that progress opens its way, it is through differences—deeply inspired sincere differences—that the human soul has made all of its conquests." Further criticizing the notions of racial purity that characterized U.S. Social Darwinism, Vasconcelos asserted that the Europeans who populated the United States were themselves an amalgam of European stocks.[62]

The U.S. system of categorizing Native peoples by blood quantum functioned, along with the creation of geographically separate reservations, as a counterpoint. Sáenz argued, for instance, that biological heritage, the characteristic on which the United States relied for racial categorization, was inaccurate when considered alone. It should instead be considered alongside differences in language, forms of governance, and artisanal and artistic practices. Doing so would no doubt make it difficult to separate Indians and mestizos, and that difficulty would be amplified as economic forces erased differences between ethnicities and cultures. Racial mixing and acculturation, Sáenz observed, would put "the subtlety of ethnographers to the test." If Native peoples spoke Spanish, rode in trucks, and sold their goods in the cities, then specific policies aimed at them would be unnecessary even if they were by other measures Indian.[63] This institutional solution rejected categorical difference in favor of a sliding scale of indigeneity.

Sáenz's observations on such challenges built on long-standing debates within Mexico. The country's 1895 census had eschewed racial labels altogether, and the 1910 census had used language as a proxy for race and culture. In the aftermath of the revolution, indigenistas remained wary of unilateral measurements. Gamio repeatedly observed that many people classified as white on the census because they spoke Spanish in fact lived like Indians. In urban areas, many supposed Indians possessed, like whites, the "characteristics of modern culture." Millions of people spoke both Spanish and a Native language but refused to tell the census enumerator that they were bilingual. Rather than the approximately 2 million people categorized as indigenous in the 1895 and 1910 censuses, Gamio believed that perhaps as many as 8 million to 10 million Mexicans should be categorized as Native. Sáenz estimated 4 million in 1932 and then more than 2.25 million in 1936, based on the 1930 census.[64]

Given the difficulties of categorization and Mexicans' inability—or lack of desire—to definitively resolve the issue, it is not surprising that the SEP's Departamento de Cultura y Educación Indígena eventually came to handle all rural schools, becoming the Departamento Rural de Incorporación Indígena (Department of Rural Indigenous Incorporation), also referred to as the Departamento Rural y de Incorporación Indígena. The shifting nomenclature itself suggested uncertainty about whether "rural" and "indigenous" were interchangeable.[65] Schoolteachers and local administrators did not find it easier than census officials to figure out who was who. At Mexico City's Casa del Estudiante Indígena, the pure Indians that the SEP hoped to recruit were allegedly crowded out by rural mestizos. And once the casa's Native residents learned Spanish and urban ways, they were loath to return to their communities.[66] They had become mestizos. As Sáenz noted, inhabitants of the Native community (*fundo*) could easily cross over into the valley of the *ejidatarios* (non-Native members of the ejido). And since campesinos and Native peoples were culturally equidistant from urban lifeways, indigenous incorporation could easily become campesino incorporation.[67]

To the extent that indigenistas could claim that Native peoples were part of an impoverished rural majority, they articulated a strategy of inclusion compatible with liberalism and differentiated themselves from U.S. intellectuals, who could marginalize Native peoples because they were a minority. By defining Native peoples as a majority, postrevolutionary indigenistas also placed the solution to the problems that Native communities faced within broader programs aimed at rural peoples. Paradoxically, this definition also made indigeneity, and the cultural attributes of rural peoples, more central to the project of forging a nation.

Child Welfare, Population, and Immigration in the Age of Eugenics

Efforts to ameliorate the Mexican population racially, economically, and culturally extended beyond rural reform to encompass policies toward urban residents and immigration. Mexican physicians, educators, and public health officials concerned with these groups participated in Pan-American and global circles that debated reforms related to hygiene, health care, and education, but Mexicans were aware that U.S. scientific measures and paradigms, and anthropometric and intelligence tests especially, might reinforce ideas regarding Mexican and "Latin" inferiority, and they therefore used those concepts with caution. Most Mexican experts distanced themselves from U.S. eugenics.

It appears that no Mexicans attended the 1912 First International Eugenics Conference in London but did participate in the international eugenic conferences held in New York in 1921 and 1932, as well as the First Pan-American Conference on Eugenics and Homiculture, held in 1927 in Havana, and the Second, held in 1934 in Buenos Aires.[68] The International Union for the Scientific Investigation of Population Problems, formed in 1928, provided another forum for debating eugenic policies, as did organizations devoted to child welfare in which feminists played key roles. The First Pan-American Child Congress in Buenos Aires (1916) was organized by Argentine feminists after two failed attempts to form a global child protection agency; subsequent child congresses took place in Uruguay (1919), Brazil (1922), Chile (1924), Cuba (1927), Peru (1930), Mexico (1935), and the United States (1942). Mexico held its First Child Congress in 1921 and a second in 1923.[69]

The year of Mexico's First Child Congress, 1921, was the same year that the SEP began to function. The 1921 congress led to the establishment of a private Commission to Study the Mexican Child and a short-lived School Hygiene Department of the Department of Public Health. Eventually, the SEP itself set up a Departamento de Psicopedagogía e Higiene (Psychopedagogy and Hygiene Department) that continued the anthropometric measurement of schoolchildren that had begun during the Porfiriato.[70] Officials from the SEP attempted to gauge the abilities of large numbers of individual schoolchildren through tests. By identifying physical abnormalities and illnesses, they hoped to correct them, for instance by providing eyeglasses to students whose families could not afford them. They also sought to accommodate children by giving teachers special instructions. If children had circulatory or cardiac problems, for example, they were not to exercise vigorously. When correction or accommodation did not seem feasible or deviations were extreme, SEP officials believed that students needed be segregated and given special instruction. Education was more efficient when it took place in homogeneous groups, the educators believed.[71]

To make determinations about ability, physicians and other experts sought out non verbal tests that were easily applied to large groups and could adequately measure Mexican schoolchildren, such as the Army Beta test, developed to select U.S. military recruits, or the Otis intelligence test. On a trip to California, Rafael Santamarina, who would later head the SEP's Departamento de Psicopedagogía, learned that U.S. medical norms needed to be adjusted: he saw the problematic fashion in which tests were applied to Mexican American children, who were judged—erroneously in his view—as deficient.[72] He had already begun this process of adjustment, and he presented results at Mexico's 1921 Child Congress.[73] Gamio, echoing Santamarina in his study of Mexican migration to the United States, counseled that tests created in the United States and administered in English could not adequately measure the intelligence of Mexican children. He labeled these tests racist: "The mental capacity of a Mexican child is probably normal, although some investigators conclude that he is mentally inferior to an American child of the same age—a conclusion probably affected by racial attitudes and by a translation into terms of mental competence of differences in economic and cultural position."[74] In general, tests would need to be not only chosen carefully and translated into Spanish but also adapted. Norms for Mexican students needed to be determined.

While serving as assistant secretary of the SEP, Sáenz was similarly concerned with adapting norms to Mexico and its diverse populations. To this end, in 1926–28 he authorized Montana Lucia Hastings, who had studied at Columbia University, to carry out intelligence tests among students at the Casa del Estudiante Indígena as part of her broader study of Mexico City secondary schools. Hastings had first come to Mexico in 1922 to adapt and develop tests for the San Diego public school system, which was trying to classify its Mexican student population. In Mexico, she worked with colleagues at Mexico's National University and in the SEP to figure out whether existing tests worked for "different nationalities and different races." She was especially concerned with the effects of language proficiency on performance on the Army Beta test and the arithmetic portion of the Otis intelligence test. In the United States, the growing presence of immigrant children in the schools, along with employers' need to select workers whose aptitudes were aligned with the work they would perform, made evident the need for intelligence tests for those with limited English-language abilities. Language was of course an issue at the Casa del Estudiante Indígena as well, but as Hastings soon learned, that was not the only obstacle. Casa residents also tested poorly because they were not familiar with the format of the tests Hastings applied. Hastings concluded that indigenous students' intelligence could not be adequately measured by the same tests as that of non-Native children. But because no other tests were available, Hastings administered the same test to each Native student twice and took the improvement in scores as an indication of the students' capacity to learn.[75] Hastings and her SEP colleagues thus struggled to adequately compare intelligence across nations and ethnic groups—Native children in Mexico, Mexican children in California and Mexico City—using a presumably universal measure. They bumped up against the difficulty of applying tests initially developed to study Euro-U.S. students who spoke their country's national language.

Following the neo-Lamarckian view that environments shaped bodily health and development, the SEP focused not just on the students themselves but also on their living and studying conditions.[76] School inspections, for instance, focused on ensuring that schools provided healthy physical and moral environments. School buildings were subjected to intense scrutiny: Were they clean? Sturdy? The right temperature? Were there vermin? Bathrooms? Was there running water? And what about the children themselves? Did they attend school regularly? Were they able to wash their hands and bathe? Did they have lice or infectious diseases of the skin? Had they been vaccinated? Did they get proper nutrition? Exercise? Nurses made home visits to ensure that children's home environments were materially and morally sound as well—though the hygienists complained that there were too few doctors and nurses even within Mexico City. School hygiene efforts involved instructing children, teachers, and mothers regarding cleanliness. Physicians and educators also advocated the cultivation of "physical culture" and cautioned that too much mental effort, if not balanced with proper physical exercise, would exhaust children's fragile bodies.[77] The goal of school hygiene was, Dr. Carlos Jiménez said in a radio address to teachers, "to form a strong and healthy race by caring for children's health and seeking a harmonious physical, intellectual, and moral development."[78]

Biologically determinist eugenic perspectives also found a place within efforts to fortify Mexican children and the Mexican race. For instance, the Second Mexican Child Congress, held in 1923, included sessions on "normal and pathological family inheritance so as to . . . be able to avoid or cure degenerations and illnesses." Participants looked for ways to discourage antieugenic marriages. Thinking about whether Mexico should encourage immigration, participants studied "the character of—and biological adaptations between—mestizos of Mexican and of other races."[79] (They characterized Europeans as mestizos rather than pure races.) Some of the eugenic measures proposed were quite radical. One participant in the First Child Congress argued for a resolution against procreation with black or yellow races: "The world owes the most to white men and we therefore deduce the utility of favoring his immigration in order to incite crosses that favor our race." This resolution failed to pass, but a proposal for the castration (*asexuación*) of criminals was endorsed, albeit after vigorous debate and by a slim margin. The congress's rapporteur downplayed the vote, noting that it "revealed the discordant opinions on such a thorny issue."[80]

As the Pan-American Child Congresses moved from Uruguay, Brazil, and Chile to locations closer to the United States (Cuba, Mexico, and the United States), proposals for negative eugenic measures and harsh immigration restrictions became more prevalent. Yet Latin Americans spoke out against the harshest measures, and at the First Pan-American Congress of Eugenics and Homiculture, held in Cuba in 1927, Latin Americans defeated a measure that *required* countries to refuse entry to "individuals classified as unhealthy." They also voted down a proposal that the American nations could pass immigration laws that denied access to "representatives of races with which they considered association to be undesirable." Those two proposals were downgraded to recommendations rather than the binding resolutions for which the U.S. delegates hoped.

Rafael Santamarina spoke out against a U.S. proposal for the testing of all entering immigrants.[81]

As eugenics and child health figured more prominently in international debates in the 1920s, Gamio also wrote copiously on population, health issues, demography, and reproduction. Gamio broached these issues in 1923 in a short story titled "Sterility" and a scholarly companion essay, "Celibacy and the Development of the Mexican Population."[82] Both pieces condemned the sterility of urban women of European descent, who by failing to bolster Mexico's demographic strength weakened Mexico's position within the international consort of nations. Both pieces praised the prolific nature of indigenous and rural women. Gamio argued, albeit with some caveats, that the rural and lower classes were a resource for the nation and that the country's evolution lay in following indigenous traditions that were healthier and closer to nature—an anti-Malthusian view that would later become a hallmark of Latin eugenics.

In "Sterility," Luisa, a young city woman, visits a pregnant sister living in the countryside. Seeing that her sister—like, perhaps, the prerevolutionary Mexican countryside itself—has suffered a grave physical decline, Luisa becomes terrified of pregnancy and once back in the city avoids her husband's sexual advances. Finding life unbearable without his attentions but not knowing what to do, she confides in the nursemaid who raised her, and the nursemaid puts her in touch with an indigenous healer who can make her sterile. The healer brings her to the brink of death. Once recovered, she tires of her carefree life in the city and returns to her sister's home for a visit. There, she finds her sister recovered from the pregnancy and once again radiant, like the countryside revitalized by a hard rain or by a postrevolutionary agrarian policy. Disturbed by the realization of her error, Luisa becomes even more frenzied when on her way home she stops at the rustic house of a poor rural family with eight children. The chubby hostess answers a friendly question about whether she wants more children with a hearty "yes." Children bring happiness amid poverty, the woman tells Luisa, and avoiding them would make the woman a traitor to her race (*descastada*). Luisa, now realizing the folly of her visit to the Native healer, takes her own life.[83]

Gamio's academic essay reiterated the story's message. Celibacy did not exist among Native peoples, he wrote there. Native women had a "normal sexual evolution" and desired children. Women of the white race, by contrast, ignored their legitimate bodily desires and became crazed as a result. For indigenous people, money—the scourge of the

Anglo-Saxon race—was not an obstacle to marriage and child-rearing, while for whites economic concerns dictated decisions regarding marriage, thereby contributing to the overall stagnation of Mexico's population. Although modernity had improved well-being, Gamio concluded, it had also led to the denaturalization of physiological life. Nutrition, housing, dress, and sexual functions had become molded by economic, social, and political considerations rather than organic, bodily needs.[84]

In both pieces, Gamio hinted but did not overtly argue that Mexico's population needed to be more culturally or racially European. White women should reproduce. Native peoples represented demographic vigor but also illness and death, as personified by the backward indigenous healer who by seeking to defy nature had brought Luisa to the verge of death. Still, Gamio suggested, Mexico's population could evolve harmoniously if it stayed close to its indigenous roots and the Mexican soil.

Gamio wrote these pieces not long after serving as second vice-president of the 1921 Second International Eugenics Conference in New York. *Ethnos*, a journal Gamio created and edited, proudly reprinted Charles Davenport's invitation to serve in that position.[85] *Ethnos* also reported a preliminary conference program. According to *Ethnos*, the program would include sessions on the prior First Universal Races Congress, held in London in 1911, and the works of William Ripley and Madison Grant. Grant's work was deeply racist. The 1911 Universal Races Congress was a cosmopolitan antiracist meeting aimed at generating understanding among the diverse peoples of the world. Were participants in the 1921 eugenics congress going to discuss the 1911 antiracist meeting? Or was the 1921 conference in fact going to discuss the First International Eugenics Congress of 1912? Perhaps *Ethnos* conveniently conflated the Universal Races Congress of 1911 (praised in a previous issue of the journal) and the First International Eugenics Congress of 1912, both held in London. The latter is quite possible, given that the proceedings of the Universal Races Congress had been published as *Papers on Inter-Racial Problems*, and after his return from the 1921 conference, Gamio stressed that he had participated in the anthropological discussion of "inter-racial problems" but not, he said, in the merely eugenic discussion of the biological betterment of the human races. Gamio was apparently uncomfortable with more hard-line biological views he encountered at the 1912 meeting.[86]

In part because they were uncomfortable with those views, Mexican indigenistas began to participate in the Latin eugenics movement promoted by the Italian Corrado Gini, who, like the Mexicans, opposed "Nordic" eugenics.[87] The Mexican demographer Gilberto Loyo studied with Gini in Rome,[88] as did the Mexican agronomist, statistician, and economist Emilio Alanís Patiño, who later directed the Mexico's national census office.[89] In the early 1930s, Gini collaborated with a team of Mexican researchers to study race mixing and demographic changes in several regions of Mexico. They measured almost two thousand individuals to determine whether the physical isolation of biologically mixed populations would lead to racial genesis or cause the extermination of very small populations through inbreeding.[90]

Was it preferable, Gini asked, to breed like with like and let the weak die out or to attenuate damage through racial crossing? Hybridity, he suggested, might lead to a greater number of more exceptional individuals, especially if a population was on average inferior but had a high variability and therefore many exceptional individuals. Gini's research in Mexico replicated his earlier research on European populations. Gainsaying U.S. efforts to restrict immigration and its isolation of Native groups, both of which hampered genetic intermixture and could therefore lead to degeneration, Gini's work sat comfortably with Mexicans and other Latin Americans who sought to redeem the mixed nature of their populations and bring isolated peoples into contact. In fact, Gini's Latin eugenics replicated key aspects of Latin American ideals of mestizaje, and Gini openly praised José Vasconcelos for proclaiming the superiority of the mestizo Latin American race.[91]

Gini's Latin eugenics also built on and modified Vilfredo Pareto's notion that there were exceptional individuals in all social strata. An Italian, Pareto was a laissez-faire Social Darwinist who believed that natural selection would itself lead to social betterment and therefore rejected artificial eugenic selection. Gini disagreed and argued instead that the environment was as important as heredity in determining a person's capacity. From Gini's perspective, governments could and should manipulate environments. This view resonated with a Mexican neo-Lamarckian meliorism grounded in education and hygiene. Revamping neo-Lamarckian views in response to an increasingly popular Mendelianism, Gini insisted that intense use of a given function might lead to modifications of the germ plasm, and the germinal characters of a population might evolve over time as groups of individuals were exposed to similar environments. This was a nondeterministic view of biology, which Gini made compatible with the new theories of hereditary transmission by invoking mutation theory and arguing that environmental factors could spur mutations that would then be passed down.[92]

At the 1931 International Congress on Population Problems, organized by Gini in Rome, Gamio took up the topic of international migration to Mexico and the rest of Latin America.[93] His paper lamented the relative lack of demographic growth in Latin America, which he attributed to the physical unsuitability of potential European immigrants to the region's agriculturally rich tropical climates. The anthropologist further argued that the population increase in Latin American countries might appear normal, but once one looked at the spectacular demographic growth of Canada, Argentina, and the United States, it became evident that most Latin American countries had not evolved normally. This was particularly dangerous for Mexico, which bordered on "a gigantic country," whose population had grown a hundredfold in a century—an "intolerable excess of population." For Mexico and Latin America, Gamio suggested, demographic growth seemed of the utmost urgency. "What direction," he asked, "is best for the Indo-Iberian people of Mexico at this time when the white race has not only invaded a good part of the American Continent but also is effectively on its way to occupying all of it?" Given the U.S. designs on Latin America and the need to augment the national population, Gamio favored increased immigration. Cultural mixing, he added, would quicken the evolution that Mexicans might otherwise achieve by educating its Native peoples.[94]

Conclusion

Mexican indigenismo and Mexican eugenics were neither univocal nor static. Gini's Latin eugenics, like the views of Santamarina, Gamio, and Vasconcelos, constructed rather than merely reflected differences among nations. Gamio and his fellow indigenistas recognized heterogeneity, and they argued for a science adapted to Mexico's geography and history. Yet their desire for a strong nation led them not just to desire a degree of homogenization among the population but also at times to posit the sort of homogenizing categories that would allow Mexico and Mexican intellectuals to participate in the international fraternity of science. Gini's Latin eugenics and its Mexican supporters provided another route for escaping the predicaments posed by North Atlantic claims of superiority. Harnessing Mendelian genetics without jettisoning the notion of a hereditary germ plasm, Gini and his collaborators focused on how culture and environment shaped heredity. Intentional separation and mixing, as well as the effects of geographic environments that were themselves mutable, could modify a people's genetic makeup. Latin eugenicists sought improvement: better health leading to bigger populations, stronger and more intelligent workers, a harmonious citizenry. But they saw diversity and mixing as constructive rather than destructive.

In general, Gamio and Mexican intellectuals, along with Mexican policymakers, clearly saw that the injustices that had bred revolution could not be fully addressed within a liberal social order that posited a kind of race-blind equality. And as heirs to a popular revolution they felt compelled to address grievances without violence or coercion. Science, they argued, would show the way by accelerating natural evolutionary processes or reversing the degeneration that had been caused by the imposition of lifeways that did not blend harmoniously with existing customs. But if science might guide an artificial cultural evolution, it could not be the same science deployed in the United States. Evolution might proceed along different paths, albeit heading perhaps in the same general direction. Even central tenets of liberalism such as private property or political representation might need to be adjusted, at least in the short term. Mexican civilization would not be identical to that of the Europe or the United States. At the same time, the writings of these postrevolutionary scholars and politicians were littered with judgments regarding superiority and inferiority—judgments based largely on the needs of a liberal capitalist modernity, the parameters of which these Mexican intellectuals never fully escaped.

2

Migration, U.S. Race Thinking, and Pan-American Anthropology

After completing his book on Tepoztlán, Robert Redfield received funding from the Carnegie Institution of Washington for ethnographic research around the Maya archaeological site of Chichén Itzá. He wrote two books on the nearby village of Chan Kom. In the second book, *A Village That Chose Progress* (1950), Redfield argued that Chan Kom villagers were ready to embrace industrial civilization as it existed in the United States. "'The Road to Light,'" Redfield wrote, "starts out toward Chicago rather than toward Mexico City."[1] Redfield's quip reversed the actual and conceptual paths he had followed. Redfield's road to Chan Kom had started in Chicago's immigrant neighborhoods, where two years before his initial fieldwork in Tepoztlán, Redfield had participated in a study of Chicago's Mexican community. Redfield initially went to Tepoztlán in 1926 to learn about the kind of village from which Chicago's Mexican migrants departed.[2]

Redfield was not alone in looking abroad to shed light on dynamics in the United States. The University of Chicago Department of Sociology and Anthropology, where Redfield studied and then worked, was located in a largely immigrant city, and many of his teachers conducted research on immigration. Sociologist W. I. Thomas produced a path-breaking transnational study of Polish migrants, domestically and abroad. Professor of sociology Robert E. Park, who had worked with Booker T. Washington at the Tuskegee Institute, drew on the Darwinian notion that immigrant and ethnic groups competed with one another to map the urban geography of what he termed the race relations cycle: contact, conflict, accommodation, and assimilation. Redfield attended Park's course on "The Mind of Primitive Man, Race, and Nationalities." He married Park's daughter, Greta.[3]

Redfield believed in the unity of humanity, and he plotted domestic and foreign examples along the same evolutionary vector. This allowed him to relate research on the folk culture of urban Chicago to investigation of evolving primitive peoples in Mexico. The presence of immigrants in the United States made the nature of foreign places—immigrants' evolutionary starting point—relevant to domestic politics and allowed

Redfield to envision continuities between Mexico and the United States. Racial concepts and ideas regarding evolution helped him understand immigration to the United States and indigeneity in Mexico. Other scholars writing from other immigrant cities like Boston and New York also tacked back and forth between domestic and foreign locales: from the U.S. black slums, Native reservations of the Southwest, and tenant farms of the South to Pátzcuaro, San Cristóbal de las Casas, Tzintzuntzán, and other Mexican localities.[4] Researchers rode these circuits in the hopes of understanding U.S. immigrant, African American, Spanish American, and Native American groups.

By the 1930s scholars openly referred to Mexico as a laboratory for understanding the kind of race mixing and separation that might take place in the United States. Yet U.S. scholars rarely acknowledged what they borrowed from Mexican intellectuals or what they learned from the people they met in the field, insisting instead on their own ability to create controlled comparison by selecting conditions. In reality, they mostly went where their Mexican colleagues told them to go. Manuel Gamio had first suggested that Robert Redfield study Tepoztlán.[5]

Mexican scholars were mobile, too. Franz Boas's trip to Mexico City was preceded by Gamio's boat ride to New York. Moisés Sáenz and José Vasconcelos both spent considerable time in the United States. And Redfield's 1926 journey to Tepoztlán was likewise preceded by the travels of Elena Landázuri, a Mexican social worker who worked with Gamio at Teotihuacán, studied at the University of Chicago (1918–20), worked at Hull House, and grew close to Robert Park. Landázuri would later work in Tlaxcala and Actopan, in the Mezquital Valley. She became Redfield's guide in Mexico City. She may also have opened doors for him in Chicago, since he followed her into that city's Mexican immigrant community. Landázuri went on to assist Gamio in his research on Mexican immigrants in the United States, a study funded by the Social Science Research Council as a complement to Redfield's own work on Mexican migrants.[6]

The networks from which Redfield's Tepoztlán research emerged demonstrate that U.S. studies of Latin America arose in the 1910s and 1920s out of domestic U.S. concerns regarding race and immigration, and not from Cold War foreign policy concerns.[7] Anxieties regarding immigration were tightly connected to economic and geopolitical concerns in the early twentieth century. Boas cited the importance of U.S. commercial expansion abroad in arguing for his International School, and Gamio wrote in the U.S. weekly the *Nation* that anthropological studies of foreign others would fortify U.S. commercial and strategic interests.[8] But some of the earliest U.S. academic studies of Mexico and Latin America emerged out of public debates regarding U.S. immigration and assimilation, in addition to debates regarding African American migration to the urban North from the rural South. Subsequent Cold War foreign policy concerns, and the Latin American studies of the 1960s, would be grafted onto these prior concerns.[9]

Racial paradigms pervaded U.S. discussions of immigration, and as a result the social scientists who first considered the study of Latin America collaborated closely with biologists and psychologists interested in morphology, the criteria of bodily and mental classification, and the inheritance of bodily and mental characteristics. Especially before the 1920s, participants in discussions regarding immigration tended to conflate biological amalgamation and cultural assimilation. But in the 1920s, the boundaries between biology and culture hardened, and the natural and social sciences consequently grew apart. Biologists increasingly discounted the effects of culture on biology and the body, taking a more determinist and hereditarian point of view. This was a period when a virulent U.S. racism denied that Native Americans, African Americans, Mexican Americans, and Latin Americans had, or could develop, the attributes necessary for full citizenship. Mainstream U.S. policy and intellectual circles supported the use of racial criteria to determine who had rights and who did not, who belonged and who should be rejected or expelled. This was especially true for immigrants. Those scientists who supported immigration restriction searched for easy, sharp racial demarcations— although they did not always find them, as detractors were quick to note.[10]

Still, against Vasconcelos's claim that Social Darwinism was hegemonic in the United States, many U.S. academics eschewed doctrines of Nordic superiority and sought to equalize rather than exacerbate the struggle for scarce resources. As eugenicists turned toward biological determinism and psychologists combined studies of biological instinct with studies of socialization and parenting, social scientists increasingly championed less determinist explanations grounded in culture. As early as 1909, in research carried out for the U.S. Immigration Commission, Franz Boas had refuted the determining role of biology. Yet Boas's efforts to undermine fixed ideas about race and its impact on intelligence, culture, and bodily form took place during a period of heightened eugenic and hereditarian thinking, and they took hold slowly and partially. On questions of race and immigration, the U.S. academic community was decidedly divided.

Eugenics and the U.S. Immigration Debates

One important locus of debate regarding race and immigration was the Division of Anthropology and Psychology of the National Research Council, and it was here that Mexico and Latin America appeared within academic programming. The NRC was established in 1916 by the National Academy of Sciences at the request of President Woodrow Wilson. Its mission was to assist the U.S. effort in World War I and the federal government more generally by facilitating the application of the natural sciences to engineering, agriculture, medicine, and other useful arts. It worked with disciplinary professional organizations such as the American Anthropological Association and the American Psychological Association by vetting and funding proposals and shaping scholarly agendas.[11]

One of the NRC's earliest projects, carried out by a psychology committee, was to create the Army Alpha and Beta intelligence tests, used to screen recruits for the armed forces and determine their aptitudes.[12] An anthropology committee formed around the same time planned a study of the "normal physical conditions of the American people of different descent, admixture, education, social class, occupation, and environment." This study would follow protocols set out by a similar British committee and measure military recruits' physiques, including eye, skin, and hair colors. The British effort had moved from classifying individuals toward ascertaining the condition of the entire national population, and the U.S. anthropologists hoped to compare the British data to the data they would collect on the United States, where "the bulk of the population . . . has a British ancestry."[13] The search for antecedents and roots was on. The data would provide a baseline against which to measure the biological mixing that immigration was promoting.

In 1919, the NRC anthropology and psychology committees fused into a Division of Anthropology and Psychology.[14] The division harbored a wide array of academics and researched a range of topics. Boas served in the division, having been elected by the membership of the American Anthropological Association with the highest number of votes and then selected for the division's executive committee.[15] He was forced to resign almost immediately after his censure by the AAA council. At the same time, the division provided psychological personnel for a eugenics committee, set up at Charles Davenport's behest, to help plan the Second International Eugenics Congress in 1921. The earliest research proposals submitted to the division attest to the importance it gave to a series of related topics that addressed racial differences, the biological conditions of national and colonial populations, and cultural concerns. The anthropological proposals included plans for the anthropometric measurement of college students (proposed by Boas); motion picture and phonographic recordings of industries, ceremonies, languages, and songs of North American Indians and Negroes; an expedition to the Philippine Negritos; the typing of Hawaiian and Samoan physiques; and archaeological surveys of the Midwest. Psychologists proposed analyses of army intelligence data; the inheritance of musical ability or intelligence; the effects of hypnosis on memory, habits, and glands; and the predictive value of both college intelligence tests and tests for selecting industrial personnel. In varying ways, these disparate researches sought to measure and understand differences in talent and inheritance. The different proposals used distinct terminologies: "two to four racial stocks, "five community groups," "the Negro," "White and colored."[16]

In addition to these topics, the executive committee also considered—it was the second of twenty-two items—contributing to a project on the tropics already under way in the Division of Biology and Agriculture: "Anthropological research in South America. (Part of a comprehensive project now before the Council for scientific research in South America. Ethnological and linguistic studies are stressed.)" Research on Latin America thus emerged as part of a broader interest in the physical, mental, and cultural traits of populations. In December 1919, the South American project, now renamed "Archaeological, Ethnological and Linguistic Research in Tropical America," was recommended for funding, pending elaboration, as was a study of recordings of Native peoples. Neither was carried out.[17]

Shortly thereafter, and prompted in all likelihood by debates in the U.S. Congress on limiting immigration, Mexico and Mexican Americans entered the NRC discussions. Clark Wissler, a psychologist-turned-anthropologist who worked at the American Museum of Natural History from 1902 to 1942 and served as chair of the Division of Anthropology and Psychology in 1920–21, developed what would become one of the division's most overarching projects, an investigation of five immigrant communities, referred to as Project #1 and later rebaptized as "Anthropological and Psychological Study of Selected Racial Groups in the United States." It would be carried out by a Wissler-led NRC Committee for the Study of the Peoples of the United States.[18] Wissler clearly intended to contribute to congressional debates by comparing Northern and Southern European immigrants to one another and to Asian immigrants.[19] He proposed psychological, cultural, anthropometric and medical studies, including studies of growth, among Finnish, Japanese, Danish, Italian, and Slavic immigrants.

Mexicans were, as Katherine Benton-Cohen has shown, for the most part absent from early legislative debates regarding immigration. While Wissler was developing his proposal, limitations on immigration, though hardly new, were reaching a crescendo. The United States already had laws excluding individuals who were deemed liable to become public charges, infirm, disabled, or otherwise unfit for work. It also excluded entire national groups, including Chinese immigrants and later other Asians as well. From 1907 to 1911, the U.S. Congress Joint Immigration Commission chaired by Senator William P. Dillingham investigated the impact of immigration on the country with the aim of establishing further limitations, and in 1917, Congress enacted a literacy requirement, followed in 1921 by an emergency act setting national immigration quotas. The Reed-Johnson Act of 1924 would make those quotas permanent. Because few Mexicans migrants stayed in United States permanently, however, their presence seemed less pernicious. (Ironically, as Benton-Cohen argues, the lawmakers saw temporary migration from Southern and Eastern Europe as harmful since the European migrants showed little interest in adopting U.S. culture.) Agricultural employers from the Southwest successfully lobbied the executive branch to exempt Mexicans from the 1917 literacy requirement, arguing that Mexican laborers were more hardworking and morally upstanding than Chinese workers. Although U.S. border officials could still turn away Mexican and other Latin American migrants by declaring them unfit, the 1921 and 1924 quotas did not apply to immigrants from the Western Hemisphere.[20]

Lawmakers and public officials in the United States thus responded to labor market demands and to racialized views regarding labor and assimilation by deploying both national restrictions and individual selection. When the NRC's Division of Anthropology and Psychology held a "Conference on Anthropological Problems" on the eve of the 1921 International Eugenics conference, the biologists and physicians in attendance sought to refine national restrictions by advocating the application of standardized basic mental tests that would allow comparison of "races and other social groups." In addition, they backed the establishment of a "preferential list" allowing immigrants from Northern European countries to exceed the national quota proposed in the 1921 law. The scientists also called for research aimed at choosing the fittest prospective immigrants from among those selected to fill quotas.[21]

When psychologist Walter Van Dyke Bingham reformulated Wissler's NRC project, he added Mexicans and Mexican Americans to the mix. Hence, more than a decade before Stuart Chase compared Middletown to Tepoztlán, the NRC sought to compare Mexicans and whites. Bingham's goal was to determine the "essential characteristics of the more important stocks in the American population" by investigating the large number of Mexican immigrants along with New Mexico's large population of "Mexican stock." They were to be studied with Japanese, Sicilian, and Scandinavian communities, perhaps later comparing them with "a typical township with a population wholly native American, in Indiana, Pennsylvania, or elsewhere." Wissler himself linked his domestic concerns to foreign policy. The United States, he wrote, suffered "constant tribulations with Mexico," and there was the possibility of "taking over control of her people."[22] Racial categories and questions about race linked all these foreign and domestic concerns through the immigration debates.

Wissler's project on "lowly peoples" sought to determine when and how immigrants amalgamated (blended) or assimilated (adopted Euro-American culture) and to pinpoint the relation of cultural dynamics to biological race mixing. Immigrants, Wissler observed, often lived in areas popularly referred to as "colonies." These physically separate settlements constituted a menace, he said, to "our own culture and national existence." Anthropology could help effect an advantageous cultural and racial engineering by providing information regarding the proclivities of these peoples.

> The problem is not merely one of culture, for the zoological factor is evident in the "race question." The leveling down of differences in culture means increased contact and eventually amalgamation. It is highly important, therefore, that we study the inherent factors in the population of these colonies. We must also take up the problem of race-mixing; someone must be able to tell us what kind of men are being produced by this inevitable crossing of racial elements. Here are great groups of problems:
>
> 1. The identification of racial characters.
> 2. The inheritance of morphological and mental characters.
> 3. The effects of external conditions upon individual development.
> 4. The psychological factors involved in culture change.
>
> These problems appear in another question of large proportions, viz., the Negro question, or rather the mulatto problem. The

psychologists have made a good beginning with their tests upon soldiers and great things are to be expected from them in the future. What we need now is a start on the anthropological phase of the problem.

Wissler linked biology and culture. Because labor markets were often racially and culturally stratified, Wissler remarked, anthropologists could also participate in the psychological investigation of issues related to industrial management. Anthropologists had not yet investigated immigrant "colony cultures," he further noted, but they had studied the "Indian colonies" of the United States and Canada as well as "the native tribes of South America, Africa, Australia, etc." "It seems high time, therefore," Wissler wrote, "that we formulate some knowledge of the 'foreign culture' colonies in our midst, before we set out gaily upon a great program of Americanization."[23] Wissler and the division thereby tied together immigrant communities, South Americans, Indians, and Negroes, all of which Wissler referred to as colonies. He then linked all of these to questions of industrial management, labor supply, and immigration.

A similar connection of foreign and domestic concerns took shape within an NRC Committee on Race Characters, which sought to build knowledge of race traits and the effects of race mixing so as to "assist the American nation toward her goal of developing civilization" and avoid "ceaseless warfare with the stubborn biological forces of nature." The committee considered Negro migration alongside that of earlier U.S. immigrant groups—the "White races." Again, the committee looked to Mexico and Latin America, with Paul Popenoe, a West Coast leader of the eugenics movement, suggesting the study of Latin America for its "Black x White and Black x native Indian" crosses. Since there was, in his view, "no race prejudice and discrimination" in Latin America, experiments there could show that the failure of U.S. Negroes and mulattoes to "come into their own" could be attributed to their inherent and innate qualities. At the same time, members of the committee called for the study of the Mexican race "flooding" the South and Southwest as Negroes moved north.[24]

The Committee on Race Characters eventually foundered, but the division continued to study immigration, in 1922 forming a Committee on the Scientific Problems of Human Migration.[25] Chaired by Robert Yerkes, who had helped develop the Army Alpha and Beta tests, and funded by the Laura Spelman Rockefeller Memorial, the migration committee formed as anti-immigrant sentiment and debate on immigration reached its apex. Yerkes's committee sought to rank and compare different national groups and focused on developing tests that might shape a border eugenics aimed at excluding individuals who were mentally unstable, affectively or intellectually defective, physically infirm, or morally or educationally backward. His committee sponsored projects to pinpoint which groups and individuals should be allowed to enter the United States as well as to help personnel departments determine potential employees' vocational utility. Human migration committee members favored the Downey Group Will-Temperament Test to rate individuals and, despite "wide individual variability, . . . perhaps also races."[26]

Biology and the Rise of Mendelian Theories of Inheritance

Franz Boas's work countered these arguments by demonstrating that the U.S. social environment shaped immigrant bodies—notably height. Boas also argued that differences among individuals within a group were larger than differences among groups, an idea that undermined national quotas based on the notion that a biological, racial inheritance, rooted in place of origin, determined the quality of immigrants or their ability to assimilate.[27] The latter argument was nonetheless compatible with individual selection. Scientists associated with the NRC Division of Anthropology and Psychology increasingly saw racial differences as biological and/or inherited, and they moved away from explanations that foregrounded social and environmental factors. In so doing, they distanced themselves from cultural anthropology and the social sciences and from the neo-Lamarckism of their Mexican counterparts.[28]

The NRC emphasis on migrants' biological racial differences was propelled by staunch hereditarian racists like Robert DeCourcy Ward, a well-connected Harvard University climatologist and eugenicist who in 1894 had founded the Boston-based Immigration Restriction League. A letter from Ward to the chair of the Division of Anthropology and Psychology argued for the selection of the fittest immigrants using the military's physical standards. Mocking Congress's rejection of those standards, Ward noted that he and his allies "at once ran into the argument (poppy cock, of course) that our poor dear alien immigrants, especially the Jews, had lived for so many years in congested districts, and on bad and insufficient food, that it was not their fault that they were undersized, and that we could not properly exclude them for conditions over which they had no control!" Similarly, a lengthy memorandum from eugenicist Paul Popenoe to the Committee on Race Characters was a smorgasbord of determinist racist terminology and concepts: "genetics of any *normal* character in man," "bi-racial crosses," "inheritance of head form," "disharmony in crosses," "racial mongrels," "intelligence of mongrels," "glandular differences." Popenoe urged the "immediate and thorough re-examination ... [of] the alleged modifying effect of environment on morphological and anatomical characters." Even Wissler derided Boas's "special point of view," "veiled attack on eugenics," and opinion regarding the influence of environment. Wissler did, however, praise Boas's "discussion of methods of measuring race differences."[29]

This NRC human migration committee, like the human sciences in the United States generally, was shaped decisively by Mendelianism. Emulating biologists who were turning away from observation and toward laboratory studies in which they could control and isolate variables, psychologists and anthropologists sought to identify specific racial traits, or "unit characters," that could be tracked across generations and used to compare racial groups. Although the contributions of parents to characteristics like height that were continuous could not be determined, Wissler felt that scientists should persist in their efforts to find the inherited "units of size." Studies of blacks and Indians would, he felt, help identify the genetic mechanisms of the inheritance of qualitative anatomical characters. Only after understanding all the mechanisms of inheritance and how different characteristics behaved when pure races were crossed, could one ascertain whether immigrants would degenerate or become stronger and more efficient in the United States and address Boas's arguments regarding environment.[30]

Biological determinism, however, did not rely merely on Mendelian genetics. At a 1922 NRC conference on migration, for instance, a Dr. Williams argued for a novel explanation grounded in a geographically determined "endocrinology of races." Williams asserted that people migrated when they became physically uncomfortable, and they bathed not because of ideas regarding cleanliness but because of oily or dry skin. Both were related to endocrine function, as was the proclivity for work:

Professor Seashore: Hamlin Garland ... speaks of "milking in the morning" as the highest type of suffering, and a New Yorker reading it would probably shudder at the idea of milking in the morning. On the other hand, I happen to know a number of people whose greatest wish is to get up at sunrise and milk in the morning—this difference is probably due to endocrines.

Dr. Williams: This is an excellent example of the point I have been making. The willingness with which one gets up in the cold to milk is not necessarily determined by one's moral qualities. For the individual whose endocrine system was such that his circulatory system responded slowly to changes in temperature getting up in the cold may be a matter of real distress, while the individual whose endocrine system produces a ready response is stimulated and finds real pleasure in the process.[31]

Different bodies would respond differently to the same cold environments, but it was the bodies and not the environments that made the difference here. Immigration and immigrants' segregation into hard, undesirable manual labor was thus reduced to a biological impulse related to their geographical place of origin.

Some researchers admitted that racial groups might shape the character of individuals not just through shared bodily characteristics but also through shared cultural practices. For Wissler, who combined physical and cultural anthropology to study race mixture and cultural assimilation, "the biological and the cultural problems of migration . . . [were] interwoven." In a 1924 project, for instance, he argued for anatomical studies of inheritance and race mixture that included measurements of Negroes and mulattoes—the latter being the best U.S. example of hybridization—as well as Hawaiians, which would presumably yield data on the assimilability of Asians. He also proposed a study that would "break new ground" in studying how individuals reacted when moving from one culture to another and whether and how they became habituated. In a report issued after the start of his research, he called for research into Mexican, Indian, and Negro children and hybrids thereof, and began work at Indian schools in Arizona.[32]

The psychology subcommittee of the human migration committee likewise targeted an ill-defined combination of individual (intrinsic) and social (acquired) characteristics as researchers searched for criteria that would help predict assimilation potential and economic suitability. Tact, for these researchers, offered the "intriguing possibility of having an innate or dispositional basis" that nevertheless became "conventionalized" early in life in distinct ways by different groups. Those "conventionalized forms" seemed to "vary greatly among races as well as among social groups." They would therefore be useful to salespeople or successful executives in determining the occupations for which distinct racial groups might have certain proclivities—such as, for instance, agricultural workers whose bodies craved getting up before dawn. In other words, there might be a culturally inspired, but deep and racial, embodied penchant for certain kinds of work. Originality, however, was notably individual, according to the committee. Energy—an easily measured and therefore objective criterion—varied within "racial and cultural limits."[33]

Scholars more squarely lodged in the social sciences forcefully challenged biological and hereditarian explanations and questioned the veneer of impartiality that the Mendelian study of traits seemed to offer. For instance, some participants at a 1922 conference organized by Yerkes's human migration committee challenged Henry Laughlin of Charles Davenport's Eugenics Record Office when Laughlin rehashed the findings of his report to the Committee on Immigration of the House of Representatives. Laughlin's report had shown that many immigrant nationalities were disproportionately represented, compared to native whites, in the population of the state institutions for the "socially inadequate." Others questioned his finding, asking whether differential rates of institutionalization in different states might be attributable to divergent state policies. "Miss" Kate Claghorn of the New York School of Social Work—Dr. Claghorn was a Yale sociologist specializing in immigration and crime, a feminist, and a founding member of the National Association for the Advancement of Colored People—pointed out the minute absolute numbers Laughlin and others had measured and suggested that laws might be enforced at different rates in different places. More men migrated, too, and men tended to commit more crimes than women. Laughlin dismissed these questions by saying that he "could only give facts and figures."[34]

Bingham likewise waved away criticisms when he presented results of the army tests, which had found "striking differences in intelligence" among white officers and both white and Negro draftees. This prompted Claghorn to ask whether intelligence tests really measured the skills people needed to "deal with the problems of life." Newer tests of temperament and character that measured persistence, common sense, moral courage, conscientiousness, self-control, bravery, and law-abidingness were not better since those qualities might or might not be deemed positive depending on who was deciding and under what circumstances. What use was a test that used a tennis set as an example, she asked, if the person being examined was a peasant? In fact, the tests Bingham used were culture-bound in the extreme. They asked, for instance, whether pinochle was played with rackets, cards, pins, or dice; whether the most prominent industry of Detroit was automobiles, brewing, flour, or packing; whether the Wyandotte was a kind of horse, fowl, cattle, or granite; and whether food products were made by Smith & Wesson, Swift & Co., W. L. Douglas, or B. T. Babbitt. Other questions related to Bud Fisher, the Guernsey, Marguerite Clark, an advertising slogan, and salsify. Bingham did note that those who had been in the United States longest did best on the tests, but he dismissed the implication that environment mattered by arguing that those who had immigrated earliest were in fact smarter, so that there was "a gradual deterioration in the class of immigrants."[35] These maneuvers were in stark contrast to those carried out in Mexico by Mexican physician Rafael Santamarina or U.S. scholar Lucia Montana Hastings, both of whom immediately recognized the biases of tests and worked to overcome them.

Claghorn argued that what was needed was not a static cross-section of a group but a dynamic view of how social relations developed over time. With patience, researchers would be able to tease out environmental factors that social workers and others might then influence.[36] But Claghorn found it hard to assert the importance of such research in the face of the laboratory studies that seemed to be more scientific.

Under the leadership of Albert Jenks of the Sociology Department of the University of Minnesota (1923–24), members of the NRC Committee on Race Characters insisted on the fundamental, scientific, and disinterested nature of their investigations. Committee members sought to produce "objective definition and exhaustive exposition," moving beyond what was subjectively exhibited to the eye and toward a scientific definition of race; the committee's "fundamental researches" and "scientific results" inhered in "unbiased observation and presentation of . . . facts in unevasive language without exaggeration or argument."[37] Jenks further believed that the committee ought to make available to the entire world a comprehensive collection of all data on racial characteristics, classified, filed, indexed, and permanently housed: "a body of accurate and scientific facts." The committee aimed, in other words, for a global racial science. That science would stretch beyond data about Negroes or Indians or Mexicans, subsuming the knowledge about them being amassed in Latin America. All the while, Jenks's private correspondence hardly hewed toward a neutral scientific stance. He conspired with Ward of Harvard to impose the will of those who he defined as being *"of America"*—they no doubt thought of themselves as prime exemplars—against those who merely "happen[ed] to be in America." And he told Ward that they would need to fight "propaganda" with "counterpropaganda." To Wissler, he wrote that it was "only fair for me to say at once that I believe the so-called races greatly differ."[38]

Given these dynamics, social scientists such as Claghorn found it hard to assert their agenda within the NRC, which was after all an organization devoted to the natural and physical sciences. Mary Van Kleeck of the Russell Sage Foundation, who headed up the social science subcommittee of the NRC human migration committee, insisted on numerous occasions that migration studies should be broadly interdisciplinary. She succeeded in getting the NRC to fund a social science research project on labor demand in the United States and another using International Labor Office statistics to explore European factors leading to emigration. Her subcommittee considered projects that took up the effects of immigration on political institutions and citizenship. At Van Kleeck's request, the initial meeting to consider these projects included representatives of disciplinary professional organizations identified by the Social Science Research Council, which had been created in 1922 by the professional organizations. Yet the social sciences fit uncomfortably within the NRC, and the NRC human migration committee wished to focus its energies on the biological research, seeing social science as not within its purview. It therefore asked the SSRC to take over the social science investigations, but the SSRC, having formed only recently, felt that it could not take on the task. The NRC committee members then considered inviting SSRC representatives to its committee or forming a joint committee. In any case, the committee's work was cut short when the Laura Spelman Rockefeller Memorial gradually withdrew funding for research that it believed had little immediate relevance for the perceived problems of migration, especially basic research in psychology. One research project the memorial singled out as particularly inappropriate characterized migration as a reflex response to discomfort and pain and sought to develop a test of eyelid reflexes that might provide clues to why people migrated.[39]

At this time as well, definitive legislation on immigration passed in Congress, and in 1924 Yerkes resigned his position as chair of the migration committee to pursue his own research more intensively. The committee urged its own dissolution, arguing that its mission had been met, but the NRC council declined to shut it down, saying that the study of migration was central to the mission of the sciences. By 1928, however, the committee was no longer functioning.[40]

The SSRC and Mexican Migration

Rather than working with the NRC, the SSRC set up its own migration committee in April 1924, inviting Yerkes, Van Kleeck, and Wissler to join. The SSRC committee considered "Negro migration" within the United States as well as migration across national borders; race differences and labor demands tied the inquiries together. Although it used race as an organizing category, the SSRC committee eschewed biological determinism. At its first meeting, Wissler, who had just returned from Mexico, spoke approvingly of Mexican investigations of its "special racial groups." One participant in that meeting suggested "consideration of some aspects of the general problem of racial conflicts," but the emphasis here was on racial *conflict* and the nature of interracial relations rather than on the intrinsic characterization of races and peoples.[41]

Among the projects undertaken by the SSRC migration committee was a preliminary survey of "antecedents and conditions of the Mexican population of the United States." The project was proposed by Fay-Cooper Cole, chair of the Department of Anthropology and Sociology at the University of Chicago, at a 1925 SSRC meeting held at Dartmouth College. Cole's purpose was to secure funding to send Redfield, who was studying under his direction, to Mexico. The city of Chicago itself had inspired the topic. Mexicans, brought in by the Santa Fe Railway, were living in boxcar communities along the rail lines and displacing the Jews and Greeks who had previously worked on the lines. The social workers who worked with the Mexicans did not speak Spanish and had asked the University of Chicago for help. Redfield had spent time in Mexico, and he had some Spanish. He was sent to make a preliminary survey. In the end, he had spent seven months researching conditions in Chicago's Mexican community. However, the Mexicans distrusted him, and the work went slowly. Redfield believed that to gain the Mexicans' trust, he would have to live in the camps or go to Mexico. Cole proposed that he do the latter in order to learn the "social, economic or mental background" of the people. The suggestion would eventually take Redfield to Tepoztlán.[42]

Cole's idea was novel. There had been social surveys of immigrants, but anthropological fieldwork was reserved for isolated communities of Native peoples. What Cole and Redfield were proposing was different. They wanted to figure out what happened when "two known cultures meet." More and more Mexicans would be coming to the United States. It was imperative to avoid further misunderstandings.

The researchers assembled at Dartmouth discussed the proposed investigation at length. Members wondered whether the project should be taken up by the SSRC's committee on human migration or a separate committee on race that was being set up in the SSRC. Sociologist Howard Odum pointed out that Professor Cole's statement applied to a project on internal migration that Odum referred to as the "Negro study." Wissler counseled against mixing this project up with issues of labor and took the discussion back to his own interest in cultural assimilation. When Wissler was asked whether he defined "'cultural groups' in terms of culture or race," he sidestepped the question. Speaking for "the opinion of the younger men in anthropology" (which he decidedly was not), Wissler pointed out that each discipline might have its own "elemental group." "Let's study the group," he suggested, "and not limit ourselves to culture. I'd rather call it the Mexican problem." The door to race studies was left open.

Wissler had met Gamio—the minutes of the SSRC meeting referred to him as "Sr. Gonzales"—in New York City, and Wissler was clearly influenced by Gamio's language regarding Mexico's mestizos and Gamio's advocacy of inter-American investigations. Wissler spoke to the Dartmouth meeting of the need to study "contemporary cultural groups" and reach hands across borders. He wanted Gamio, who had resigned his post in the SEP and was looking for work, to carry out the Mexico research. "Mexico is a little sensitive," Wissler pointed out. "It is not everybody who can go poking around, especially if he is a United States [citizen]." The Mexico research, as another committee member pointed out, would be just a starting point for studying the "industrial revolution" among Japanese, Indians, Chinese, and other groups. The underlying question that concerned them seemed to be whether any non-Western peoples could adapt to industrial society. The study of foreign countries might shed light on domestic U.S. dynamics—an idea based on the assumption that political, economic, and social conditions mattered little or that they could be separated out as in a controlled experiment.

In this discussion, Mexico once again stood in for mixed cultures generally, a culture in transition, part industrial, part non-white. It was also *part of* the United States. As Guy Stanton Ford observed, "Mexico has revealed congeries of tribal groups. Is not that after all, what has brought us to the establishment of a Committee on Human Migrations within this Council? We have discovered that we in the United States are more or less a tribal group, some speaking one language and some another." From this viewpoint, studies of "contemporary peoples" around the globe should remain tied to studies of immigrants in the United States. Researchers might begin by examining the United States, but in the end they should preserve the unity of international and U.S. researches.

The project was ultimately referred to the SSRC's committee on human migration, where it was approved, along with five others, including a project that considered international migration alongside Negro migration within the United States. A third project responded to the growth in Negro and Mexican migration prompted by restrictions on European unskilled labor by asking whether labor shortages could be addressed through mechanization, which was presumably preferable to welcoming more migrants. Redfield received funding for his fieldwork in Tepoztlán. Gamio drew up a research proposal, transnational in scope, that he presented to the SSRC committee for approval.[43] Gamio's proposal broached questions of race by inquiring into the racial background—white, Native, or mixed—of Mexican migrants. He also wished to investigate their current "state of civilization," and its historical development, including the effects of the Spanish conquest, and "economical and biological backgrounds." But, all in all, Gamio took little interest in inherent biological qualities and focused instead on the "economic, social, political, and other factors" leading to emigration.[44]

In Gamio's proposal, questions about the United States were underdeveloped, although they ultimately became more central to the book he published on the topic. The initial proposal called instead for new studies in other Latin American countries. "The object of such an investigation," he wrote, "should be to determine the real nature of the problem presented by the contact between the Indo-Spanish and Anglo-American races, and by what means the relations between these two races may be made more harmonious and mutually helpful than they have been heretofore."[45] Like many U.S. contemporaries, the Mexican scholar viewed his work as shedding light on the general issue of how two different civilizations interacted. By making Mexico stand in for Latin America as a whole, as he often did when in the United States, and by counterposing it to the United States, he affirmed a Mexican–Latin American distinctiveness and Mexican nationalism.

Ultimately, however, Gamio's researches led him to denounce U.S. racism against Mexicans. In his 1929 book, Gamio asserted that he did not have enough data to allow conclusions regarding "race contact." Defining race "as real physical differences," he argued that the discussions taking place in the United States had "really to do with social, cultural, or economics facts and not with the actual racial problem." He nevertheless took the time to address those who might deem Mexicans physically inferior. "Deficient or diseased" migrants were not allowed to enter the United States, he remarked, and in any case, the proportion of Mexican migrants that border inspectors turned away was not larger than the proportion of migrants of other nationalities. Why then, he asked, was there prejudice against Mexican migrants? That prejudice afflicted even Mexican Americans who had been U.S. residents for generations and those who were relatively light skinned. All people of Mexican ancestry were, he concluded, tainted by the stigma of Mexicans' Native descent and the U.S. obsession with color.[46] The questionnaires Gamio and his research assistants used to conduct interviews asked Mexican Americans questions about racial attitudes and discrimination, as well as about living and working conditions and cultural traditions: "Do the Americans show sympathy with you? Do you have the same opportunities as Americans?" They asked about loyalty to both countries and opinions about "Washington, Hidalgo, Lincoln, Juárez." Who did Mexican Americans consider to be part of "'The Race,'" and how did their own views about Mexico differ from those of "Americans"? Gamio also queried his presumably male informants about whether they would prefer to marry a Mexican, a Mexican American, or an American and whether they found white women beautiful because "of their White skin, because they are more beautiful than the women you know, or because you think your social position would be improved?" Presumably, answers to this question would help him determine whether discrimination was based on physical differences, culture, or class distinctions. Would an "American" or a "Negro" want to marry a Mexican? Did the Mexican Americans live in segregated districts? Did they enjoy economic, political, and social rights? What did they think about immigration quotas? Overall, these questions pointed to the availability of social mobility and access to rights and addressed diverse forms of possible discrimination. Mexican migrants were also asked about their reactions to "the big buildings, the trains, the many automobiles, the factories, the moving-picture houses, and schools." They were to compare their lives in Mexico and the United States and reflect on their future plans. Would they stay or leave? And were they interested in becoming Americanized?[47] The focus was on Mexican animus toward the United States, which Redfield did not seem to believe was necessarily related to the racism they experienced.

A second book, edited by Redfield, contained summaries of the interviews Gamio and his team had collected. Redfield acknowledged the widespread evidence of discrimination contained in the stories but also cast doubt on Gamio and the value of the findings, which he ultimately deemed unscientific: "These documents do not constitute a scientific study of the Mexican immigrant," he wrote in his introduction to the work. They did not adhere to the life history method developed by his mentors at Chicago. It might be possible to collect such life histories and "with outside data, to gain insights into the mechanism of development of racial pride and sensitiveness. . . . The present documents, however, are not sufficiently related to the whole cultural milieu." Redfield had to admit, however, that the stories were "in many ways . . . alike" and seemed to provide a picture of a "sort of generalized Mexican immigrant. . . . A generalization is, therefore, built up by a mental procedure hard to describe adequately." In the introduction to a chapter on "Conflict and Race-Consciousness," Redfield cast further doubt on the data, writing that "we do not know how they really feel about it; and where their attitudes are expressed, we do not know what experiences gave rise to those attitudes. . . . In some instances one is tempted to ascribe the intense, even bitter, racial feeling that is expressed to certain personal experiences."[48]

Back to Biology?

Gamio's study of Mexican migration was part of a more generalized movement toward a greater recognition of the importance of cultural and social factors in shaping the experiences of migrants and other non-white groups. The creation of the SSRC was itself a manifestation of the growing importance of the social sciences and of their growing institutionalization in universities and as adjuncts to state policies. Yet biology remained a component of studies of social groups within the SSRC and even more so within the NRC. As immigration restriction passed the U.S. Congress and research on the topic waned, both institutions turned more squarely to the study of race per se; in 1926 the NRC's Division of Anthropology and Psychology created a Committee on the Study of the American Negro, and the SSRC formed an Advisory Committee on Interracial Relations. These committees formed a joint Committee on Racial Problems. These committees' efforts, like those of the previous migration committees, were framed within debates regarding cultural-cum-racial contact. Their discussions ranged broadly across the experiences of immigrants, African Americans, Mexicans, and Native Americans.[49]

With many of the psychological studies that had previously preoccupied the prior NRC human migration committee now proceeding outside the

NRC, its Division of Anthropology and Psychology renewed its commitment to physical anthropology. Boas rejoined the NRC as part of the Committee on the Study of the American Negro, where he served alongside eugenicist Charles Davenport and Robert J. Terry, an anatomist from Washington University in Saint Louis and chair of the committee. Terry believed that individual development depended on both descent and the social environment, and he called for collaboration with the SSRC. Yet the NRC committee's proposal for research focused on the body and intrinsic psychology rather than social factors. It included studies of full-blooded Negroes and their African ancestry—a new topic being studied by Boas's student Melville J. Herskovits—which the committee saw as a prerequisite to understanding racial mixing. In general, Negroes were to be studied alongside whites and Indians.[50]

The SSRC Committee on Interracial Relations differed from its NRC counterpart in important ways. It proposed research that was clearly aimed at addressing inequalities, and its focus on "interracial relations" at least implied that racial problems were not intrinsic to racial groups but emerged from social relations among them. Along with studies of Negro folksongs, it proposed studies of Negroes in industry, organizations that worked with Negroes, urbanization, legal justice, and attitudes in racial contacts. It was chaired by Will Alexander, who had headed the Committee on Interracial Cooperation, an antiracist organization formed in the wake of the white attacks on blacks that had rocked dozens of U.S. cities in 1919. It included notable African American intellectuals Carter G. Woodson and Charles Johnson. Perhaps most important, it made the novel suggestion that blacks be trained in greater numbers to study racial issues. In fact, it urged its own dissolution, recommending that the study of blacks be taken up by Negro researchers—a recommendation the SSRC leadership rejected.[51]

Still, even within this group of social scientists, biological and hereditarian approaches were evident. That is not surprising, given that its membership included Todd Wingate, who also served on the NRC committee, and Joseph Peterson, who had received funding from the NRC human migration committee for a study of Negroes in the South. Peterson now proposed an SSRC study of the distribution and heredity of mental traits. Though he was generally critical of the biased nature of existing intelligence tests and believed that mental faculties might be developed, he was also interested in possible limitations on that development and open to the idea of inherent racial differences. In addition, the committee considered a study of the anthropology of Africa and another on the Negro family and child welfare, both of which focused on the transmission of racial character. These studies had initially been proposed together, as a study of the African origins of the Negro family in the United States, with the implication that the family was a key transmitter of a heritage that was grounded, like the major races, in continental origins.[52]

At a joint meeting in 1928, the NRC and SSRC committees carefully sorted through questions of social and physical environment and individuals' anatomical and psychological inheritances. They focused on blacks and immigrants. Cole opened the proceedings by alluding to the "difficulties raised by this term 'Race,'" explaining that the concept could refer to biological, national, religious, and linguistic differences. The difficulties, in Cole's view, were the result of social and natural scientists' engagement with Mendel's notion that the result of genetic crosses would replicate the characteristics of the parent races in precise proportions. Mendelianist experts had become fixated on "pure" parent races, but even simple observations, Cole observed, led to the conclusion that many traits did not follow the Mendelian rule. He hypothesized that clusters of traits that held together and might therefore be termed race—hair form, skin color, or shape of lips and nose—might be inherited along Mendelian lines and might be the ultimate signs of race. But he had to admit that there was no agreement either on that matter or on Boasian or neo-Lamarckian claims for environmental influence. It was plausible that adjustments to environment would lead to physical changes, and natural selection also implied a relationship to environment. Herskovits's innovative NRC- and SSRC-funded studies of blacks were showing, furthermore, that social mores, including black men's preference for marrying lighter-skinned women, could lead to racial changes in their progeny. If biology shaped culture, then the converse was also true.[53]

Behind all these issues was Wissler's old question about whether immigrant races would assimilate or separate. Would the United States become more homogeneous, or would new generations simply replicate the differences of the parents' or grandparents' generations? If inheritance did not follow Mendelian lines, replicating one or the other parent, then perhaps populations would blend together over time. If adaptation to social and physical environments prevailed, then populations were also likely to converge—although different races might react differently to the same environment. In this context, the conference returned to the old question of family lines. Eugenic studies going back to the nineteenth century had focused on defective families: Robert Dugdale had studied the Jukes, and Henry Goddard the Kallikaks.[54] Boas, too, had insisted on the importance of family lines as part of his attempt to reconcile the concept of inheritance with his refusal of the concept of race. "The term 'racial heredity' is not precise enough," Boas had asserted some years earlier, noting that only a few characteristics like hair form and pigmentation were present among clusters of family lines that were grouped as races.[55] Boas, however, did not dismiss the issue of how biological traits passed from parent to child, and at the 1928 conference, he argued that though this inheritance might not be racial because it did not necessarily cluster into groups, it might still be biological and inherited. To elucidate the nature of the interaction between bodily inheritance and environment, the study of parents and their children would not do, since each generation might grow up in a different environment. Instead, what was necessary was study of the life course, the development of the child. Here it would be useful to study different races and family lines in the same environment, and the same family lines in different environments.[56] Though Boas emphasized environmental influences, he tried, like the Mendelians, to isolate distinct traits.

In suggesting studies of the life course, Boas focused on changes in the individual. Over time, he had increasingly seen this as the main target of investigation. According to anthropologist Herbert S. Lewis, Boas followed Charles Darwin in seeing individual variations as in part at least fortuitous rather than determined. Natural selection (the environment) operated not on races but on infinitely variable individuals, favoring certain traits and not others. By the end of the conference, these Boasian precepts had made it into a proposal for studies of white and Negro children from gestation up to fifteen years. By looking at several communities, environmental factors could be gauged. The development and application of psychological tests would reveal "individual and family differences."[57]

The question of African ancestry in U.S. Negroes, which had preoccupied the SSRC committee, also resurfaced in a proposal for studies of African cultural and physical ancestry. Though conference discussions had raised the possibility that African heritages were themselves mixed, the conference's resolutions seemed more intent on tracking African "cultural remnants" in the United States by taking "actual samples of West Africans" and comparing them to "isolated groups of Negroes in America." This proposal was not dissimilar to Corrado Gini's interest in tracking isolation and mixing in Mexico and Europe, but conference participants figured

Africa as a site of pure blackness, in contrast to hybrid Latin American and Caribbean populations: U.S. investigations into the West Indies and Central and South America, like Gini's foray into Mexico, would allow experts to track "variability where race crossing has occurred." Herskovits spent a good deal of his conference presentation explaining that while crosses in the United States would be incorporated into the Negro racial group, in Brazil they would enrich the non-Negro population.[58] The racial categories and the social separation that constructed pure race in the United States were not absolute or universal. But this argument regarding the social construction of racial categories, along with the view of Africa as hybrid, foundered on notions of pure races linked perpetually to their places of origin.[59]

One of the most interesting outcomes of the conference was to split off the social research from the anatomical research, including anthropologist Aleš Hrdlička's studies of old-stock white immigrants, Charles Davenport's suggestions for physical anthropology studies of immigrants, and proposals for enhancing the techniques for measuring cadavers. Although these subjects were in no way deemed insignificant by conference participants, they were no longer seen as providing evidence that biology determined cultural outcomes. Studies of biology and culture could each proceed separately.[60] Hence, even as conference participants noted that culture and biology might work in tandem, culture was being split off from biology.

However, as a second SSRC-NRC conference on race differences revealed, the separation was partial. In fact, this 1930 conference, held in Detroit, produced an especially bizarre and racist proposal—albeit one that was ultimately set aside. The proposal emerged immediately after the first conference. Black children, perhaps Native American children, too, and perhaps even a control group of white children were to be placed at birth in something akin to an orphanage, where they would be given the best possible nutrition, medical care, and education. If they turned out well, biology would be proven insignificant. The project had the backing of SSRC president Edwin Wilson, who noted the "fuss about child growth and development" and wanted to set up control groups that could push past the "lunacy at large on the question of heredity and environment." Culture could be brought into the laboratory for examination. Cole, in a subsequent letter to the NRC anthropology and psychology committee chair, opposed the proposal. His letter quoted an unidentified source as saying that the differences between a Negro child and a white child cared for in equivalent institutions could not be the same because the wardens and nurses would, based on their past experiences, react differently toward black and white skins. Furthermore, the two groups could not be isolated from "the world of prejudgment and prejudice." Boas viewed the research as "highly desirable" but recommended that it be sent to a new committee that was "in touch with the Negro problem" and that this committee should include a Negro among its members.[61]

Anthropology and psychology committee chair Knight Dunlap, who also served on the joint SSRC-NRC committee on race differences, did dances to try to salvage the planned investigation, which seemed likely get financial backing. With the SSRC-NRC committee, Dunlap convened a child research conference. What if they had black nurses and wardens, too, as well as white staff, with black and white children to serve as controls? (That black nurses might care for white children was not considered.) Harold E. Jones quoted anthropologist Alfred Kroeber regarding the "possible availability of Indian children," though Kroeber warned that it might be difficult to get "the Indian children away from their mothers at a sufficiently early age." Kroeber was also of the opinion that Mexicans were "too mixed" to take part in the experiment. But he did suggest an interracial institution to compare children of different races—although decorum might dictate that they "not all be under the same roof." The orphanage idea was dismissed with the question, "How would the native White groups . . . respond to such investigations?" Maybe it could be done in Jamaica? Some participants urged the more modern option of using nursery schools and educating parents or simply using sampling techniques to isolate environmental factors. But the methodological obstacles to statistical analyses seemed too great. The project was shelved. Shortly thereafter, the joint SSRC-NRC committee disbanded, as did the NRC Committee on the Study of the American Negro. By 1931, the SSRC Committee on Interracial Relations had also folded.[62]

Overall, cultural anthropologists increasingly jettisoned biological approaches but continued to face and debate determinist racial theories rooted in biology. The Boasian anthropologists had moved away from notions of biological immutability or inevitability, but they never dismissed outright the importance of biology. Some, including Boas, suggested that many characteristics did not seem to be inherited along Mendelian lines and that biology did not always congeal into racial groupings. African Americans might, like Native Americans, become more distinct through intermarriage or geographical separation. But this process depended—as

Herskovits recognized—on sociocultural factors. It also depended on culturally determined forms of racial categorization. "Mulattoes" in Brazil might be white. In the United States, they were black. In general, though, scholarly debate tended to portray Africa as a site of racial origins and racial purity, whereas Latin America was figured as a laboratory for racial mixing that might hold lessons for the United States.

Studying Latin America: Mestizaje and Acculturation

In 1932, anthropologist Robert Lowie of the University of California at Berkeley, while serving as chair of the NRC's Division of Anthropology and Psychology, commissioned the *Handbook of South American Indians* to complement the existing *Handbook of Indians North of Mexico* and the recently published *Handbook of Indians of California*. When the editor that Lowie and his collaborators had commissioned died unexpectedly, a conference of noted experts was convened in early 1934 to discuss the parameters and organization of the *Handbook*. Ostensibly South America was the object of study, but the United States, Mexico, and the West Indies repeatedly crept into the conference discussions. One unnamed participant stressed the relevance of Latin America for the United States, calling for "a Pan-American point of view." Anthropologist Leslie Spier, who like Lowie had studied with Boas and conducted research on the Native peoples of North America, argued that the project should include Central America, the West Indies, and Mexico—thereby encompassing African-descended peoples as well as Native peoples and consequently discouraging an undesirable "local professionalism." Lowie went even further, suggesting that the project could be "Pan-world." These men saw themselves as cosmopolitans creating broadly applicable, global knowledge.[63]

This conference took place as the newfound Pan-Americanism of the Roosevelt years was opening the door not only for research south of the border but also for greater collaboration with Latin American scholars. For Wissler, the project represented "a symbol of accommodation and cooperation between the North America and Latin American countries."[64] This was precisely the point Gamio had been making for two decades and of which Wissler had perhaps become convinced in his dealings with the Mexican scholar. Perhaps now Gamio's desire for true, equal collaboration between Anglo- and Latin-America would find a way, though Spier's reference to Latin American's local professionalism cautioned otherwise.

Around the time this conference was taking place, the SSRC tasked three anthropologists with drafting a sweeping framework for future research regarding the changes resulting from face-to-face interactions across cultures. The 1935 "Memorandum on Acculturation" was written by Herskovits, Redfield, and Ralph Linton of the University of Wisconsin–Madison. The memorandum did not discuss Mexico or even the rest of Latin America. It is nonetheless significant that of the three authors, two had extensive experience there. By the time the trio of anthropologists drafted the memorandum, Herskovits had already done fieldwork among the Suriname "Bush Negroes" (1928 and 1929) and in Haiti (1934), studying African survivals. Redfield had completed his ethnographic study of Chan Kom—cowritten with the Mexican schoolteacher and ethnographer Alfonso Villa Rojas—the village that, Redfield wrote, "chose progress." At the University of Chicago, Cole had hired Redfield to teach "Peoples of the World," which included Mexican ethnology. The course was a prerequisite to "Our Alien People."[65]

Herskovits, Linton, and Redfield defined acculturation as the changes that resulted "when groups of individuals having different cultures come into continuous first-hand contact," and it distinguished acculturation from the bigger concept of culture change, which might not involve first-hand contact, and the more limited concept of diffusion, which involved tracking single traits. More significantly, they differentiated acculturation from assimilation, which they presented as a phase of acculturation only in some cases. When cultures came into firsthand contact through migration, conquest, war, travel, mass exile, or other situations, they believed, many distinct outcomes were possible, including adaptation, reaction, or selective acceptance. The memorandum chronicled the vast variety of situations that would need to be documented and studied, both apart and together, to grasp the mechanisms of face-to-face culture contact. The authors also carefully detailed the internal and external differences of power that shaped acculturation processes: On whose land did interactions take place? What was the numerical correlation of forces? What about political or economic dominance or the use for force?[66]

Insofar as Redfield, Linton, and Herskovits's memorandum did not discard consideration of physical type, the anthropologists did not depart from the precedent set by earlier cultural anthropologist. But their focus was now squarely on culture. In a rather subtle formulation, they claimed that physical type shaped "*attitudes* operative in acculturation, as well as the importance of the concomitant occurrence of race-mixture or its prohibition" (my emphasis). In other words, perceptions of physical characteristics might shape people's *choices*.[67]

Conclusion

Redfield, who ricocheted among Mexico, the world, and the alien people of the United States, re-created connections that were amply evident to experts in the human and social sciences. The connections to race, biological and cultural inheritance, and the presumed difficulties differences posed to democratic governance, were close at hand. While doing fieldwork in Tepoztlán, Redfield had written to his father-in-law, a member of the SSRC's migration committee, that locals considered the revolutionary hero Emiliano Zapata "the liberator, the Abraham Lincoln, the M[arcus] Garvey of the Indians of Morelos."[68] Redfield's mother-in-law, who accompanied him on the trip, called the village's ruling elites "'the Tammany Hall' of Tepoztlan . . . as lowbrowed as politicians in all parts of the world, only more so as they had pure Aztec foreheads."[69] She linked Tepoztlán's leaders to U.S. immigrant politicians, and both to their biological, physical, and mental inheritances.

Redfield's 1929 book on Tepoztlán did not focus on race but was concerned instead with cultural change, especially the uneven process of modernization. Drawing on categories that were presumably native to Tepoztlán, Redfield distinguished the traditional *tontos* (silly ones) from upstanding *correctos* who introduced to the village alien forms of culture. In a letter to Robert E. Park, Redfield considered and then dismissed the importance of physical appearance: "When one first comes down here everybody looks much alike, but after one has lived here awhile one sees the very great differences among individuals with respect to degree of civilization." A small group of Tepoztecan shopkeepers and artisans had "acquired considerable civilization," he wrote, and brought in jazz musicians from Mexico City for their parties. Jesús Conde, the keeper of the local shrine and an important informant for Redfield, was married to a part-Tarascan woman from Michoacán. Conde had lived for many years in the capital city and had become interested in his Native heritage while living there. "The self-conscious revival of the Indian tongue," Redfield informed Park, "is a significant aspect of the transition to urban culture. They want to study it as it *should* be spoken, as if it were Sanskrit. There are some young men here who want to study both English and Nahuatl." Conde was thus both civilized and Indian—or at least he was presumed to be able to combine the two. He was not in any way "pure" Indian, just as Tepoztlán was not purely primitive.[70]

But just as Cole pointed out the "difficulties raised by this term 'Race'" at the start of the 1928 NRC-SSRC conference on "Racial Differences," Redfield noted that some Tepoztecos could be civilized and Indian in a book that took for granted the transition from traditional to modern. The anthropologist was clearly aware of the limitations of his categories, the changes taking place in Tepoztlán, and the ways that individuals could pick and choose from seemingly modern and traditional repertoires. Yet he stuck to his evolutionary categories, projecting them simultaneously onto the distinct barrios of the village and along an evolutionary axis from ancient to modern. Presumably this understanding would help him grasp the trajectories of Mexicans in the United States and others who were also lower on the evolutionary scale.

From the time that Boas attempted to trace the peopling of the Americas and the diffusion of folktales, Mexico and Latin America had been a laboratory for understanding racial purity, cultural and racial mixing, and social change. This interest grew out of, and intersected with, scholars' and policymakers' interest in immigrants, Native Americans, and African Americans in the United States. Interest in racial and cultural contact, and the movement of peoples, tied the researches together.

Part II Science and Nation in an Age of Modernization and Antiracist Populism, 1930–1950

> The historic policy: That Indian property must pass to whites; that Indian organizations must be repressed and prevented; that Indian family life must be dismembered; that Indian cultures must be killed; and that Indians as a race must die.
>
> The present policy: That Indian property must not pass to whites; that Indian organization must be encouraged and assisted; that Indian family life must be respected and reinforced; that Indian culture must be appreciated, used, and brought into the stream of American culture as a whole; and that the Indian as a race must not die, but must grow and live.
>
> —John Collier, "A Birdseye View of Indian Policy Historic and Contemporary," brief submitted to the subcommittee of the House of Representatives Appropriations Committee, 1935

When U.S. Commissioner of Indian Affairs John Collier presented his Indian policy to the House of Representatives Appropriations Committee in 1935, he outlined a stark difference between the federal government's "historic policy" and his Indian New Deal, which rolled back allotment and instituted more culturally sensitive policies.[1] Collier's characterization of the Indian New Deal as an unequivocal gain or a definite break from the past was later challenged by a number of scholars and activists. More recently, some historical accounts have tried to reconcile these divergent viewpoints, primarily by noting variations among and within Native communities. The historiography of Mexican indigenismo and postrevolutionary Mexican Indian policy has followed a similar path, from praise to revisionist critique to postrevisionist scholarship attuned to variation and ambiguity. New Deal and postrevolutionary programs were implemented by local officials who could be more or less sympathetic or effective. Native peoples themselves varied in their lifeways, beliefs regarding national cultures and national governments, and ability or desire to create alliances with government actors. Even within one community, not all members had a shared outlook.[2]

The chapters in Part II look at the understudied knowledge practices that shaped state policy in the 1930s and 1940s, including the Mexican emphasis on ethnographic knowledge, which became a touchstone for Collier. I am concerned with the ways that scientists served as mediators. When they visited settlements to observe, survey, question, photograph, test intelligence, or assess imagination and creativity, they became the human faces of the nation-states they served. Their reports depicted conditions within Native communities—and at times the opinions of Native peoples—for interested state officials. The knowledge they produced emerged from the dynamics they confronted in the villages they visited and from their participation in national and international conversations. Researchers' individual aptitudes, personalities, and trajectories mattered as well, along with their schooling within disciplines and their experiences working for growing state bureaucracies.[3]

Of course, Native peoples and anthropologists both faced many constraints, and for the Native peoples especially, they could be grave. Take, for instance, the 1936 visit of ethnographer Miguel Othón de Mendizábal to the Mezquital village of Santa María Tepeji. Mendizábal arrived in the village as the envoy of President Lázaro Cárdenas, who sent him to investigate residents' urgent claims that townspeople were being assassinated by members of the right-wing *defensa rural* (rural militia) of the town of Ferrería de la Encarnación in the neighboring municipality of Zimapán. Zimapán leaders apparently wanted to incorporate Santa María within their own municipal limits, perhaps because Santa María collected taxes from the nearby mine of La Bonanza. With the support of the state government and local political officials, the defensa rural chief had not only murdered Santa María villagers but also taken land from local residents and compelled them to work in his fields. The villagers entreated Cárdenas for help, and Cárdenas sent Mendizábal. Mendizábal's presence in Santa María as Cárdenas's envoy no doubt made a statement that both the villagers and their foes understood.

In return, Santa María residents tolerated, and perhaps even welcomed, Mendizábal's questioning, which did not stop at the political conflicts that concerned village residents. In five days in Santa María, Mendizábal collected information on the terrain, waterways, rainfall, vegetation, climate, language, ethnicity, occupations, demography, agricultural products, production per hectare, production costs, irrigation systems, agricultural salaries, ranching, the cost of living, and more.[4]

Both in Mexico and in the United States, Native communities did not always cooperate with ethnographers, however, and residents of any given community might offer differing opinions about whether to cooperate, with whom, and when. At Zia Pueblo in New Mexico, Native authorities halted research sponsored by the U.S. Indian Service that was conducted with local schoolchildren. At the same time, they recognized the jurisdiction of the Indian Service Agency. "Please accept and observe the Zia Pueblo's rules," the Zia governor wrote in a letter to schoolteachers. "1. Any person or persons who have not done any business previously in the Zia Pueblo, must have a written introduction from the United Pueblos Agency, officially signed. . . . 2. All important business must be transacted in the Pueblo of Zia with the approval of the Agency and the Zia Pueblo Council. 3. Physical examinations and vaccinations must not be done before consulting for approval of the Patient and the Patient's guardian or parents." Likewise, anthropologist Oscar Lewis met with resistance during a joint U.S.-Mexico project in Tepoztlán. To avoid suggestions of impropriety, his team carried out interviews with children in the open courtyard of the village school. Despite that precaution, conservative factions of the town objected to some of his questions and sought to drive him from town. Only the intervention of the Cuernavaca state governor secured his research.[5]

The following two chapters track state-sponsored efforts to acculturate Native peoples. I examine the hemispheric convergences, divergences, and connections that shaped those state efforts as well as global phenomena, including the Great Depression, the Good Neighbor policy, and World War II. Definitions of indigeneity and race, along with views regarding the relation of culture to economy and the colonial politics of governing difference, shaped experts' thinking about the state policies and processes of modernization and acculturation. So did scholars' experiences in local communities. Mexico did not have a powerful centralized state agency akin to the Indian Service, and Mexican officials were reticent to develop national policies aimed specifically at indigenous peoples, so local experiences exerted a particular pull over Mexican indigenistas, who learned to tailor policies aimed at rural people generally to specific locales. Meanwhile in the United States, Collier promoted ethnographic research, but as both the state and the sciences grew in importance during World War II, universalizing and predictive theories increasingly guided policies toward Native peoples and other so-called minorities and peoples abroad.

IN MEXICO, REFORM of state policies toward Native peoples gained force as the postrevolutionary state consolidated itself in the 1930s. From 1926 to 1929, the Mexican government faced an armed revolt. The Cristero Rebellion was inflamed by Catholics unhappy about state efforts to displace Catholic schools, limit the teaching of religion, and stamp out raucous, heavy-drinking saints' day fiestas. Cristeros took up arms, forcing state officials to devote resources to quelling the insurgency and thereby limiting the state's ability to improve rural communities. The revolt also forced government officials to recognize that they had to deliver immediate and tangible improvements if they wished to head off further insurgency. In that context, a group of self-styled socialist politicians reanimated social reforms and took the revolution in a more popular-democratic direction. Mexico's peculiar "socialism" was not radically anticapitalist. Rather, it promoted rational, secular state intervention and economic development. Cárdenas built on this legacy. By the time he left power in 1940, the state had transformed land tenure through the massive redistribution of land, increased the numbers of ejidos, and stepped up the provision of services in the countryside.[6]

In the 1930s, Mexican state officials also worked to institutionalize political support. In 1938, Cárdenas created the Partido de la Revolución Mexicana (PRM, Party of the Mexican Revolution), building on the precedent of—and supplanting—the Partido Nacional Revolucionario (Party of the National Revolution), which had been created in 1929 by former President Plutarco Elías Calles (1924–28). The PRM displaced powerful mestizo and white elites and cemented alliances among Cárdenas, regional elites, campesino and labor organizations, and middling state officials such as schoolteachers. Mendizábal's visit to Santa María Tepeji was the result of precisely this type of alliance.[7]

Officials in the Cárdenas administration, like prior policymakers, were ambivalent about policies for Native peoples that diverged from those for rural peoples in general. While renewing efforts to address the specific needs of Native peoples, they wavered on this path. For instance, in 1936,

Cárdenas formed the Dirección de Asuntos Indígenas (DAI, Department of Indigenous Affairs), which reported directly to him. But though the DAI oversaw the provision of services to Native communities, it depended on the programs and resources of government offices with broader national mandates, such as the SEP and the Departamento Agrario (Agrarian Department, the main land reform agency). The DAI's first director, Graciano Sánchez, was a pro-Cárdenas agitator for agrarian reform who went on to head the Confederación Nacional Campesina (National Peasant Confederation). His interest was not primarily in Mexico's indigenous peoples. His successor, historian Luis Chávez Orozco, was a left-wing cultural pluralist who more actively promoted Native autonomy. Under Chávez Orozco, the DAI amassed more power and funding: it took over the administration of local boarding schools for Native peoples as well as the cultural missions run by the SEP. With the support of the DAI, educators and linguists formulated bilingual education projects.[8]

These pluralist measures drew force from earlier indigenista arguments for pluralism. They were fueled as well by experiences in the prior decade when policymakers and intellectuals traveled around Mexico and took stock of just how heterogeneous the country was. The revolution's first efforts to modernize the nation's rural and indigenous masses had revealed, moreover, the difficulty of rooting out practices deemed backward. Socialist policymakers were inspired, in addition, by the Soviet Union's policies toward its ethnic "nationalities." Chávez Orozco and other socialist reformers observed that the Soviet Union had industrialized while promoting Native languages and allowing non-Russian nationalities to govern themselves. Perhaps, then, this model merited emulation. Socialist intellectuals' infatuation with Soviet models passed quickly.[9] But debate about the nationalities policy and forms of incorporating Native autonomy into government put cultural pluralism squarely on the political agenda. As the tumult of the revolutionary fighting and the Cristero War receded and the postrevolutionary state consolidated itself, the need to forge a homogeneous citizenry as a means of avoiding conflict also abated. Perhaps peace did not require full uniformity after all.

Even as Cárdenas and the DAI bolstered policies aimed specifically at meeting Native communities' needs, the Cárdenas administration never abandoned efforts to address the problems Native peoples faced by applying policies toward rural poverty in general—policies more compatible with both the socialist emphasis on class and liberal notions of universal citizenship. From this homogenizing viewpoint, Native peoples were part of an Indo-mestizo rural majority, and their needs could best be met through broad economic reforms. The Cárdenas administration's efforts to reform education and land tenure often failed to distinguish between nonindigenous and indigenous peasant communities.[10] Indigenistas responded to this contradictory set of policies by carving out a novel strategy. They began to argue that economic reforms of material life were compatible with cultural differences they figured as autonomous. This approach would accelerate after 1940, when the administration of President Manuel Ávila Camacho (1940–46) intensified the developmentalist push of the Mexican state.[11]

In the United States, New Deal reformers' efforts coalesced with the June 1934 passage of the Wheeler-Howard Act (or Indian Reorganization Act, IRA)—the backbone of the Indian New Deal. Building on suggestions in the 1928 Meriam Report, the bill abrogated prior policies. The IRA also included provisions for drafting new tribal constitutions and creating Native governments recognized by the Indian Service. The Indian New Deal sought to secure Native peoples' economic autonomy and self-government; promote economically viable handicrafts and other industries; give Native peoples access to local schools, clinics, and hospitals; and show greater tolerance for cultural difference. Under Collier, the IS curtailed efforts to root out Native religions; provided Native communities with land and credit; closed the boarding schools that had yanked young people from their families and communities; and created new local schools that permitted the use of Native languages alongside English. But Collier and his cohorts never questioned the ultimate authority of the IS, even when it fell short of its stated goals.

Collier, like Manuel Gamio, became a major figure bridging the worlds of policy and academia. He played an important role in U.S. policymaking not only at home but also abroad, especially in relation to Mexico. The commissioner was a romantic critical of the modern mass culture spawned by industrialization and partial to anthropological theories of cultural relativism. More than his close collaborators, Collier searched for ways of making pluralism compatible with the modernization of Native agricultural and economic practices, health care, education, and governance. Especially in the later years of his administration, Collier combined cultural relativism with functionalist frameworks that, in contrast to Mexican approaches, linked culture and technology to politics, economics, family, and spirituality. Functionalism made it harder for U.S. reformers to envision transformations of Native communities that did not undermine them.

The functionalist perspective, which would increasingly shape U.S. policy and thinking, was succinctly summarized by one of Collier's collaborators, physician and anthropological researcher Dorothea Leighton: "A coherent culture represents a very delicate adjustment between people and environment which has been arrived at by countless generations of trial and error," she wrote. "If it be thoughtlessly and undiscriminatingly interfered with, the disruption and the loss to human happiness and human safety may sometimes be incalculable." Leighton illustrated her point by providing the example of "Tom," whose Navajo family was "as much white in their way of living as one is likely to find among The People." Tom's family farmed using "modern" irrigation and heeded government officials. Family members built a "good house" rather than living in a flimsy hogan and did not attend Navajo ceremonials. But the family nonetheless disliked whites. Leighton wondered why and suggested that they had acculturated too quickly.[12] This kind of functionalist viewpoint provided little concrete guidance for administrators, besides admonishing them to know Native cultures deeply and proceed cautiously. It made modernization (premised on rationality and science and hence universal) and indigeneity (premised on unthinking tradition and difference) seem like a perilous combination.

INTERPRETATIONS OF NEW Deal and Cardenista Indian policies written by participants generally emphasized the success of those policies in halting the most punitive assimilationist measures and redistributing land. Subsequently, in the 1960s, interpretations became more critical of these reforms. Revisionist historians accepted that Mexico's postrevolutionary governments had neutralized local powerholders who paid substandard wages, gobbled up the most productive lands, and gouged Native peoples in local marketplaces, but they pointed out that postrevolutionary governments had also created new local and regional strongmen who became as authoritarian as their predecessors.[13] Revisionist historical accounts of the Indian New Deal noted that Collier foisted policies of self-government on Native groups with little respect for existing forms of communal authority. The Indian Service dictated policies throughout the country for reservation schools, clinics, and other services that were implemented in a top-down fashion that failed to account for local conditions. Russell Barsh has put forward an even less sympathetic view of Collier, suggesting that his rejection of termination, which Congress continued to place before him for consideration, was a ploy to retain IS control and perpetuate the IS bureaucracy.[14]

As revisionists note, following the passage of the IRA, Collier toured Native communities, encouraging them to vote in favor of drafting constitutions and to elect their governments as stipulated by the IRA. During these visits, the commissioner offered veiled threats along with the enticement of credit for productive enterprises. Communities felt compelled to align their tribal governments with the provisions of the IRA, even when that meant abandoning prior forms of collective decision making. Collier's efforts often failed or had paradoxical results, notoriously so among the Navajos, where the IS forced stock reduction measures aimed at combatting overgrazing but in the process harmed some of the poorest Navajos. The stock reduction measures deepened rifts among tribal members, some of whom were for compliance and others against. After all, not all members of a given community or tribe had similar interests or perspectives. In certain situations, women benefited more than men (or vice versa); in some situations, youth benefited more than elders.[15]

But although reforms often aggravated existing divisions within groups, this was not in every case the intent of the reforms, as postrevisionist scholarship acknowledges. Responsibility for divisions within communities cannot be placed only, or primarily, on white or mestizo powerholders. Postrevisionist scholarship has also suggested that reforms did not always proceed in a straight line. Policies initially implemented in ways Native groups saw as unfavorable sometimes yielded long-run benefits as Native peoples learned to use the imposed techniques, tools, and methods. On the Blackfeet reservation, studied by Paul Rosier, the establishment of the tribal governments following IRA rules initially generated conflicts between traditionalist "full-breeds" and more Westernized "half-breeds." But IRA-induced tribal governments ultimately allowed the tribe to gain control of lucrative oil contracts and to exercise effective economic and political decision making.[16] The historiography on Mexico has come to similar conclusions. Historian Mary Kay Vaughan has suggested that certain Mexican communities, especially those with greater proximity to white-mestizo culture, were able to bargain more effectively with local and regional powerholders and to manipulate government mandates to their own benefit. Shane Dillingham argues that the Mexican government's recognition of Native governments and Native intermediaries paradoxically helped stimulate the indigenous movements that took shape in the 1970s.[17]

Indian policymaking, and more generally the applied social sciences, as I analyze them here, developed within the broader field of power that included the actions of influential stakeholders unconcerned with Native welfare and covetous of Native lands and resources. Collier's arguments against termination of IS protection and control over Native communities may have been a self-serving maneuver to perpetuate the IS, but the liberal notions of individualism that had guided allotment in the United States and disentailment in Mexico had produced massive loss of land, overseen and sanctioned by nation-states that favored large-scale capitalist interests. In a context of overall state expansion, Collier's contention that government should take responsibility for righting this state of affairs seems consistent and logical as well as fair. The IS was indeed paternalistic, as were the scholars who supplied the IS with the data it needed. But federal control of Native policy also implied recognition of the special status of Native peoples and of the rights and privileges they had established, as nations and through treaties, with the government. Similarly, Mexico's local *agraristas* and indigenistas who supported Cárdenas could be as authoritarian as their Porfirian predecessors, and postrevolutionary federal attention to Native peoples was clearly a bid to establish central control over heterogeneous regions and political economies. But federal control did displace some of the most powerful and forceful, and least democratic, local and regional elites, and it often did so with the help of local communities. In these broader political struggles, anthropologists—as well as schoolteachers, geologists, and agronomists, many of whom lived in the communities they produced knowledge about—were crucial translators and mediators.[18]

THE CHAPTERS THAT FOLLOW place the knowledge practices behind Native policy in a transnational framework. Experts did not just mediate between local communities and national states; they also translated across national borders. Beginning with early twentieth-century Pan-American conferences, the development of new knowledge practices bolstered U.S.-Mexico relationships, and indigenismo became a plank of Roosevelt's Good Neighbor policy, itself a reflection of the broader political changes that spawned Cardenismo, the New Deal, and less punitive policies toward Native peoples. Mexican indigenistas contended with the disparaging U.S. views by intensifying comparisons but reversing their valences, as we have seen. By contrast, Commissioner Collier called into question U.S. exceptionalism by placing the United States within a broader continental and global context. Along with many of his collaborators, Collier showed a willingness to see U.S. struggles with its racial and cultural diversity as part of a broader American pattern.

As a member of the American Indian Defense Association, Collier had established connections with Mexican experts on Native policy even before taking office. As commissioner, he worked with his Mexican counterparts to encourage collaboration among Indian agencies across the Americas, an effort that culminated in plans for an Inter-American Indigenous Institute. The process that led to the founding of the IAII began in 1933, at the Seventh International Conference of American States in Montevideo, where delegates called for a Pan-American conference on Native issues. When the conference repeatedly failed to materialize, participants at the 1939 Americanists Conference in Mexico City hatched a plan for a conference in Mexico. Moisés Sáenz worked with Collier and his envoys to plan what came to be called the Inter-American Conference on Indian Life, which took place at Pátzcuaro, in Cárdenas's home state of Michoacán. The conference was attended by government delegates, along with a few dozen indigenous delegates, mostly from Mexico, and a good number of social scientists from throughout the Americas. Cárdenas gave the opening speech. Collier delivered the response. The conference resolutions called for the constitution of a governmental institution focused on generating knowledge that could be deployed by governments throughout the continent. The IAII would function as a knowledge clearinghouse for policymakers; staff a news service; collect and distribute data on population, government budgets, and the history of Indian policy; and make U.S. and Mexican achievements intelligible for other countries. Each member country was expected to create a national Indian institute to devise national policies.[19]

The formation of the IAII helped Sáenz, Collier, and Gamio cement their importance within national and international indigenista circles. Sáenz directed efforts to seek the necessary government ratifications, and he remained acting director until he died unexpectedly in 1941. In the United States, Collier worked to demonstrate that indigenismo was an important flank of Pan-Americanism and of the broader war effort, and the U.S. Senate passed the Pátzcuaro Convention in May 1941.[20] As required, Collier set up a U.S. National Indian Institute to coordinate the Pan-American work. Sáenz was slated to become IAII director, but after his death, Gamio became its leader. Collier served as president of the governing board.[21]

The U.S. entrance into World War II, which augmented the nation's power and, eventually, its imperial pretensions, shifted the Pan-American knowledge project. Policymakers increasingly sought to identify regularities within and across borders that foreign and domestic governments might effectively manipulate. Rather than seeing the United States as one American nation among others that sought knowledge regarding diverse societies so as to guide local practice—a viewpoint closer to that of the Mexican indigenistas and to Collier's earlier formulations—the social and human sciences increasingly sought broadly applicable knowledge regarding modernization. They now deployed the examples of Native governance from abroad they had been collecting, along with the U.S. experiences with its domestic minorities, to shape possible postwar policies overseas.

This shift became evident after the Japanese attack on Pearl Harbor, when Collier and the IS signed on to run the prison camp at Poston, Arizona. Initially, Collier became involved in conversations regarding the Japanese American confinement when the U.S. Army identified a site on the Colorado River Indian reservation as a possible location for a camp. The commissioner wanted to ensure that the land the government occupied would be returned to the Native Americans when the camp closed. He ended up agreeing to run what would become largest of the "internment camps." Collier believed that he could engineer a more humane experience for the imprisoned Japanese Americans by drawing on his knowledge about how to govern more democratically across ethnic differences, including the lessons he learned from Mexico. He also believed the camp would generate lessons that the United States might apply in an eventual postwar occupied Japan.[22]

In the 1930s, Collier had taken lessons from Mexico. In the 1940s, he posited his Indian Service as a model of administration to be emulated, perhaps imposed, around the world. The IS, he now argued, was a repository for knowledge regarding governance across ethnic difference that might serve as a basis for shaping policies toward the disparate local peoples the United States might face during the war and after. The United States, the commissioner suggested, would now export models based on its own experiences of governing democratically across differences that he termed "colonial." The notion that the United States would provide models for the rest of the world thus developed alongside the view that the United States could collect and systematize knowledge from around the globe as part of its global hegemony. The United States now had the means to build an unbiased, comprehensive file of knowledge about race—a goal that some had advocated in the 1920s.[23]

Collier and his allies embraced a more global, universalizing perspective but did not abandon cultural pluralism. Like many other intellectuals, they believed that they could touch the essence of humanity by arraying its diversity. At the Museum of Modern Art in New York, Edward Steichen's photographic exhibition *The Family of Man* (1955) would put cultural diversity on display while positing universal human strivings and emotions: courting, parenting, eating, playing, dancing, singing, hunting, planting, grieving.[24] Laura Thompson and others who collaborated closely with Collier moved in circles influenced by Bronislaw Malinowski, who propounded the universal psychic and physiological needs of the individual. Thompson, who married Collier in 1943, linked these ideas about universal humanity to liberal notions of individual freedom.

In Mexico, too, cultural pluralism partially gave way to more unilateral approaches to modernization as Ávila Camacho succeeded Cárdenas. By 1940, political mobilizations had been largely subsumed to state needs by the creation of popular organizations tied to the ruling party. The Ávila Camacho administration and those that followed were more interested in consolidating state power and modernizing the economy than in the redistributive efforts that had characterized the Cárdenas years. The stage was set for the cooptation of popular petitions, the rightward political turn of governing elites, and the push for economic modernization. Demands for improved access to land would be met by technological fixes aimed at enhancing efficiency rather than the redistribution of property and wealth. Intellectuals increasingly subordinated questions of race and ethnicity to questions of economics and class, seeking data that could be readily measured, counted, and ordered on a scale of modernity. Antiracism, which had always been intertwined with the difficulties of racial categorization, would shade into a denial of race, as policymakers and experts accepted the persistence of only those non-Western cultural attributes that did not obstruct economic modernization.

3

From Cultural Pluralism to a Global Science of Acculturation in the United States

Historian Natalia Molina has demonstrated the "relational" nature of race and racism. The racial scripts used to discriminate against Los Angeles's Mexican American community drew from practices that had been deployed earlier against the city's Chinese community. Those scripts, however, also breached borders, as is shown by the trajectory of Commissioner of Indian Affairs John Collier, who began his career working with immigrants in New York City and California; took up the cause of Native Americans; brokered Indian Service involvement in the internment of Japanese and Japanese Americans; and, on leaving office in 1945, founded the Institute of Ethnic Affairs, devoted to bettering conditions for Spanish Americans and blacks, as well as colonized peoples, notably Guamanians.[1] Collier looked abroad for lessons he could use at home. He surveyed contemporary colonies, the history of Spanish colonialism in New Spain, and postrevolutionary Mexico. In the 1930s, he worked to create Pan-American circuits of knowledge.

Throughout his career, Collier sought to preserve the integrity of Native societies and other marginalized communities while helping them incorporate aspects of modern Euro-U.S. culture. He paid particular attention to the role of Native intermediaries, who might translate modernity into Native idioms while preserving difference. Just as important, Collier and his collaborators used fieldwork as a vehicle of acculturation within and across the borders of the United States. They found that IS administrators, Native intermediaries, and field researchers could all set in motion processes of acculturation that would change everyone involved.

As a number of historians have noted, Commissioner Collier deployed models based on British colonial rule and other examples of indirect colonialism that aimed to preserve and use Native leadership. Yet the historiography on Collier has been mostly silent regarding the commissioner's fascination with Spanish colonialism. That fascination grew initially from his interest in the Pueblo people of the Southwest, whose cultural integrity had, in his view, been preserved by methods of Spanish colonial government. Collier's contact with Mexico and Mexican scholars furthered his attachment to the Spanish colonial model. He insisted that the kind of indirect rule that Spain had implemented could promote local democracy by creating nonhierarchical forms of interaction across cultures and horizontal forms of leadership within cultures. To develop his ideas, Collier drew from philosophical pragmatism, social-psychological theories of leadership and influence, and theories of acculturation, all of which were concerned with similar issues. He also drew from anarchist ideas regarding local democracy that he had embraced in his youth. Yet in insisting that models of indirect colonial rule were compatible with the local democracy of face-to-face groups, Collier suggested, perversely, that his ideal was a reality. And he made local democracy stand in for democracy tout court. In the process, he papered over some unsavory aspects of both U.S. and Mexican governance of Native peoples.

Collier saw colonial governance not as an exception to democracy but rather as a form of potentially democratic governance across ethnic, racial, and cultural differences—whether domestic or foreign. National and colonial governance, foreign and domestic, were not for him opposites. Both could be part of a U.S. democratic imperial formation. In fact, Collier and his colleagues often studied peoples who themselves bridged foreign and domestic or who challenged distinctions between colonial subject and national citizen, including Native Americans, Hawaiians, Spanish Americans, and Guamanians.[2] Collier imported foreign and imperial experiences to fortify democracy. Increasingly, as U.S. power manifested itself during World War II, he also sought to export U.S. lessons abroad, spreading democracy via empire.

In some ways Collier's thinking was unique, and many contemporaries considered him eccentric. Few politicians would have recognized U.S. colonial and imperial ambitions in the way Collier did. Rather than work in isolation, however, Collier drew from and contributed to an extensive network of academic allies, including University of Chicago scholars such as anthropologists Robert Redfield and Lloyd Warner. He also collaborated with former students of Franz Boas such as Ruth Benedict and Margaret Mead. Other trusted advisers included child study expert Lawrence Frank, psychoanalysts A. A. Brill and Jacob Moreno, and social psychologist Kurt Lewin. Among his closest collaborators were psychiatrists Dorothea and Alexander Leighton, who had worked with Native groups in the United States and were immersed, as were Benedict and Mead, in the field of culture and personality studies. Laura Thompson, an anthropologist of the Pacific Islands who had been raised in Hawaii, was a key confidante from the time they met in 1941 until they divorced in 1956.[3]

From Immigration Policy to Indian Policy

Because Collier and his contemporaries came of age in the aftermath of massive international migrations, they were greatly concerned with the potential difficulties that cultural diversity posed for democracy. Collier worked from 1907 to 1919 with immigrants on New York City's Lower East Side and later briefly in Progressive Americanization efforts for the California State Housing and Immigration Commission, until conservative opposition forced his resignation. In this early work, Collier rejected assimilationist efforts at Americanization, arguing that immigrants could maintain the traditions of their homelands while embracing U.S. customs. He helped organize a New York City pageant of nations in which immigrants paraded in the costumes of their homelands. Collier's goal was to teach their "proudly, blatantly, intolerantly American" children to enjoy Old World traditions, while enriching the immigrants' culturally impoverished adoptive nation.[4]

According to historian Kenneth Philp, Collier was a devotee of the anarchist Peter Kropotkin, an evolutionist who rejected the Social Darwinist mantra of competition and marshaled biological evidence to argue that the essence of human nature was cooperation. In line with this anarchist intellectual matrix, Collier favored spontaneous, cooperative self-organization over hierarchical leadership.[5] He therefore downplayed his own role in organizing the pageant of nations, claiming that "all the initiative, the planning," had come from the people. Collier likewise referred to community centers he was organizing as self-governing institutions in which leaders would use their power sparingly if at all and direct neighbors to take initiative themselves. Collier called these community centers "clearinghouses" for community services—the same term would later be used to describe the IAII—places for the horizontal exchange and transmission of information. In discussing immigrant children's games, he likewise argued that teachers would not need to teach the rules of play because they would pass spontaneously from one generation to the next. As Kropotkin might have predicted, there was little conflict and no hierarchy.[6] Here, in a nutshell, was the theory of culture and government action Collier would espouse as commissioner, one that wishfully elided the power of leaders and cultural translators and that blinded him to the paternalism of his own policies.

Collier's work with New York's immigrants focused not on race but on culture. His efforts were nevertheless part of an ongoing discussion regarding Americanization, cultural transmission, and acculturation that harked back to race, biology, and reproduction. Collier occasionally employed the language of biological inheritance, and his focus on children and community life also looked to arenas of experience that, as we have seen, had helped define race.

Collier was a close friend of Luther H. Gulick, an educator and specialist in physical education, who with his wife, Charlotte Gulick, founded the Campfire Girls. Luther Gulick was a follower of psychologist G. Stanley Hall, who argued that individual growth and development mirrored social evolution. Gulick and Collier talked at length about "heredity, growth, and the growth of the mind." Because the Gulicks so admired Native Americans' supposed "intensiveness of group life" (as Collier put it), they wove Native symbolism into the Campfire Girls. Group life and individual development were thus linked to Native Americans in Collier's mind as early as 1910.[7]

Collier was pulled into advocacy on behalf of Native Americans around 1920, after resigning from the California State Housing and Immigration Commission. Mexico played a starring role in Collier's accounts of this transition, which invariably mentioned a camping trip to Mexico with his family and five dogs. But it appears that instead of Mexico, Collier went to Taos, New Mexico, to visit his friend Mabel Dodge. There, he became entranced by Pueblo ritual, and his lifelong fascination with the Pueblo people began.[8]

One of Collier's first publications on Native issues, titled "The Red Atlantis," drew from his work with immigrants. It also presaged his work as commissioner. Collier addressed the theme of acculturation and Americanization by noting that at the Spanish church in Cordova, no one hurried and no one spoke English. Collier contrasted its relaxed, cooperative premodern culture to the hurried and harried modern white culture. Whereas a "severe individualism" prevailed in the Taos artists' colony, the nearby Indian artists were "intensely social." Drawing on anarchist currents, Collier advocated channeling the Pueblos' communal spirit into modern cooperative arrangements.[9]

Observing a Pueblo initiation ritual, Collier was no doubt reminded of his conversations regarding adolescent growth and socialization with the Gulicks. In that ritual he saw an alternative model of creating social bonds: "Of all the contrasts between primitive and modern life, none is more complete . . . [than] this one," Collier remarked.

> Primitive groups in all continents have utilized the adolescent crisis as a means to the perpetuation of social heritages and to the building of

powerful citizenship. Within and through the public crisis, they have brought into being mental complexes, sentiments and habits which in negative and positive ways have controlled attitude and conduct through the remainder of life. The methods and results have been endlessly varied, but the broad result has been to insure recurrent flowerings of emotion, conformities of behavior and adequacies of effort. . . . Through suggestion and autosuggestion, through travails, fastings, lonely marches and group-assemblages, the youth prepared himself. . . . All that was deepest, most awful, most romantic, most energizing in his emotions, rose within this social setting and discharged itself toward social ends.

Although this group spirit was not a bodily racial inheritance, as both Darwinians and neo-Lamarckians might have it, it was nevertheless deeply embedded in a developing self that was an echo of the group. Collier invoked William James's essay "The Moral Crisis of War," which praised the character-building elements of the military and the ideal of selflessness that military service elicited. Native rituals could serve as alternatives to the group loyalty the military inspired, he believed.[10]

By 1922, Collier had become an activist on behalf of Native peoples and a staunch opponent of U.S. government policies. He was a founding member and executive secretary of the American Indian Defense Association, created in 1923 as Congress debated whether to grant U.S. citizenship to Native peoples and terminate the federal government's responsibility for administering Native affairs. In response to the Bursum Bill of 1922 and other legislation that legitimated non-Indian claims on lands occupied by Native groups, Collier and his associates in the American Indian Defense Association worked with the Pueblos and others to make their voices heard in Congress. Collier helped create the political climate that led to the 1928 Meriam Report, which provided the blueprint for reform of U.S. Indian policy. "The Indian Bureau," Collier wrote in 1929, "is the nexus of a conspiracy of robbery under quasi-legal forms."[11]

Collier, the Colonial, and Mexico

Curious about why Native culture among the Pueblos was so resilient despite white efforts to extinguish it, Collier sought out experts, including Charles Lummis, who had written about Mexico and Central and South America. Collier began studying Spanish colonialism in New Spain, and in 1930, he traveled to Mexico for the first time. Over the next decades,

Collier would commend Mexico's postrevolutionary social engineering and praise postrevolutionary policies inspired by the colonial era friars and by the colonial Laws of the Indies. A 1932 essay by Collier in the journal *Progressive Education* lauded Mexico for recognizing the "corporate embodiment" of its Native peoples, eschewing "authoritative guardianship," and considering Indians as citizens. It applauded Mexico's local schools for broadly serving community needs.[12]

On a 1931 trip to Mexico City, Collier made the acquaintance of the country's indigenista intelligentsia. In Moisés Sáenz's Taxco home, Collier and Mexican indigenistas scrutinized the condition of Native peoples in the Americas. They became convinced of the importance of a hemispheric approach to Native politics, Collier remembered in 1942. Considering the idea that all Native peoples were part of a continental Red race, they asked: "Will the time come when the Indians can be united, when the Republics can pool their experience with Indians, when hemisphere-wide programs for the release of Indian spiritual and economic powers can be set upon their way?" They also discussed how "the good-will of white men" such as the Jesuits, Franciscans, and Dominicans had unified Indian history and created a framework for understanding the effects of the Spanish conquest. Collier, Sáenz, and their colleagues wanted their governments to build on this globalizing perspective.[13]

Collier's 1942 account of that visit inevitably reflected the desire for hemispheric unity that guided wartime U.S. foreign policy. His recollections also reflected the universalizing, generalizing predictive social science that was taking shape during the war. But Collier's use of a colonial model repeated a theme he had been playing on since the 1920s, when he had been introduced to theories of indirect colonialism and wrote articles comparing U.S. Indian policies to those of France and Belgium in the Congo. (The Congo had also made an appearance in "The Red Atlantis.") Around the time he visited Mexico, he read *Africa View*, by the British zoologist, eugenicist, and left-wing humanist Julian Huxley. The book asserted that indirect colonialism sought "'to maintain and support native rule (within the limits laid down) *and not to impose a form of British rule with the support of native chiefs, which is a very different thing.*'" Collier read a 1928 article on the Maori of colonial New Zealand by Felix Keesing, who claimed that the "New Zealand experiment in racial adjustment from Stone Age to civilized manner of life" could produce data relevant to the study of "racial contacts." Collier felt that Keesing's insights regarding the Maori could be "transposed almost wholly to apply to the American

Indians . . . [and suggested that] comparative study of the history of the present situation of 'primitives' might have averted many blunders by dominant governments in the past. It might point toward unguessed solutions for the future."[14]

Collier saw parallels among Spanish colonial, Mexican national, and British indirect colonial administration. Each sought to bolster Native forms of leadership. Each sought to govern through—rather than against—Native social structures. Theories of indirect colonial rule allowed Collier to sidestep troublesome questions about territory and sovereignty generated by Native peoples' anomalous place within liberal polities—the very issues that made separation along the lines of the Laws of the Indies troublesome to Mexico's heirs to the liberal tradition. Indirect rule sought to administer territory by facilitating political autonomy, but political autonomy was always circumscribed to localities. Theories of colonialism could thereby help justify the U.S. system of reservations.

Invoking colonialism, Collier referenced a form of governance that was then both pervasive and global. By the time Collier reached Mexico in 1931, he was alive to the importance of global and comparative knowledge of both Native peoples and administrative strategies, facilitated by the worldwide extension of colonial empires. Collier's interlocutors at Taxco were perhaps less attuned to the comparative history of colonialism but still familiar with the idea of applying anthropological knowledge to policy decisions. Indeed, Gamio had been touting that theme for more than a decade. Mexican intellectuals viewed colonialism as part of a history that provided positive models to follow and negative models to avoid. They valued the more humane and enlightened ethnographic aspects of Spanish colonialism even as they recognized Spain's colonial land and labor policies as exploitative.

Expertise and Native Agency

As commissioner of Indian affairs, Collier repeatedly championed Mexico's land and education policies and sought to emulate indigenista efforts to understand, catalog, and sustain cultural difference. He referred often to Mexico in his speeches and articles. For instance, in a 1936 address to the Council of Women for Home Missions, he argued that the monastic orders of New Spain tried to mitigate Spanish cruelty in Mexico, and he called the Laws of the Indies "one of the wisest bodies of law for Indians yet achieved." When Collier addressed Native American leaders at a large public meeting in western Oklahoma in 1934, he told the audience that the Mexican Indians had been landless and "practically slaves" before the revolution but that now their landholdings, wealth, and power were increasing. Why? Because Mexico governed its Native peoples in a form that was more democratic and less authoritarian than the past U.S. Indian Service administrations. Mexico followed colonial precedent in basing its administration on local knowledge and on the tolerance of difference, he said.[15]

Just as Collier's claims regarding immigrant self-organization had constituted a tactically useful misapprehension, he fancifully portrayed Mexico's indigenista institutions as vehicles for Native leadership, free of bureaucratic red tape. With great hyperbole Collier praised the "ejidas" [sic], describing them as "cooperative societies of mutual aid, which practically are land-holding and land-using corporations." The ejido, and not the government, would act in loco parentis, thereby ending government paternalism. He further characterized the ejido as a form of "indirect government," "the liberalizing, the democratic, and the economical and productive government." Moreover, in Mexico there was no centralized, "authoritative" Bureau of Indian Affairs. All was "coordinated locally— within neighborhoods of Indians—not centrally at the capital." And all this had been planned by a "sociologically informed statesmanship . . . [and] tested out through controlled and carefully recorded experiments and demonstrations." Already in late 1933, Collier had sent IS personnel to Mexico to see the new rural schools, which served—as he had hoped the New York City schools would—as community centers.[16]

Following the supposed Mexican model, Collier worked to make the IS less authoritarian. It would convince and cajole but not impose. He insisted that Indians themselves should solve Indian problems, and by the end of his term, the number of IS personnel of Native heritage had increased from about 30 percent to 65 percent (in Collier's accounting). Speaking to an assembly of social workers, Collier asserted that in Mexico "the fullness of Indian participation is noteworthy above everything else. Indeed the whole operation is Indian-made, and Indians are holding in the Mexican Indian Service every class of technical position to the highest and most professional."[17] He later noted in the 1934 Oklahoma meeting that Mexico's Indian Service was operated as he hoped to operate the U.S. Indian Service: "The Indians, themselves, hold nearly all of the positions right up to the top."[18]

Ernest Thompson of the Oklahoma Kaw people, perhaps suspicious of Collier's continual touting of Mexican examples, asked whether foreigners or aliens were working for the U.S. Indian Educational Bureau. Collier's reply to that xenophobic question implied that the presumed foreigners were Indians and therefore Native and not foreign. "The man who has had most to do with the development of this very successful Mexican Indian program is a man call[ed] Sions [Sáenz], a Mexican Indian," Collier responded.

Last autumn our American Government invited Dr. Sions to come up here as its guest and to advise us about Indian matters and he came. It was very interesting to me, there in Washington, after he had finished going around the Indian country, to see Dr. Sions meeting with the high officials, including the members of the cabinet in Washington. Dr. Sions, himself an Indian, and telling our own highest officials the story of how the Indians of Old Mexico are recapturing their lands. . . . Dr. Sions . . . has now gone back . . . but I wish it were possible to take one of you Indians down to Mexico and enable you to see that the Indians are capable of doing anything and of holding positions up to the very top of the profession and of being President of a great country and of running their own Indian Service.[19]

Sáenz came from a wealthy Sonoran family. He did not consider himself Indian, and Collier might easily have known this. When Sáenz died in 1941, Collier's memorial statement alluded to Sáenz's Indian blood. But the cover letter written by Collier's son asked whether Sáenz's family would object to his being called "Indian." Did the elder Collier attribute a lingering importance to a biological inheritance? Did he buy into Sáenz's own view that to be Mexican was to be in some way Indian, at least in part? Or was it simply convenient for Collier to portray Mexico's policy as "Indian-made"?[20]

Some months before Sáenz's death, in a letter to a U.S. scholar studying the ejido in Mexico, Collier made it plain that he understood the limitations of Mexican indigenismo but intentionally downplayed them. Mexican land policies were, he wrote, "far beyond attainability," and the ability of the government to carry out policies was limited by "the personnel operations of the government down there." There was indeed "red-tape"—or at least ineptitude. "But," Collier added in his letter, "don't pass these thoughts of mine along. And we here must always recognize that the big thing for us is to acclaim the philosophies and the purpose." In portraying Sáenz and the Mexican Indian policy as Indian, Collier likely saw himself as proclaiming a principle rather than describing a reality.[21]

The assertion nevertheless allowed Collier to claim that Mexico's influence on the U.S. government was, at least indirectly, the influence of Indians on a white European nation—not a foreign influence but the influence of a Native American and, perhaps, transnational, Pan-American subject. Like Chase, he used Native America to assert a continental American identity, one that Mexico embodied more fully than the United States, and also one that white civilization might emulate. Collier's overly optimistic view of Mexican indigenismo helped him press the point that government policy could activate Native agency. In describing Sáenz, Collier portrayed the Mexican indigenista as a "Dr." who consulted with U.S. cabinet members, thereby reaffirming both Indian agency and expertise. But in speaking of Sáenz as both an Indian and an expert, Collier sidestepped thorny questions regarding the role of the IS in shaping relations with Native peoples whose own forms of expertise were often not recognized. Collier felt that enlightened leadership on the part of government officials would empower Native peoples and renew lifeways understood as "traditional." But he never stopped believing that Native peoples might need expert help.

Since Native culture was not static, that help should come in the form of dialogue between Natives and non-Natives, and so Collier sought Native allies to serve as intermediaries, forging alliances with the less traditionalist factions within a number of Native groups. Yet Collier also felt that enlightened leadership would be scientific. By imagining Native intermediaries, who were, like Sáenz, also Native intellectuals, Collier avoided facing the possibility of conflict between science and the democratic empowerment of Native peoples or between modernity and Native lifeways. Collier's Mexican counterparts, however, could not avoid these dilemmas. Their ambiguous position as scientists made them more cognizant of the difficulties of using science to forge consensus.

Collier turned again to a Mexican example to illustrate how Native intermediaries conversant with modernity might harmoniously blend scientific knowledge and Native tradition. Young Indian men and women who attended normal school in Mexico later returned to their communities, he wrote: "Thus, in these Mexican schools the wisdom of the folk and the right instinct of the folk are fertilized and somewhat guided by first-rate sociological, anthropological and esthetic minds of cosmopolitan backgrounds."[22] Acculturation would not be teleological. It would be not simply biological mixing—although "fertilized" implied biological mestizaje—but a process shaped by an expertise grounded in cosmopolitan access to the diversity of the globe. Here again, Collier's perspective echoed that of Gamio and other Mexicans, although Gamio was more skeptical of claims of universal expertise.

Collier spoke in similar terms to a group of Navajo children returning to their communities from boarding schools. Addressing them as intermediaries who might bridge the best of white and Native worlds, he hoped that they would help solve Navajo problems by bringing to bear the "the incalculable power and value of knowledge, and of mastering of machinery and facts, and of technology." He nonetheless reminded his audience of the values maintained through the ages by Native peoples:

> It is the policy and duty of the Government to cherish and reawaken, in the mind and soul of the Indian, not only pride in being Indian, because all Indians have that, but hope for the future as an Indian, and love and ardor toward the rich, many-sided values of Indian life as expressed in the arts, the songs, the dances, the rituals, the cooperative institutions and forms which are yours as your heritage and have come down to you out of your past, and which the American nation needs just as much as you possibly can need the American nation. That is the point of view of the Indian Bureau today, along with an increased determination to bring to you science, modern ideas, and all that goes into making of practical effectiveness and of personal power. . . .
>
> You must—you can—as Indians take to yourselves the heritage of universal man—the gift of the modern world. You must—you can—use that new heritage to save your own native hope.[23]

Collier refused to draw a stark contrast between past and future, Native and European, traditional and modern. He nevertheless associated Native peoples with the past and with localized "folk" communities, in contrast to the cosmopolitan sensibilities of indigenistas. Collier both universalized the Native heritage and figured it as lodged in the past. He viewed the past both as part of the present and as something that had to be left behind. He separated and elided. Long a critic of the depersonalizing nature of industrial capitalism, Collier nevertheless harbored no doubts about the benefits of scientific animal breeding and range management, Western medicine, or book learning. He assumed that indigenous people wanted or needed the "American nation."

Even as Collier saw Native intermediaries as bridging Euro-American and Native lifeways, and even as he assumed that these intermediaries could, with IS guidance, preserve a changing tradition, he also knew that whites' ways must change, and IS personnel were also—and perhaps the primary—objects of change. Consequently, he sought to create a new sort of IS employee. Collier viewed most IS employees, especially those working in the field, as ignorant and steeped in paternalism, and he called for a new type of bureaucrat knowledgeable about local politics, able to transfer technological know-how, and willing to "surrender initiative" and yield power. He convinced the Rockefeller Foundation to create a pilot project to train new personnel who could more effectively implement his Indian New Deal. To achieve IS goals, Collier felt that IS personnel must transform their inner selves and their disposition toward others—emulating, perhaps, Sáenz's efforts to "Indianize" mestizo Mexico. What was needed was not just tolerance, Collier told Native American students at the Baptist Bacone College in Muskogee, Oklahoma, but sympathy, a "back and forth" action between groups of different races and religions. That sympathy would paradoxically intensify differences.[24]

Collier also felt that to make good policy Indian Service personnel needed more and better knowledge. Soon after taking office, he enlisted social scientists and other experts from the Soil Conservation Service of the Department of Agriculture to address soil erosion on Native lands, and in 1935, he convened an advisory board of anthropologists. An Applied Anthropology Unit (AAU) functioned from 1935 until 1938, when it was shuttered by budgetary constraints. Anthropologists with the AAU worked with tribal authorities on drafting tribal constitutions as stipulated in the IRA, although as Akim Reinhardt has noted, among the Pine Ridge Sioux and other tribes, the constitutions enacted were more often boilerplate than culturally sensitive documents.[25]

To illustrate IS success in empowering Native leadership while deploying social science, Collier repeatedly returned to successful efforts at soil conservation at Acoma Pueblo. The IS-appointed superintendent of the pueblo had legal authority to impose stock reduction measures aimed at preserving Southwest landscapes eroded by drought and overgrazing. But rather than impose her will, Collier argued, the pueblo superintendent shared the facts as she knew them. After months of debate, the people of Acoma finally approved the plan to drastically cull their sheep from 33,000 heads to 8,500. For Collier, the IS profited from waiting patiently "until the Pueblos' own central will took a painful task unto itself." As a result, Collier asserted, the people of Acoma did not become bitter but instead learned to cooperate with the IS, and the IS saved "probably millions by using social science and relying on the principle of democracy."

Among the Navajos, by contrast, the IS failed to understand that the tribal council lacked the authority to carry out stock reduction. As a result, stock reduction deeply divided the Navajos. The IS, moving hastily and without knowledge of local conditions, had only limited success. Just as important for Collier, IS policy among the Navajos had produced splits between old and new rather than blending them or translating the new into the old language.[26]

In the wake of the AAU's closure, Collier formulated a new research initiative that combined the many strands of his thinking about democratic leadership, Native intermediaries, and administration as acculturation. Collier's first version of this project envisioned an "Indian group from our tribes" going to a community in Mexico and vice versa. The U.S. Indians visiting Mexico would become informants for the IS investigators, and their presence would set off a process of acculturation that investigators could in turn analyze. In this proposal, the presumed similarities between Mexico and the United States would facilitate research across borders. Collier envisioned working with either the Papagos (today Tohono O'odham), who lived on both sides of the U.S.-Mexico border, or the Pueblos, who had at different times lived under Mexican and U.S. sovereignty. But the proposed investigation also depended on differences between the United States and Mexico, differences that would lead to acculturation and allow the Indians to observe a (changing) other. The proposal presented indigenous people as agents who investigated and stimulated acculturation rather than passive objects observed by an outsider. Yet Indians remained objects of study, both standing in—and serving as intermediaries—for the white experts. With some condescension, the commissioner wondered whether having Indians as researchers would lead to oversimplification, but he concluded that it would be useful to get rid of technical verbiage.[27]

In the end, however, Collier did not use Indians as researchers. Instead, schoolteachers and nurses did much of the field research for what became known as the Indian Personality Project, of which Laura Thompson was the coordinator. Although the project's ostensible goal was to understand how to engineer favorable changes in Native societies while minimizing disruption, the fieldwork became a formidable instance of acculturation in its own right. Reflecting on the completed project, Thompson remarked on one unexpected outcome: ironically, it was perhaps the Anglo-U.S. researchers who were most changed. Prior research coming from IS headquarters, Thompson noticed, had often antagonized local residents and local IS administrators alike. The personality project had instead tried to draw in local Indians and non-Indian residents on the reservations. "Certain Indians considered it just one more field project which, like countless others in the past, would disturb and exploit the Indian for the benefit of white scientists." But for the teachers, the research was eye-opening. Their knowledge of Native values and lifeways had been limited to the "superficial observations" made in the classroom or on the playground. Many had never before been inside a Native home, and their first home visits were full of "surprises and even shocks." The firsthand knowledge helped them professionally. Applying intelligence tests, they learned not only to appreciate their students' aptitudes but also "a great deal of value to themselves," and participation "fostered their personal growth." Thompson concluded that the participants' experiences "tended to deepen their awareness of, and respect for, societies and cultures different from their own."[28] Thompson believed democratic consensus demanded respect for others' cultural differences.

Two Visitors and a Turn toward the Pacific, 1941

In the early 1940s, with World War II casting doubt on the future of colonial dependencies, Collier rekindled his interest in colonialism. According to the commissioner, two visits in 1941 from scholars familiar with Pacific dependencies "completed a cycle" in his thought. The first visitor was Felix Keesing, the anthropologist whose work on the Maori Collier had read many years before. The great-grandson of one of the earliest British missionaries to Fiji, Keesing had been born in the Federated Malay States and raised in New Zealand. After graduating from the University of New Zealand in 1928 with a master's thesis on the Maori, he went to the United States and did graduate work with Clark Wissler at Yale University. Keesing then moved to the University of Chicago before taking a position with the Institute of Pacific Relations, where he visited and wrote on Samoa and the Philippines. From there, he studied for a year with Malinowski at the London School of Economics and then headed to Honolulu, where he became chair of the first department of anthropology and sociology at the University of Hawaii.[29]

In 1941, Collier read Keesing's *South Seas in the Modern World*, a synthetic survey that described the adjustment of Native peoples of the Pacific to modernity and Western encroachments. At their Washington meeting, Collier and

Keesing had discussed parallels between the Maori and the U.S. Menominee Indians, whom Keesing studied at Yale. Collier took *South Seas* as a model for the research he wanted to carry out on Native Americans. He would echo the geographic scope of *South Seas* by focusing on North and South America.[30]

The second visitor Collier received in 1941 was Laura Thompson.[31] This young anthropologist would become Collier's closest collaborator and his second wife. Thompson was born and raised in Hawaii. Her father was British, her mother from Nevada and San Francisco. She first came into contact with anthropology after college when she worked briefly at the Bishop Museum in Honolulu. The museum, Thompson would later recall, was inhabited by people who transgressed literal and figurative borders: translating, masquerading, cross-dressing, and, like spies, taking on false identities. This experience prepared her for the liminal position she would occupy as a woman inhabiting the tribe of (male) anthropologists. Bishop Museum curator Edwin Bryan was rumored to appear once a year at the museum dressed as a woman; Peter Buck, who later became director of the museum, was part Maori; Mary Kawen Pukui, a folklorist and an authority on Hawaiian culture, was in Thompson's words an "expert informant and translator of Hawaiian texts." And retired Vassar College professor Martha Beckwith, another Hawaii expert at the museum, was a "white-haired lady" who Thompson described in her memoirs as having a "fragile, feminine appearance [that] belied her disciplined approach to her subject." Beckwith, who was fluent in the Hawaiian language and had lived in California for a time, boasted that she could slip across the border into Mexico "as a little old lady innocent of the ulterior motives of an inquiring scientist and collector of tales, or other suspicious activities usually associated with spies and other doubtful characters."[32]

Thompson began graduate studies in anthropology at Radcliffe College, but she was put off by the sexism of the Harvard professors, one of whom suggested she really wanted to marry an anthropologist, not become one. Thompson transferred to the University of California at Berkeley, where the anthropology department was considered fairer to women doctoral students. There, she met and married a German graduate student in German literature, Bernhard Tueting. Having completed her doctoral degree, Thompson won a competitive Bishop Museum fellowship, which supported her first sustained fieldwork, in Fiji's Southern Lau Islands, with Tueting at her side. After the two returned to the United States, Tueting had a nervous breakdown and lost his teaching job, and the couple decided to move to Germany. Hitler was on the rise, and Tueting's mental health continued to deteriorate. He became abusive. In spring 1938, Thompson escaped fascism and her first marriage, securing a divorce in Reno.[33]

Passed over for a full-time teaching position at the University of Hawaii, Thompson wrote up her research on Southern Lau and completed a book on Fiji. Subsequently, she received a commission to study the U.S. Naval Administration on Guam. Keesing supervised this research. From there, she visited Shanghai and Tokyo. Thompson was becoming a world denizen. She began writing and speaking on the dangers of fascism, which she had observed in Germany and in the Far East. It seemed to her that no one was listening until an IS anthropologist who had worked at the Bishop Museum told her that John Collier was interested in bright young women. (Thompson later noted that Collier was a native of Atlanta who "had the manners and the roving eye of a southern gentleman.")[34]

Collier and Thompson met, and in the weeks following Collier sent her a sampling of his writings on American Indians. Thompson liked what he had to say. Collier read *Fijian Frontier* and was equally taken with what Thompson had to offer. Thompson's stance toward colonial administration jibed with Collier's ambivalent efforts to empower Natives by directing them and to revive Native traditions by modernizing them. In her work on the Pacific, Thompson, like Keesing, stressed the various forms of colonial administration and the diverse ways in which colonial administrators and settlers interacted with local societies.[35]

In Keesing's dissection of colonial rule, the missionary, the trader, and the government official each had a distinct agenda and way of interacting with local cultures. Their effects were therefore different. As the nature of cultural contact changed over time, the changes did not always lead to a linear progression toward Western modernity. Trade ebbed and flowed, affecting local patterns of labor and consumption. Colonial administrators bought land, surveyed it, sold it, and redistributed it. Missionaries and administrators imposed moral and legal norms, but those norms were not applied consistently, and Native peoples blended and adapted them according to their desires and needs. Keesing and Thompson stressed the importance of Native actions. "Numbers of the natives themselves were active instruments of change," Kessing wrote. "The contact situation has been anything but just an imprinting by outsiders of new patterns upon passive native groups." In his introduction to *Fijian Frontier*, Bronislaw Malinowski summarized Thompson's stance: "She is in full sympathy with the attitude of the British authorities. She gives them due credit. . . .

But she makes it quite clear that the main adaptations, the creative phase of change and transition must be achieved by the natives themselves."[36]

Neither Keesing nor Thompson would likely have accepted that they were in "full sympathy" with colonial powers, yet they accepted colonialism as a fact of life. Their criticisms of it were generally mild, and they were optimistic about the ability of colonial powers to do good. If colonialism was diverse, it might be made better. Keesing suggested that colonial authorities would eventually respond "to the moving forces of democracy and philanthropy by assuming a more positive form." Colonialism would then become "enlightened and successful," improving material well-being and education and fostering self-government. Unfortunately, there was also "ample room" for less favorable "alternatives"—outright economic expropriation, land grabs, violence.[37] Although colonialism might soon be overthrown, Keesing did not fear this. In fact, he rejected the view that nationalist leaders were "'communist agitators'" or "discontented or perverted individuals," seeing them instead as "products of the times" and of "social unrest and political domination." Nationalism emerged, he said, because of "pressure of alien will, feelings of uncertainty and frustration, a sense of resentment at being looked down upon, a reaction against following Western models as a result of disillusionment as to the benefits to be gained, a desire to build up once more the group status and integrity, contact with ideas of freedom and self-determination stirring widely in the modern world."[38]

Keesing was nevertheless worried—here his paternalism became evident—about whether nationalism would take the proper form. Colonial administrators should let "the people work out their political destiny themselves, though, of course, with every guidance that is feasible." Native leaders might not yet be "fully competent," but they would, unfortunately perhaps, learn from their experiences. This was, Keesing had to admit, idealistic given the strategic and commercial interests of "dominant white groups." In that context, anthropologists might use "sympathetic cooperation and ameliorative measures" to avoid conflicts between settlers and Natives. Protest could be channeled into forms of self-expression that were palatable. In the future, international agreements might allow Native peoples to "continue their march to self-government outside the limits set by imperialism."[39] The IS, Collier surely noted on reading this book, faced a similar dilemma when considering whether to terminate federal protections—although most advocates of termination favored liberal property rights rather than national sovereignty.

Keesing, like Collier, contrasted his own position to those of assimilationists, which Keesing equated specifically with U.S. policies of immigrant Americanization. Keesing also objected to the opposing viewpoint of those who drew a cordon sanitaire around the Pacific Islands. His own view was premised on the notion that adaptation to modernity had been difficult even in the West and that Native cultures included "rich accumulations of human experience that are well worth preserving, as well as efficient adjustments to the local island environments." In reality, colonized peoples "nativized" Western culture into a "cultural blend infused with the indigenous spirit."[40]

Keesing addressed the question of race in another section of *South Seas*, in which he aligned himself squarely against biological or hereditarian arguments. Despite racial variations among individuals, he said, there was no evidence of intrinsic differences among groups. "Neural systems" were plastic, he wrote, and any observed differences in temperaments or traits among groups should be attributed to "patterns of personality and conduct," an allusion to Ruth Benedict's *Patterns of Culture*. Keesing also noted the "realistic fact" that cultural differences worked out over millennia could be very difficult, but not impossible, to overcome.[41]

In an essay on applied anthropology, Melville J. Herskovits laid out a critique of colonial powers' use of anthropological knowledge. Applauding efforts to "cushion the clash of cultures to any degree possible," Herskovits noted that although there was no reason to question the motivations of anthropologists who contributed to colonial projects, the results of their actions might harm those they wished to aid. The anthropologist might end up like a defense lawyer who was compelled to give evidence against his client. Herskovits was especially critical of Keesing's mentor Malinowski, who had begun by trying to make colonialism less disruptive to Native peoples but too often ended up making colonial exploitation more efficient. This was especially problematic because, unlike physicists, anthropologists owed allegiance to the people they studied. The U.S. Indian Service, Herskovits concluded, was at the time "unequivocally on the side of the native," allowing anthropologists to work "wholeheartedly" with it. But even so, an emphasis on short-term applied thinking might lead to the abandonment of the long-term intellectual projects on which intellectuals ought rightly to focus.[42]

Here in a nutshell was Collier's conundrum. Even as he valued and sought to protect and preserve Native lifeways and to serve Native peoples, his office gave him the power and resources to manage Native affairs. Were stock management plans, new schools, or better-trained IS personnel what Native peoples really needed or wanted? In the short term, for some, perhaps the answer was "yes." Policies that improved conditions in the short run, however, pushed aside more deep-seated issues and problems. Moreover, the emphasis on science and rationality was doubly problematic because science was intimately bound up with modernity, which was still defined as non-Native. Collier's thinking, like that of Thompson, Keesing, and the Mexican indigenistas, was no doubt an earnest and creative effort to come to terms with these contradictions. They understood the complexities of both Native administration and Native societies, and they grappled with ways of characterizing the complex outcomes they observed. But Collier and his allies also made unrealistic plans, including plans for expert intermediaries, Native and non-Native. They sought a reconciliation based on a vision of colonialism that the objects of their studies did not necessarily share.

Democracy, Leadership, and Community

World War II shifted the terms of engagement between the United States and Mexico and between U.S. and Mexican indigenistas. The U.S. government, worried that Axis powers might take over the American colonies of France, Holland, or Britain, intensified its efforts to court the American nations. At a July 1940 meeting of foreign ministers, the American states had agreed to mutual hemispheric defense against possible outside aggressors. A month later, President Roosevelt appointed Nelson Rockefeller to head an Office for Coordination of Commercial and Cultural Relations between the American Republics (later renamed Office of the Coordinator of Inter-American Affairs, OCIAA) within the Executive Office of the President. The new agency was to use cultural diplomacy to foment hemispheric solidarity and ensure that the United States retained access to vital natural resources and goods coming from Latin America. Some six months later, Roosevelt's Four Freedoms speech defined the Americas, North and South, as lands of democracy. As the war rekindled the discourse of democracy, Collier confounded the local democracy he had previously advocated with the Allies' wartime ideal of antiracist democracy.

As new sources of funding related to the war appeared, Collier saw an opportunity and focused increasingly on Pan-American projects. At home, Collier's Indian New Deal was suffering. Emergency funding for IS programs provided from the Civilian Conservation Corps and other sources was now drying up. Hostile members of Congress repeatedly denied Collier funding for his projects. The Pátzcuaro conference, however, had reenergized Pan-American organizing around Native issues. The commissioner argued that Pan-American efforts to address issues of concern to Native peoples were part of hemispheric defense. Collier reminded U.S. government officials that "30 million Indians and 45 million people of Indian heritage" in the Americas created "important bonds between the American republics which can never be shared by any European or Asiatic nation."[43]

Furthermore, Collier argued, drawing on concepts articulated at Pátzcuaro, that democracy was not a modern Western invention but a long-standing practice within Native societies. Understanding democracy as the ability of individuals to participate in forms of local self-government and become "social creators," Collier presented as a model for the world the Pueblo Indians, whose local democracies supported their discussion of whether, how, and when, to adopt Western technologies. Repeating his earlier positions, he insisted that the Spanish imperial policy of indirect administration had allowed these forms of local democracy to persist. Even more, Collier suggested that the Indians' "deathless local democracies . . . [were] the material out of which a triumphing democracy of the West could build itself." The Pátzcuaro resolutions, he wrote, had called on national offices of Indian affairs to "work indirectly with the Indians through their organized group or community—organized for self-help, mutual aid, and mutual defense." Collier extended this line of argument: "Indirect Administration—the British in Oceania supplied this name—was recognized at Pátzcuaro to be a fundamental principle of Indian work by governments." The Pátzcuaro delegates, Collier reiterated, had counseled "governmental policies of knowing inwardly the Indian groups, using the groups, executing national as well as local purposes through the groups." Collier related Native administration inspired by indirect colonial rule to a Pan-American democracy linked to Native heritage. One of the first projects approved by the Inter-American Indigenous Institute was a historical study of Indian democracy in Mexico, to be carried out by historian Luis Chávez Orozco.[44]

Over the next few years, Collier repeatedly contrasted the life-affirming local democracies of the continent's Native peoples to the erasure of individuality and difference by German authoritarianism. In April 1941, he spoke in Chicago on Pan-American Day. Projecting local democracy globally, he asserted that Native democracies were "a Western world solidarity reaching from Arctic Alaska to Cape Horn." Speaking to IS personnel later that year, Collier linked this democracy to the individual freedoms fascism was trampling. "We are emphasizing as far as we can, in every policy and every procedure, the concept of local democracy, of the fullest participation of the individual Indian's personality in the life of his tribe, the life of the jurisdiction, of the community; the fullest participation of the individual Indian, the group, the neighborhood, the family, the tribe, in their own affairs and in the larger affairs of the world. The keynote of all we are doing is democracy conceived . . . as the giving of the self ardently into the hopes and the travails of the community. And we are discovering that democracy conceived in that way has never died from Indian life."[45]

Collier's thinking on democracy had been shaped since the 1910s by discussions within social psychology about how groups or leaders influenced individuals and how group belonging gave meaning to individual lives. Collier followed the work of sociologist Charles Horton Cooley, who had studied the community-building functions of primary social groups and face-to-face interactions among children. He was influenced as well by Austrian émigré psychologist Jacob Moreno, creator of sociometry, an approach to mapping and measuring the strength of interpersonal relations. Moreno pioneered the use of psychodrama, a group therapy that sought to forge spontaneous social bonds within a group as it re-created events in an individual's life. In the 1940s, Collier and Thompson both looked for ways that communities might shape individual conduct to oppose unthinking fascism. They turned to Cooley and, more quietly, to Moreno.[46]

Collier and Thompson also collaborated openly on research regarding personality and acculturation with Eugene Lerner and two German émigré psychologists, Kurt Lewin and Erich Fromm. Lewin and his students, inspired perhaps by Moreno, sought to understand the psychological underpinning of authoritarianism and the racism of ordinary Germans. They looked at leadership in face-to-face groups. In a famous series of experiments, Lewin and Ronald Lippitt used psychodrama-like playacting to investigate "democratic" and "autocratic" leadership in mask-making clubs of ten- and eleven-year-old boys. The leader of one group exercised strong, directive, autocratic leadership, while the other let the boys decide for themselves how they wanted to work. Analyses showed that the autocratic group was more hostile and prone to scapegoating. In the democratic group, there was more friendliness, praise, cooperation, we-ness, and a more objective, constructive attitude. The democratic group also made better masks![47]

As Thompson and Collier began to develop research on personality, leadership, and acculturation among Native American communities, Thompson read Lewin's work and traveled to his Iowa laboratory. The notion of local democracy and the small scale of Native American communities, as well as the presumed importance of face-to-face groups in shaping broader social processes, shaped Thompson's plan to set up similar controlled social experiments among Native groups. Thompson and Collier considered that the research, like psychodrama, might have a therapeutic effect, stimulating the back-and-forth sympathy for which Collier had called. Thompson later explained that the Indian Personality Project was "action research . . . [in which] scientists involved normally function both as scientist-technicians and as integrative or 'democratic' leaders in Kurt Lewin's sense of the term. That is, they endeavor to stimulate, draw out, and foster the talents and leadership qualities of the participant group's members, and to minimize their own roles except as catalysts of group potentialities."[48] This was a goal Collier had first articulated in his early work with New York City immigrants. It was as utopian in the 1940s as it had been in the 1910s.

The "action research" methodology drew as well on insights by psychologist Jean Piaget that Harvard Business School professor Elton Mayo had subsequently used in research at the Hawthorne Western Electric plant, just outside Chicago. Piaget pioneered a form of interviewing that give interviewees ample leeway to direct conversation, and Mayo and his team of researchers had discovered that the interviews they conducted using this method had a significant impact on morale and productivity. Collier and Thompson envisioned a project in which IS personnel would similarly open lines of democratic communication with the Native people they interviewed.[49] Here again, science and expertise functioned as the neutral ground on which presumably democratic—albeit small-scale—communication took place. Mayo's research had sought to disarm potential industrial conflict, and Collier's research implicitly sought a similar goal or at least a similar outcome. The Native intermediaries, Collier imagined, might perform a similar harmonizing function. Nevertheless, as Melville J. Herskovits had warned, anthropological knowledge created to mitigate the worst excesses of colonial situations might in the end simply make colonialism more efficient.

From Native Americans to Japanese Americans: "Colonial" Difference at Poston

As the U.S. military rounded up Japanese Americans from the West Coast, they looked for lands owned by the government to hold them.

This brought the Department of the Interior, which also housed the Indian Service, into the conversations regarding the internment camps, and in March 1942, Collier agreed to have the IS run a Japanese American confinement camp at Poston, Arizona.[50] From the start he imagined the camp as self-governing. Wartime shortages of money, personnel, and supplies made self-government and self-sufficiency a practical necessity. Federal officials also felt that self-government would help the United States avoid potential embarrassment caused by running the camp as the nation waged war against totalitarianism and racism.[51] Collier, believing that the IS could mitigate the worst abuses of authority and create more effective and less coercive forms of leadership, made of these necessities principles. On a visit to Poston, he told the prisoners, "Our people are not here to tell you how to do these things internal to your own community. Still less to do these things for you. . . . Most of you are here in the capacity of full citizens of the American Commonwealth. Being here in that capacity, it is for you, within the limitations which are in the nature of the facts, to determine your own fashion of life. And our function here is to facilitate your action in any way that we can and then to protect your liberties in so far as we have the power."[52] Collier understood that the confinement was unjust, yet he believed that IS control over the camp would ensure that the Japanese Americans were treated respectfully, protected from civilian racism, and prepared to reintegrate into U.S. society after the war. He pragmatically sought to mitigate the worst effects of a confinement that he took as a fait accompli—"in the nature of the facts." But whereas Collier's work among Native Americans had been based on existing forms of community, at Poston he and his collaborators were building community from scratch. As Collier translated lessons learned from other contexts, he seemed unaware of how imprisonment shaped not just community within the camp but also its prisoners' relationship to the IS personnel who were running it.

Even before the Japanese Americans prisoners began arriving at Poston, Thompson and Collier had made plans for research on group dynamics and acculturation among them. In a letter to Collier, Thompson laid out research into "autocratic," "laissez-faire," and democratic leadership (Lewin's terms) in the camps; the research on autocratic leadership should be carried out, she wrote, only "if circumstances permit." Collier responded that he had told War Relocation Authority head Milton Eisenhower "that I was sure that there would be one or more of these colonies whether he wanted it or not, where dominating management would be in the saddle—in other words we will have our control group without artificially arranging it, perhaps." (Collier inserted the word "perhaps" into the typed letter by hand.)[53] Collier tapped psychiatrist Alexander Leighton, a U.S. Navy officer with anthropological training, to head Poston's Bureau of Social Research (BSR). The bureau would provide ethnographic knowledge to help administrators find less coercive and more culturally appropriate ways to govern. It would also generate knowledge that might be applied in a postwar occupied Japan. Dorothea Leighton, also a physician and Alexander's wife, helped with the BSR research.[54]

Collier believed that the Indian Service's "long experience in handling a minority group" equipped it, as one of Collier's longtime IS collaborators noted, to soften the blow of the confinement.[55] In line with this thinking, the Poston BSR applied procedures that had been part of prior research with Native Americans. Collier called Poston a colony and sought to foment democracy or self-government in this presumably colonial setting. The camps were similar to indigenous communities in their geographic isolation and ethnic homogeneity. The questions regarding acculturation, leadership, and group coherence that guided research concerning colonial rule were relevant to the Japanese Americans. In both cases, there were generational differences, conflicts even, between more acculturated youngsters and more traditional elders. Moreover, just as Collier had sought to recruit Native peoples as bureaucrats and researchers, Alexander Leighton sought out college-educated second-generation prisoners to act as intermediaries and participate in research. By providing the Japanese American researchers with additional training, Leighton noted, the BSR would "do for this little group what the Administration was trying to accomplish for all 18,000 evacuees." In other words, it would make the incarceration less onerous and prepare the confinees for life after the war.[56] Again, research itself emerged as an acculturative process, one that would not just help reconcile differences but also avoid conflict. Of course, the confined Japanese Americans saw things differently, often believing that the researchers were government spies, a suspicion aggravated by the fact that the Leighton's research outfit was, like the Federal Bureau of Investigation, a bureau.[57]

The concept of democracy that Collier and his collaborators deployed at Poston foregrounded communication as the key to acculturation. Effective communication could overcome differences, connect people, and develop group morale—a view that built from philosophical pragmatism.[58] Free communication generated efficiency, which the BSR researchers saw as crucial to modern democracy. Conrad Arensberg, who had participated in

Mayo's Hawthorne study, lectured to the camp researchers on his work at the Western Electric plant, and he developed a research plan for Poston, where, he believed, the institutions of self-government would, like trade unions, mitigate potential conflicts by acting "as sounding boards for complaints and as outlets for collective emotion."[59] Poston researchers saw their work as developing models of transparent communication and antiracist collaboration along the lines of what Thompson sought to accomplish through action research on Native Americans.

Collier and his collaborators knew that the confinement of Japanese Americans was unconstitutional as well as immoral. When the commissioner addressed Poston's residents in June 1942, he characterized the removal and confinement as "loaded with injustice." But the same pragmatic thinking that led him to view IS tutelage of Native Americans as being in their best interest led him to conclude that the IS under his leadership would administer the camps more fairly and more democratically than other government agencies or the army, albeit within narrow limits.[60]

Administration, Colonialism, and Postwar Governance

In the quest for a sound world view which will meet the needs of our time, there are two principles on which I think most of those who believe in some sort of a democratic or free world still agree. These are respect for individual personality and respect for cultural diversity. By respect for personality I mean we, in contrast with the fascists, believe that the individual rather than the state is the focal point of society and we envision the chief function of the state to be the creation of the optimum total environment for the development of individual personality. By respect for cultural diversity I mean, in contrast to fascist ethnocentricity, we believe in maximum consideration and tolerance for the unique and persistent patterns of culture found in different parts of the world. We believe that cultural diversity has a dynamic positive value in the enrichment of life and a vital function in the world of today and tomorrow.

If we can agree that these two principles are basic to democratic thinking toward a sound post-war world order, then we have a firm foundation on which to build colonial policy. . . .

Referring to the two democratic principles already stated, namely respect for individual personality and respect for cultural

diversity, I submit the following basic goal as axiomatic: The final aim underlying democratic colonial planning should be to help the natives help themselves to fit into the world in which they live. This means that it should be to attempt strategically and experimentally to manipulate the total environment of the society so that the individuals who comprise it will have the optimum opportunity for the development of personality within their interactive nature-culture patterns. But this is not all. The aim should also be to stimulate the initiative of the individual and will-to-life of the group toward actively meeting their own problems—not only problems which rise within the society itself, but problems which develop out of the necessity of adjustment with other societies, above all with modern industrial civilization.
—Laura Thompson, "Some Essentials for a Democratic Colonial Program," ca. November 1942

Collier and the Poston research team believed that their experiments in the camps would provide "an opportunity, in a completely inconspicuous way, to draw from the Japanese colonizing job scientific results which might be important in our post-war job in the Far East."[61] Thompson made a similar suggestion in December 1942 in the Inter-American Indigenous Institute journal *América Indígena*. Materials from a pilot study she was carrying out among the Papagos, she wrote, would provide guidance regarding not only Native peoples but also "the baffling problems of the post-war world."[62] The concept of colonialism—with its emphases on ethnic difference and the governance of groups occupying discrete territories—served as a lever that opened a door onto broader generalizations regarding administration, democracy, and work across cultural and geographic borders.

Around the time Thompson drafted her *América Indígena* essay, she was working on the paper, excerpted above, regarding democracy and postwar colonial administration for the State Department. After the Allies won the war, Thompson argued, they would have to administer "vast areas of the colonial world." The United States could not afford to take a laissez-faire attitude that abrogated its responsibility but instead needed to set in place a process of democratic planning based on strategic experiments on the effects of state action—the kind of experimentation in which the IS had been engaging. In the past, colonial efforts had either "insulated" minority groups and made them into "museum exhibits," tried to assimilate and Westernize them, or left them to themselves—the laissez-faire approach. None of these strategies, she argued, was adequate on its own. The United States needed a plan of action in which science would lead the way. It would be a modernizing science of acculturation: "Our task as administrators is not to rush in and try to force people to accept modern methods of hygiene, medicine, agriculture, cattle breeding or soil conservation (as has so often been done in the past) even though we are convinced of their superiority." Rather, administrators needed to combine "modern scientific knowledge ... [with] local mores, attitudes and values."[63]

Thompson suggested that postwar colonial administration should adapt the British principles of indirect rule to the Allies' "democratic aims." Democratic colonial leadership would use indirect methods such as public opinion and individual conscience—propaganda and the internalization of social sanction—rather than law or force. Socialization should aim to guide and direct rather than punish and withdraw affection. Following Lewin and Lerner, she advocated integrative rather than authoritarian leadership. Ultimately the goal was to develop "a form of government which will eventually be run entirely by natives."[64] In the interim, of course, self-government would not be at hand.

Collier and Thompson now sought to project lessons from U.S. work with small-scale local communities onto larger national and global stages, but they refrained from spelling out how the local would articulate with the national and global. Mexico no longer provided a model for Collier; instead, he now applied U.S. lessons to Latin America. For instance, in 1943 Collier predicted that in postwar Latin America, "there will be brought to bear the principles of administration, the methods and the content of education, and the psycho-social methods, which our own U.S. Indians have demonstrated and which are identical with the principles and methods on which world reconstruction will have to be based once the Second World War has ended. They are the principles and methods of democracy, total and local—the essential ingredient in world order. Our Indians today are furnishing a laboratory and a demonstration ground on behalf of the world's reorganization ahead."[65] The contours of U.S. postwar ascendancy were already visible. It would involve asserting U.S. authority democratically while respecting local realities.

Collier and Thompson championed cosmopolitanism among U.S. policymakers and citizens but recognized the danger that U.S. involvement in the world would turn into an imperialist attitude. As early as

December 1942, Collier had convened an informal group, referred to colloquially as "Peace and Democracy," composed of key government officials and academics, including Keesing, who was now working for the Office of Strategic Services, the precursor to the Central Intelligence Agency. Other members were Emil Sady, former U.S. representative to the IAII in Mexico City (and later an administrator of occupied areas for the marines and in the State Department), Eugene Lerner, Clyde Kluckhohn, a Harvard University professor and specialist on the Navajos, and Clarence Senior of the Office of the Coordinator of Inter-American Affairs, a historian and political scientist who had written on Mexico. Thompson presented her State Department position paper on postwar democracy to the group, and Collier's advocacy of local and global democracy framed its enterprise. At a meeting in New York City, Collier explained that in the aftermath of World War I, democracy had failed to win the imagination of people around the globe, leading to the rise of fascism. To prevent this from happening after World War II, the Peace and Democracy group would need to ensure that the "little man" did not retreat into provincialism, pulling his government with him. Using the press, radio, visual culture, and face-to-face community meetings as propaganda tools, the group should work to shape public opinion so that the common man might learn to relate his "local geographic community to larger areas of life, to interests larger even to the world scale."[66]

Senior advocated establishing an Institute for the Study of Colonialism that, eschewing imperialism, would deal with "darker peoples both here and abroad," including "such semi-colonial areas as Latin-America." Other participants worried that this would eventuate in a "missionary attitude toward colonial peoples" and asserted that it was best to focus on combating both isolationism and imperialism at home. As Collier seemingly recognized, the term "democracy" had become associated with the imposition of U.S. values and lifeways, not to mention economic arrangements. In one document—apparently influenced by Saul Padover, assistant to Secretary of the Interior Harold Ickes—Collier and Thompson wrote that the United States should not dictate or lead unilaterally. In fact, the country would sometimes need to follow and would need to know more about other countries. "We are woefully ignorant," they wrote, "and yet so cock-sure." Arguing for "ordered heterogeneity," they cautioned U.S. leaders not to impose U.S. forms of representative government or create a bland "undifferentiated internationalism." People should be able to continue their unique lifeways, unless of course they used force or abrogated the rights of "minority or deviant groups."[67]

These goals were to be achieved through research, the training of administrators, and the shaping of public opinion, all of which could not only put the brakes on wrongheaded U.S. imperialism but also be applied domestically. Initially, Collier and his allies planned as part of their Peace and Democracy initiative to create an ethnic institute or institute of ethnic administration in the Department of the Interior. The institute should deal, according to one of Collier's collaborators, with the "whole minorities problem: Indians, Japanese, Negroes, Eskimos, Puerto Ricans" as well as "class stratification in the growth of farm tenancy [and] the poll tax disfranchisement." In the wake of the 1943 Zoot Suit Riots in Los Angeles and race riots in Detroit, administrative solutions to domestic troubles seemed especially urgent, and Collier and Padover proposed a government-sponsored institute of ethnic democracy devoted to minority issues at home and abroad. They used the term "ethnic," they said, because it was "less weighted with emotion than 'racial,' 'minority,' or 'colonial.'" Suggesting that the Detroit riots might have been averted through "democratic social engineering," they advocated for future training of democratic administrators-cum-researchers so as to prevent "explosions": "disgraceful race clashes and humiliating race discriminations."[68] The initiative did not prosper, and in March 1945, Collier resigned as commissioner, though he continued to serve on the governing board of the IAII and as head of the U.S. National Indian Institute.

Later in 1945, Collier and Thompson created a private agency, the Institute of Ethnic Affairs. Its work was the summation of their search for democratic social engineering through indirect rule, and its steering committee included most of their collaborators from the past decade. One major plank of the institute concerned the "non-self-governing peoples." At the end of the war, Ickes secured an appointment for Collier as consultant to the U.S. delegation on trusteeship at the first session of the United Nations General Assembly in February 1946. Collier and lawyer Abe Fortas drafted a "Resolution on Non-Self-Governing Peoples" that was approved by the assembly. But the federal government wanted to avoid placing itself under the Trusteeship Council that had been set up to oversee the trusteeships, and it backtracked on its pledge to work on behalf of self-government for the dependencies. It called instead for a strategic trusteeship for the Trust Territory of the Pacific, which it administered. As a strategic trust, the Trust Territory would be directly controlled by the United States under guidance of the U.N. Security Council, thereby bypassing the General Assembly. From their perch at their Institute of Ethnic Affairs, Collier and Thompson relentlessly criticized the U.S. approach. They actively opposed U.S. military control over the Pacific Islands, arguing that the strategic trusteeships were tantamount to annexation. They also denounced the economic exploitation of naval rule on Guam, which had been a U.S. territory since 1898.[69]

Collier suggested that the U.S. failure to admit that it was a colonial power was leading to scattershot and ineffectual forms of governance, and he insisted that the United States fulfill the U.N. Charter, which declared that trusteed territories should be governed for the good of their residents. Dependencies should be administered, he added, not by the military but by civilians trained to respect cultural and racial differences. Collier also advocated increased self-government. No longer a public official, he was vocal in his denunciation of the exploitation and discrimination that flourished under U.S. rule. But he stopped short of promoting full independence.[70]

In the case of Guam, however, Collier and Thompson, with Ickes's support, lobbied actively for five years for the devolution of power to local authorities. Hundreds of Guamanians joined the Institute of Ethnic Affairs, which published a newsletter on Guam issues. Together with Guam activists, Collier and Thompson succeeded in getting the federal government to withdraw the military from Guam, secured U.S. citizenship for Guamanians, and set up an elected legislative body on the island.[71]

In *America's Colonial Record*, a pamphlet published in London, Collier walked readers through conditions in each of the U.S. colonies. Starting with U.S. expansion across the American continent, he moved on to the Philippines, Puerto Rico, Hawaii, Alaska, the Pacific Islands, the Panama Canal Zone, the Virgin Islands, and finally the American Indians, whom he characterized as colonized, dependent peoples. Collier identified some favorable results of U.S. governance. But the headings in the pamphlet indicated a less generous appraisal: "Is There a Pattern in American Colonial Policy?" (the answer was yes), "Political Advance but Economic Differentiation," "A Feudal Society," "Domination by a Class," "Economic Dependence on the United States," "The Terms Imposed," "A Dubious Future," "Grounds for Anxiety," "Industrial Monopoly," "Economic Distress," "An Indifferent Government," "Colonial Poverty," and "A Policy of Destruction."[72]

In 1949, President Harry Truman initiated the Point Four Program of technical assistance to developing countries, a kind of scaled-down

Marshall Plan for Asia, Africa, and the Americas that laid the groundwork for the formation of the U.S. Agency for International Development in 1961. The Institute of Ethnic Affairs contributed to this effort with its expertise on aid to nominally independent "backward" peoples. Drawing models of policies relevant to the Point Four Program from around the globe, Collier returned to the Mexican example and called for additional studies of the ejido. His foremost example of collaborative work across borders was the IAII, which he characterized as a "new operative mechanism bringing the recipient country into full cooperation and seeking full basic agricultural, health, educational, and organizational improvements at minimum cost."[73] Given that in 1950 the Mexican government actually contributed more to the IAII than the United States did—$6,000 compared to $4,800, and President Miguel Alemán also promised a new building for the outfit—it was hardly a "recipient country" in regards to indigenous issues. At a meeting on the Point Four Program attended by members of the U.S. National Indian Institute Policy Board and officials of the Department of Interior, D'Arcy McNickle, a longtime IS employee and Collier confidant, wondered whether Point Four was in fact trying to modernize attitudes and values that people did not want changed. Point Four should take lessons, McNickle suggested, from the experiences of the Indian Service. Before initiating development programs, the United States should research whether people in a community actually wanted them. Programs imposed from the outside would not have the desired economic impact, and the federal government could not achieve its objectives without attending to local conditions.[74]

Alongside its work on U.S. colonial dependencies and foreign aid, the Institute of Ethnic Affairs supported improved conditions for U.S. "minorities." Perhaps most innovative was its work with "Spanish-Speaking Peoples." Nelson Rockefeller's Office of the Coordinator of Inter-American Affairs had begun working on this group in response to protests over Jim Crow segregation of Mexicans and the deplorable living and working conditions in U.S. migrant labor camps. The Mexican government had prohibited the emigration of agricultural workers that the United States needed because of wartime labor shortages, and the OCIAA teamed up with universities, employers, and Good Neighbor groups throughout the Southwest to improve conditions for the braceros. In 1945, however, the OCIAA moved to the State Department and became the Office of Inter-American Affairs. Jane Pijoan, who coordinated the OCIAA work on Spanish Americans, continued her work at the Institute of Ethnic Affairs. According to Pijoan, the problems of Spanish-speaking peoples were similar to those of other U.S. minority groups, but they took on a particular valence because of their international ramifications: "The Spanish-speaking people of the United States are a natural link with the other Americas," she asserted, and they therefore constituted a "national asset." But because Spanish-speaking peoples lived too close to Mexico, their assimilation was hampered. Pijoan wished to end this "wasteful" gulf by instantiating new forms of leadership among Spanish-speaking peoples and by promoting white efforts to generate "constructive understanding" and "broadening opportunity."[75]

Conclusion: Moving toward Functionalism and Cold War Developmentalism

Collier and his collaborators challenged U.S. policymakers to recognize colonial policies at home and abroad and to rule according to local conditions. Their views seemed not to resonate with government officials, who did not see the United States as a colonial power like France or Britain. And within the general public, the "isolationism and imperialism" Collier feared were in fact quite widespread. Collier, by contrast, drew incessantly from foreign examples to understand difference at home. His experimental comparisons and translations neither cordoned off the United States nor suggested that it was exceptional. He recognized parallels.

But he and his colleagues stopped short of creating paradigms that could travel wholesale from one site to another. Milton Eisenhower, while head of the War Relocation Authority that had detained Japanese Americans, had argued for Poston as a model for other camps. Collier resisted: "The social pattern of the colonies should not be prescribed in advance of experience, . . . and complete uniformities should not be desired but feared."[76] Having done fieldwork and documented cultural particularities, Collier and his anthropologically minded collaborators believed that those particularities had value. In general, they toggled between the controlled experimentation Thompson had advocated—the projection of local examples onto larger national and global stages—and discussion of the diverse situations from which abstractions emerged and in which they might be applied. This back-and-forth echoed the tensions between models of governance based on universal citizenship and humanity and those that recognized and valued the diversity of the people the United States would administer at home and abroad. The war itself had stimulated a need for universalizing, predictive social sciences. The arc was bending in that direction. Still, Collier and Thompson did not abandon their relativism.

Bronislaw Malinowski's premise that there were universal human needs grounded in biology influenced Thompson and the Leightons. Although Alexander Leighton saw human needs as social and psychological as well as biological, he otherwise concurred with Malinowski: "Due to the biological and psychological nature of man, one human community has fundamental similarities to all others, even though there may be great differences in customs and attitudes." Leighton believed that the Bureau of Social Research's work at Poston would support the predictions needed for U.S. postwar endeavors.[77] Yet, as Leighton knew, the process of translating research from one context to another would not be straightforward. Postwar involvement of the United States in occupation, relief, and rehabilitation would mean encountering people "different from the average American in racial descent, traditional values, and predominant attitudes." Abroad, as they had done in Poston, U.S. administrators would have to bridge a cultural gap between government and governed, and adjust government to the people. Leighton also understood that a relocation center differed from an occupied area and that "one must, of course, beware of transferring too literally the lessons learned in one to the other."[78] As he put it in a book he wrote about his Poston experiences, "Both Principles and Recommendations are offered with the reservation that there are always exceptions to general statements and that application must be tempered by the particulars of each concrete situation."[79] For Leighton, adapting lessons learned in one place to another was part of a scientific process of generating universal laws in which new data required reformulation of theory.

Leighton saw this methodological back and forth as a direct response to similarity and difference among human populations, a key conundrum for both colonial and democratic powers. Leighton's first principles of scientific democratic administration were: "Principle 1. In all the different peoples of the world there are universal, basic characteristics inherent in human nature; and Principle 2. There are profound differences in belief, sentiment, habit and custom among the various communities, tribes and nations which make up humanity." Barriers of "caste and class" were, he noted, part of "the very nature of administrative hierarchy." They were aggravated by differences of language, systems of belief, social organization, and skin color. The latter in particular could create barriers of "enormous strength and durability" that were too often deepened by administrators' prejudices. This led Leighton to pessimism regarding the ability of the United States to govern effectively abroad.[80] Leighton had learned that dictating democracy, or managing it from above, did not lead to effective governance.

Collier had always hoped to bring the best of modern ways to Native peoples without disrupting the essence of their lifeways, and he searched for state policies to achieve those goals. Many of his collaborators saw Native societies as functional wholes in which economic activities were related to culture, religion, and politics. Even small changes might set off undesired effects. Collier took a slightly different view, arguing that although Native peoples' entrance into modernity was inevitable, experts guided by science could and should engineer adjustment so as to mitigate the harms caused by modernization. After the United States entered World War II, Collier increasingly hoped to develop formulas for applying lessons learned within one set of minority peoples to policies toward another set. Yet ethnic groups and communities differed, he recognized, and policies could not effectively be applied uniformly. General policies had to be adapted locally by officials knowledgeable about those communities. Yet as commissioner of Indian affairs, there was no way that Collier could avoid being an authoritarian democrat.

Collier and his collaborators recognized that the United States was a colonial power and took on the responsibility that recognition entailed. It was a heavy burden that all too often was shrugged off in favor of acclaiming "the philosophies and the purpose." Collier, ignoring the more intractable forms of conflict borne not just of difference but of violence and historical animosity, envisioned a world where cultural diversity coexisted with cosmopolitan tolerance. In seeking to make an ideal real and to articulate compatible government policies, Collier always relied on scientific expertise, invoking the arbitrating force of a seemingly neutral rationality that in effect, if not in intent, affirmed the power of the federal government—a government that purported to represent the universal good of democracy.

4

Cultural and Economic Evolution, Pluralism, and Categorization in Mexico

The formulation "to incorporate the Indian into civilization" is a remnant of old systems that tried to hide de facto inequality. That incorporation has been generally understood as an intention to de-Indianize and to make foreign, that is to say, to do away with primitive culture, uproot regional dialects, traditions, customs, even the profound emotions of the man who is attached to his land. On the other hand, no one can still expect a resurrection of the pre-Cortesian indigenous systems or a stagnation that is incompatible with the flux of life today. What we must support is the incorporation by the Indian of universal culture, that is to say, the full development of all the natural energies and faculties of the race, the improvement of his living conditions, adding to his subsistence resources and to his work all of the tools of universal technology, science, and art, but always based on respect for his racial personality, his conscience, and his identity. The program for Indian emancipation is in essence that of proletarian emancipation in any country, but without forgetting the special conditions of his climate, his past, and his actual necessities. To better the situation of the indigenous classes, it is necessary to sketch out a campaign that will be carried out over several generations and a series of governments, all inspired by a common aspiration. . . .

We must not think that the specific, detailed programs should be rigid and dogmatic for each nation, since they are not for each jurisdiction or district within our country. Sectarian or routine subordination is prejudicial whether it be in an agrarian reform platform or in a proposal for educational or social revitalization. One may find Mexico's primitive community and that of the Inca era similar to one another, but each had to adapt to its own times, lands, and climates.

If we were to succeed in carrying out policies that benefited all of the indigenous classes, we would thereby strengthen and transform a great majority into useful citizens, at the same time abolishing differences of caste and class. The productive energies will develop more efficiently; the remnants of feudalism that have persisted despite emancipatory struggles will disappear, and we will definitively achieve a political and social unity that will be the basis for a real national organization that will make possible a true inter-American solidarity.

Among Mexico's principal needs is the indigenous problem, and to address it, the plan we develop should contemplate an intensification of the work we have begun. . . . Through rural schools, boarding schools, and cultural missions, teachers are making an effort to improve the native environment, awakening in them confidence and teaching them the road toward the satisfaction of new necessities, as well as their rights and responsibilities, so that they can enter into the national community having all the attributes and requirements necessary so that they can contribute to its economic progress and its democratic configuration.

—Lázaro Cárdenas, speech to the Inter-American Congress on Indian Life, Pátzcuaro, April 14, 1940

In his 1940 speech opening the Inter-American Congress on Indian Life, President Lázaro Cárdenas called for both "the incorporation by the Indian of universal culture," and for "respect for his racial personality, his conscience, and his identity." Equating *indios* with the global class category of proletarian, he sought the incorporation of Native peoples into a modern economy. He simultaneously gestured toward the need for ethnographic knowledge, calling on governments to know "times, lands, and climates" and to adapt government programs to local specificities.[1] The speech thus encapsulated the dilemmas of Mexican indigenismo and the contradictory imperatives that guided the Mexican state's policies toward Native peoples. Federal bureaucracies made overarching plans that were not tailored toward specific Native peoples but were applied and coordinated locally by agencies attuned to the conditions of different locales. The Mexican state wavered. At certain times it granted greater power to localized policies and the specific institutions that applied them; at other times it centralized power in Mexico City and applied universal national policies in an undifferentiated way.

Within scholarship and politics in the 1930s, there was increasing emphasis on the particular conditions of specific locales. The Instituto Nacional Indigenista (National Indigenous Institute), founded in 1949, would be explicit about its local and regional approach, setting up Centros Coordinadores (Coordinating Centers) in specific areas to study and then address local and regional (rather than just national or global) economies and politics. But this localized approach had begun earlier, and it mirrored a federal government that consolidated political control by winning over local and regional leaders one at a time. Fieldwork by researchers was not unlike the touring of politicians. Indigenista investigators visited localities, learned the needs of the people and how they lived, and enlisted local allies, including brokers who often acted as data collectors.[2]

A group of socialist reformers intent on delivering concrete material improvements gained power around 1930. Abandoning the idealism and evangelism of the 1920s, these reformers moved toward an empirically grounded, pluralist epistemology and embraced economic and cultural diversity. They did not, however, abandon economic modernization as a goal. Indeed, socialists continued to measure efficiency and community participation in markets. They simultaneously recognized that *how* precisely to modernize communities depended on regional and local conditions. As Cárdenas suggested, the long-term goal of modernization did not always line up with short-term goals or local applications. It would require "a campaign that will be carried out over several generations and a series of governments."[3] Officials therefore studied specific regions closely and within each region sought to coordinate and adapt the work of diverse national-level programs addressing needs related to schooling, land tenure, agricultural production, road building, telephone lines, credit, medical care, and more.

Along with this class-based and economic but empirical and pluralist approach, socialist intellectuals also advanced a cultural pluralist agenda, especially during Cárdenas's years in power. Perhaps most notably, the Secretaría de Educación Pública seriously considered bilingual education for the first time. But as the Cárdenas administration turned rightward after 1937–38, it set in place large-scale policies of rural economic modernization and turned away from its prior more ethnographic attention to campesino and indigenous lifeways. Indigenistas continued to trumpet pluralism as a method and goal, but they separated economics and culture and argued for an *economic* modernization that preserved *ethnic and cultural* specificity. Although culture might change, too, in the short run it was not the target of state policies.

This chapter focuses on indigenistas' pluralist epistemologies and the strategies they used to reconcile those epistemologies with modernizing evolutionary paradigms that increasingly focused on class as a universal category. I build on a scholarship that has focused on indigenismo's broadly assimilationist and racist modernizing program. Indigenistas were without a doubt devoted to a modernizing, evolutionary agenda that was all too often racist in its dismissal of Native lifeways and viewpoints. Their adherence to this agenda was especially evident in the years directly following the revolution, and it resurfaced after 1940, when the Mexican state more actively pursued large-scale economic development. But one aspect of indigenismo is often ignored by historians: the voluminous, lifeless, and insipid particulars that filled so many indigenistas publications and reports, and especially the indigenista studies produced in the 1930s.[4] Historians' dismissal of those details is not surprising. It is hard to make sense of the copious descriptions in indigenista writing, descriptions that are repetitive in form if not in content, neutral in tone, and seemingly lacking in perspective. The overflowing data nonetheless deserve attention. This chapter provides just that, looking beyond the evolutionary platitudes and generalizations that bookended indigenista publications to the abundant tables, graphs, and lists that made up their bulk—the messy, messy data. In fact, indigenistas often noted how difficult it was for them to reach conclusions. Incongruity often prevailed in indigenista work, with systematic racial orderings often failing to reflect the details the books and reports so amply documented. In contrast to their U.S. counterparts, who looked for theories that could encompass and subsume data and produce generalizations and predictions, Mexican indigenistas noted their inability to reconcile the particular and the general, and they stayed close to the ground. Especially in comparison with their U.S. counterparts, they seemed uninterested in making sweeping generalizations or in developing overarching theories.

At the same time, the chapter pinpoints some of the implicit evolutionary paradigms that organized the overly abundant indigenista data. To reconcile the parts with the whole, the data with the postrevolutionary modernizing agenda, indigenistas deployed at least three distinct forms of aggregation, separately and in combination: taxonomic, encyclopedic, and numerical. Taxonomy created a semblance of order within diversity. The processes of sorting, labeling, and making charts foregrounded the modern scientific process of categorization itself, and most systems to categorization relied on evolutionary paradigms that ranked communities along a continuum from more primitive to more civilized. But more often than not the diverse aspects of the specific communities studied failed to fit neatly into the categories indigenistas dreamed up, and one taxonomic system might challenge another, as endless inter-American debates regarding racial classification and statistics made clear. Encyclopedias and exhibits, like taxonomies, invited citizens to know one another. Just as important, they documented and contained an ungeneralizable heterogeneity. The repetition of categories in a multitude of encyclopedias gave a semblance of unity as Mexicans from all corners of the country were subjected to the same criteria of intelligibility, implying that difference did not subvert a national unity. Heterogeneity was a part of a Mexican whole harmonized by the unifying scientific gaze of indigenistas themselves and of the state they represented. People might live in different kinds of houses or make their living in different ways, but all needed shelter and food and might be helped by government programs aimed at improving housing and nutrition. In this regard the categories implied that citizens were interchangeable, a view compatible with a liberal social order. Numbers, too, implied interchangeability. But numbers also bolstered evolutionary hierarchies by focusing on characteristics, especially economic characteristics, that could be (in contrast to, say, art) neatly measured and arrayed on an evolutionary hierarchy. Indigenistas documented those practices that undermined health and economic well-being, that made indigenous and/or campesino economies inefficient and ineffective, simple and poor. Numbers allowed Mexicans to measure and rank and therefore to exchange views effectively with their peers around the world. All of these intellectual procedures accomplished the same national unity that in other contexts indigenistas secured by imagining a utopian, harmonious, evolved future.

Culture and Economy in the Era of Mexican Socialism

Especially in early indigenismo, evolution encompassed both the cultural and the material. Indeed, cultural and material were not clearly separated. For instance, in an 1923 essay, ethnohistorian Miguel Othón de Mendizábal contrasted the primitive peoples who inhabited Mexico during the "era of the American migrations" to the subsequent, more "advanced" pre-Columbian civilizations, characterizing the earlier residents as backwards in almost every way: they lived in "fleeting settlements," their "precarious" subsistence was shaped by nature, and their spiritual life involved "simple and humble veneration, almost family-like, similar to that of all people at the dawn of civilization." With the Nahua people's arrival, however, the Valley of Mexico had taken a giant step forward. "Religious needs evolved," and rituals became "more complicated and increased." Religion was now normed and enshrined in institutions. It was, like Nahua economic and political life, more civilized.[5]

The earliest postrevolutionary state policies toward Native peoples were congruent with this view of evolution. The placement of Manuel Gamio's Dirección de Antropología within the Ministry of Agriculture and Development implied that Native problems were related to land and agricultural production, hence economic.[6] Yet the program the department implemented in Teotihuacán was based on the supposition that greater economic efficiencies would be achieved through cultural interventions that could increase employment and income opportunities for residents or make them healthier and therefore more productive.[7]

With the disbanding of the Dirección de Antropología, national programs for Native peoples moved to the SEP, which oversaw museums and other cultural institutions along with education. This move implied a shift away from issues of agricultural production and toward cultural intervention, a shift no doubt endorsed by the SEP's first secretary, the idealist José Vasconcelos, who rejected a materialism that he associated with the United States. Yet many SEP programs sought to correct wrongheaded ideas—what one SEP official referred to as a "cultural delay" (rezago cultural)—because they promoted bad living conditions, poor work habits, and deficient consumption.[8] Conversely, SEP experts often characterized economic circumstances as creating the conditions necessary for cultural changes. According to Lauro Caloca, a close collaborator of Vasconcelos and later member of Congress who headed the SEP's Departamento de Cultura y Educación Indígena, Native people who possessed land tended to cooperate with the SEP's cultural missions, whereas those without land needed all the members of the family to work and therefore kept their children out of school. It was imperative to solve their economic problems first.[9] Enrique Corona Morfín, who replaced Caloca at the head of the Departamento de Cultura y Educación Indígena, likewise argued that material and cultural changes went hand in hand. The (never fully implemented) program he developed with Vasconcelos provided access to land, seed, plants, livestock, and beehives, the regulation of work conditions, and the teaching of hygiene and modern production techniques.[10]

Around the time the Cristero Rebellion was coming to an end, Marxism took hold of the intellectual imagination of prominent postrevolutionary leaders, and a materialist perspective began to shape state policy. The moralistic school programs of the 1920s, reformers began to realize, had not changed religious practices, extended the use of Spanish, or gotten rural people to produce new products in new ways. Communities had too often cast aside new agricultural techniques and advice about sanitation or failed to take part in cooperatives. A new approach was needed, one that relied less on preaching and more on providing directly useful knowledge. Within the SEP, Secretary Narciso Bassols (1931–34) promoted a socialist education that was rationalist, anticlerical, intent on routing out superstition. He emphasized productive forces, seeking to improve rural peoples' health, productivity, and prosperity. On the eve of the Cárdenas presidency, Congress wrote the socialist nature of education into the constitution.[11]

Production and consumption now took on a greater importance. In regard to Native peoples specifically, Bassols stressed the need to eradicate illnesses and to introduce modern technologies that would improve families' incomes; otherwise, he said, social and cultural interventions could not take root. It was "crystal clear," he asserted, that without the economic measures taken by the SEP and other state agencies, "the development of our educational efforts will be limited by the impenetrable border created by the efficacy of the agricultural and industrial systems." Regarding technical and scientific education, the goal was to find pedagogical methods that would allow indígenas to absorb a "solid scientific culture." During Bassols's tenure, the SEP linked rural education more firmly to agricultural production, and beginning around 1932, it took over the Escuelas Vocacionales Agrícolas (Agricultural Vocational Schools) that had been under the purview of the Ministry of Agriculture.[12] Within higher education, reformers sought to train professionals who could carry forward state-sponsored social reform. As materialist approaches took hold and the SEP focused on improving Native peoples' health and productivity, policymakers increasingly equated the problems of indígenas and campesinos, both of whom were economically disadvantaged. Bassols referred alternatively to "campesino masses" (masas campesinas) and indígenas.[13]

Mexican socialism was materialist not just in its focus on production and concrete material results but also in its epistemology, and socialist educators believed that the study of a material, natural reality was a necessary prelude to state action. This materialist epistemology spawned an empirically grounded, ethnographic approach to economic issues. Schools (and social policies more generally) would henceforth need to focus on the particularities of specific localities. When the Casa del

Estudiante Indígena folded in 1932, the SEP replaced it with Escuelas Normales Rurales (Normal Rural Schools) located in regions where Native peoples were concentrated. Students would remain near their homes, learn knowledge tailored to their specific situations, and become teachers in surrounding communities. The SEP likewise turned its itinerant cultural missions into permanent missions affixed to the new normal schools. The permanent missions would adhere to Bassols's productivist agenda by hiring agronomists and handicrafts teachers as well as doctors and other public health workers. The director of the Misiones Culturales y Enseñanza Normal (Cultural Missions and Normal Schools) under Bassols, Manuel Mesa Andraca, instructed SEP officials to make their teachings relevant, "varied according to the conditions of each region and . . . closely linked to its economic and social possibilities." He believed that the SEP needed to provide teachers with practical knowledge that was tailored to the ecological and economic realities of the specific areas where they worked.[14]

This materialist orientation countered the idealism of intellectuals associated with the Ateneo de la Juventud, which had been established to counter Porfirian positivism. Ateneo members included José Vasconcelos and Antonio Caso, chancellor of the National University (1921–23), a humanist philosopher who stressed the importance of culture as a vehicle for national unity and took inspiration from the ideas of Arthur Schopenhauer, Friedrich Nietzsche, and Henri Bergson.[15] Around 1933, in a debate regarding the National University's curriculum, these idealists publicly challenged the socialist reform agenda and its empiricist epistemology. Vicente Lombardo Toledano, a former student of Caso and the director of Mexico's most prestigious preparatory high school, the Escuela Nacional Preparatoria (National Preparatory School), defended the proposition that Mexico's universities should be required to impart a socialist curriculum. The role of Mexico's universities, Lombardo Toledano claimed, was to guide the nation so that it might solve "the problem of production and distribution of material wealth," which he defined as the "era's most important problem." The solution required efficiency, so the university's role was to train professionals to produce knowledge of "the economic resources of our territory, the biological and psychological characteristics of our population, and of our government." The state would use this knowledge to combat inequality. Lombardo Toledano also argued for a philosophy based on "nature," by which he meant scientific methods, in which ideas sprang from the perceptions of a material, external reality.

Lombardo Toledano contrasted this viewpoint to Caso's idealist conception of national values. Whereas Caso "affirmed the preeminence of religious factors and the supernatural character of the spirit," Lombardo Toledano believed that "spirit was the product of nature."[16]

In a debate that began during the First Congress of Mexican Universities in 1933 and continued in the press, Caso resisted the perceived imposition by fiat of a socialist education that he believed undercut crucial individual liberties. In imposing a socialist curriculum, Caso said, Lombardo Toledano and his acolytes would limit free speech and impose orthodoxy on the university. Defending academic freedom, Caso threatened to resign if the resolution declaring the university socialist was passed.[17]

Caso's strategy was ultimately successful in that postsecondary education was explicitly excluded from the legal codes that enshrined socialist education in primary and secondary schools. Lombardo Toledano and his left-wing allies nevertheless scored a victory. The university was not *required* to become rationalist and materialist, but it moved in that direction anyway. New schools and institutions of higher learning generated increasing numbers of experts trained to meet the government's growing need for applied knowledge. In the National University, the first students entered the newly formed economics program in 1930, and that same year the Instituto de Investigaciones Sociales (IIS, Institute of Social Investigations), a research institute that initially focused on indigenous issues, was formed. In 1938, the first anthropology program in a Mexican institution of higher learning was set up at the brand-new Instituto Politécnico Nacional (IPN, National Polytechnic Institute).[18]

Researching the Mezquital

Around 1932–33, Gamio participated in an effort to apply this socialist epistemology in the Mezquital Valley. Only a few hours' drive from Mexico City, the Mezquital's Otomí population lived in what observers deemed abject poverty. Government officials attributed this poverty to the region's arid terrain, and they crafted programs to address those conditions. Around 1926, President Calles handpicked the site for a shiny new Escuela Vocacional Agrícola on the site of El Mexe, an expropriated former hacienda. In 1932, this agricultural school came under SEP control; students from the normal school at Actopan were transferred there; the school acquired a permanent cultural mission; and Gamio joined an Institute of Social Investigation at El Mexe.[19]

In line with the socialist reformers' desires, Gamio's 1930s Mezquital research proposals focused on questions of labor and productivity. When Gamio arrived at El Mexe, Mesa Andraca wrote to him to set out the institute's goals, reminding the anthropologist that he was to produce "useful results" and warning him to avoid "exorbitant" efforts. The institute should focus on "concrete and exact knowledge" of the area's biological, economic, and cultural situation.[20] Gamio's initial reports clearly sought to satisfy his bosses. Rural and indigenous education, Gamio claimed, had to be technical and practical rather than achieved through "theoretical" book learning. In line with Bassols's and Mesa Andraca's focus on material conditions, he attributed cultural variations within the region to "economic factors [that] forcefully influence cultural ascent or descent." Yet that correlation was not direct, according to Gamio, and there was in fact less cultural than economic variation.[21] In some areas material conditions improved without a consequent change in ways of thinking and doing.[22] An outline of potential research that Gamio submitted to the SEP favored the study of "spiritual orientations" and spiritual as well as material uplift. But hewing to Bassols and Mesa Andraca, he asked SEP officials to consult with their "sociologists and experts" about whether he should study only "issues that are material in nature or serve material ends, which would make the work more concrete."[23]

Gamio's initial formulation of the Mezquital research differed from the final research plan and the research carried out, and the differences point to the growing importance of economic factors to the officials who paid his salary. In a disorganized, early draft research plan, possibly compiled with his assistants Eugenio Maldonado and Alfonso Fábila, Gamio called for investigation of intercultural social relations and Native perceptions of those interactions. He suggested not just recording how the researchers viewed the ethnicity of populations and forms of land tenure but also asking the Native peoples how they perceived those things and how they saw politics, education, economics, culture, and morality. This was in line with the research he had recently completed on Mexican immigration to the United States.[24] Higher-ups in the SEP apparently did not approve this approach—the final research plan eschewed mention of attitudes and drew instead on prior research outlines, including one that Carlos Basauri had used among the Otomí in 1930, probably as part of his research with Corrado Gini.[25]

The research protocol that Gamio and Fábila ultimately followed in the Mezquital was grounded in the evolutionary notion that peoples adapted biologically and culturally to their geographical environments. People's tools, along with their forms of social, economic, political, and familial organization, which together revealed their level of civilization, were adaptations to those material conditions. Because material conditions were diverse, so would evolution be. Gamio's research outline gave primacy to what in Marxist terms would be viewed as productive forces. The Mezquital outline began with an accounting of the geographical environment: soils, water resources, and flora and fauna. It then considered Otomí historical development and demographic strength in relation to other local groups. Unique to the Mezquital study, and reflecting the moment at the close of the Cristero war when the project was carried out, researchers surveyed associational life, asking whether people belonged to trade unions or other associations and whether they subscribed to socialist or other ideologies. Last, the protocol considered material culture, work technologies, social organization, and, finally, spiritual culture. Similar taxonomies appeared in other research outlines, whether their authors were Marxists or not.[26]

Gamio lobbied for specialists to do the research for which he and his assistants lacked training. The Departamento Agrario had already collected data on land tenure in the Mezquital as a prelude to land redistribution, and Gamio enlisted an engineer to investigate other topics related to agricultural production. The Secretaría de Economía (Ministry of the Economy) contributed a geologist who studied mineral resources that might be mined and sold, and identified other materials for possible use in manufacturing such goods as clay pots or dyed fabrics. Gamio hoped to enlist an IPN biologist to study flora and fauna as potential resources to be exploited. (He could not secure the necessary funds.) Physician Manuel Basauri (Carlos's brother) of the Mezquital cultural mission promised to look into topics related to bodies, their health, and their capacity for work. He would measure a plethora of indicators: height, weight, cephalic index, muscular force, nutrition, use of intoxicants, access to water, and housing conditions. Gamio himself undertook to understand local industry by asking schoolteachers for information about the towns where they worked, including the raw materials available and their origins and cost, and where products were sold and at what price.[27]

After Gamio left El Mexe, around 1932, his research assistant Fábila completed and later published their joint findings, which in the end focused almost exclusively on material and economic conditions. Mendizábal did further research in the region not long after, but funding was scarce and his stay in the region was brief. Gamio's final report focused on geography, economy (land distribution, work conditions, agriculture, industry), the inhabitants' ethnobiological situation and health, and material and intellectual culture. Fábila's book picked up where Gamio left off, providing information on living quarters, furnishings, domestic and industrial tools and utensils, food, clothing, and domestic economy, especially family expenditures. Mendizábal's 1936 study provided a painstaking reconstruction of family income and expenditures in two villages as well as land tenure, roads and communications, production costs, and profits.[28]

Assimilation and Pluralism in the Socialist Era

Historian Guillermo Palacios has identified two strains of reform within the SEP during the 1930s: a Marxist productivism that promoted greater efficiencies and a populist culturalism that sought to retain forms of campesino and Native culture. According to Palacios, the productivist concern with economics and efficiency was grounded in evolutionary thinking and efforts to emulate "the West." By contrast, culturalists jettisoned the rhetoric of "incorporation," which sought to civilize Native peoples into a white-mestizo Mexican culture, and instead sought the "integration" into the nation of differences, especially linguistic differences. Yet, as we have seen, pluralism could be economic and linked to local conditions of production and consumption, and assimilation to a Euro-U.S. modernity could be cultural as well as economic. As Palacios admits, the line between Marxists and culturalists was blurry.[29] Bassols, although a staunch advocate of what might be deemed a productivist agenda, agreed with Sáenz and Gamio on the cultural value of certain aspects of Native lifeways. Mexicans should embrace the West's ability to "dominate and capture the forces of nature for the material benefit of men," he wrote, but without losing the Native "soul" in the process. Despite the ill effects of conquest and exploitation, Native communities had retained valuable spiritual, moral, and artistic qualities. Native peoples were hardworking, disciplined, and cooperative; state officials should nurture these values.[30]

Other policymakers, such as Carlos Basauri, espoused pluralism as a pragmatic, short-term accommodation to lessons learned on the ground rather than an overarching orientation. While head of the SEP's Departamento de Educación Indígena under Assistant Secretary of Education

Luis Chávez Orozco (1936–38), Basauri both promoted instruction in Native languages and reaffirmed the need for all Mexicans to speak Spanish.

> If on the one hand it would be ideal for all Mexicans to speak one language, since we all understand the value of this for constructing a nationality, on the other hand, and given the material impossibility of achieving this goal and the psychological circumstances that stand in the way of imposing an official language, we have to recognize that indigenous languages also have a great cultural value and that in trying to destroy them, which is impossible, we provoke hostile reactions between the Indians and the rest of the Spanish-speaking population, and as a result, our desire to unite the population ideologically recedes into the distance. The above notwithstanding, we ... should intensify the *castellanización* campaign. We must give the Indian the official language as an instrument: first, to establish intellectual communication with the rest of the population and second, for his defense.

Basauri argued, furthermore, that the teaching of Spanish to Native peoples was akin to the teaching of English or French to Mexican intellectuals, who could then take part in scientific discussions in those languages. He thereby equated his own place as a subaltern intellectual within a global scientific community and that of Native peoples' place within the nation. Like Mexicans who spoke English, Native peoples needed to be able to translate from and into their own languages. The objective was not cultural blending or mestizaje but mutual understanding.[31]

By the 1930s, intellectuals like Basauri would no doubt have known about the obstacles that the 1920s assimilating indigenismo had faced. Along with the rise of Hitler, that knowledge made them more aware of the value of tolerating difference, and Basauri here showed an understanding of how the history of racism and exclusion generated inequality. Assimilationist policies could provoke conflict, he suggested, articulating an insight that had apparently eluded Vasconcelos and Sáenz, both of whom argued that national unity needed to be grounded in assimilation. Appreciating the ill effects of imposing a language from a position of power, Basauri promoted Spanish as a political tool rather than an instrument of civilization. Even so, he reaffirmed the inevitability of Spanish as the national lingua franca and could not fully abandon modernization as an ultimate goal: making "the Indian's culture evolve."[32]

For the Marxists who gained power during the Cárdenas presidency—including Lombardo Toledano, Chávez Orozco, and Mendizábal—Soviet policies demonstrated that cultural pluralism and evolutionary productivism were compatible. Respect for difference could hasten and smooth the application of policies aimed at economic growth. Lombardo Toledano had visited the Soviet Union in 1935, and on his return, he advocated the formation of ethnically homogeneous territorial units that would be governed by Natives themselves. At a February 1938 pedagogical conference, educators affiliated with the Mexican Communist Party sanctioned a policy of self-determination. They abandoned it only three years later, but other left-wing indigenistas continued to champion a pluralist acceptance of difference and deride "Western" assimilationist approaches.[33] For example, participants at the First Conference of Philologists and Linguists, convened by the DAI and the new anthropology department at the IPN in 1939, scorned old-style efforts to incorporate Native peoples and denounced what they saw as efforts to make Native languages disappear. A conference presentation by DAI director Chávez Orozco argued that "notwithstanding the economic, racial, and historical factors" that adversely affected the Indian "spirit," Native cultures had not been degraded to the point of being useless, and Native cultures therefore should be respected "in all their superior manifestations, without trying to change their character [*desnaturalizarlas*] or even divert them." Indigenistas should "attempt to stimulate their full development." Still, he suggested that Native cultures needed to be *developed*, and presumably only "superior manifestations" of Native culture merited this treatment. Moreover, in the same speech, Chávez Orozco defined the indigenous question "as economic above all, as well as cultural," and suggested that it "be resolved through all the means and resources that contemporary technology and science can contribute."[34]

Participants in this conference presented an innovative plan to teach Native peoples to read, write, and speak grammatically in Native languages. But following Carlos Basauri's pragmatic rationale they justified this instruction as a way to help monolingual Native peoples become fluent in Spanish. Enhancing difference in the short run would mitigate it in the long run. The future goal of evolution at times warred with present-day diversity. Evolutionary perspectives were thereby reinstantiated while tolerance was urged.

The persistence of an evolutionary subtext alongside economic and cultural pluralism within Mexican indigenismo and state policies explains some of the incongruities of Mexican policies, such as the convoluted argument for Native language instruction. Also incongruous were the repeated efforts of postrevolutionary governments to create separate organizations that addressed Native issues but making those organizations rely on mainline agencies, laws, and policies. Cárdenas himself manifested these contradictions, arguing in his 1940 Pátzcuaro speech that Native peoples had cultures and values that should be applauded while also stressing the determining role of the economy and the consequent similarity between Native and non-Native rural peoples. Indígenas, in his view, were an exploited social class. Although he emphasized adjusting educational and agrarian policies to different locales, histories, and climates, he concluded that social policies that benefited "*las clases indígenas*" would eventually favor "a great majority"—an argument premised on the belief that everyone was moving in the same direction, toward greater material prosperity.[35]

Epistemologies of Heterogeneity: Categories That Blur, Numbers That Don't Add Up

Indigenistas struggled mightily to reconcile the diverse local conditions they observed with their modernizing frameworks based on criteria of efficiency. As members of a global scientific fraternity, social scientists felt compelled to participate in creating generalizations about humanity or simply in representing their country to national and international audiences at conferences and in publications. But especially in reports and publications for internal consumption, the unruly data they collected were also proudly, and sometimes lavishly and extensively, on display. Evolution provided a yardstick, but there were so many measurements! So much data to collect! As researchers recommended what to reform and how, they also reveled in diversity. They tracked hectares of land cultivated or irrigated, school buildings and their conditions, temperature and rainfall, chemicals in the soils, latitudes and longitudes, plants and animals, roads and railroads, the goods transported on them, children who attended school, and the marital status and racial characteristics of students' parents. Indigenista reports, packed with lists and large fold-out charts, in fact were often little more than compilations of data, with text simply repeating and summarizing the data in the lists and charts.

Indigenistas readily conceded the problem: their abundant data often failed to yield ready conclusions. Perhaps, then, conclusions were not

3. POBLACION DE 5 AÑOS O MAS, QUE UNICAMENTE HABLA UNA LENGUA INDIGENA POR SEXOS EN 1930 Y 1940

Núm. de orden	LENGUA	1 9 3 0				1 9 4 0				INDICE 1930 = 100		
		TOTAL	Hombres	Mujeres	H/M 100	TOTAL	Hombres	Mujeres	H/M 100	TOTAL	Hombres	Mujeres
	TOTAL REPUBLICA	1 185 162	529 163	656 009	80.66	1 237 018	556 119	680 899	81.67	104.38	105.10	108.79
1	Amuzgo	5 779	2 809	2 970	94.57	7 540	3 688	3 852	95.74	130.47	131.29	129.70
2	Cora	900	435	465	93.54	1 724	732	992	73.79	191.56	168.28	213.33
3	Cuicateco	5 744	2 480	3 284	75.98	4 261	1 639	2 622	62.51	74.18	66.09	80.33
4	Chatino	8 208	3 713	4 495	82.60	8 586	3 807	4 779	79.66	104.61	102.53	106.32
5	Chichimeca					940	455	485	93.81			
6	Chinanteco	17 190	7 298	9 892	73.77	20 387	8 594	11 793	72.87	118.60	117.76	119.22
7	Chol	15 125	7 872	7 253	108.53	19 499	9 694	9 805	98.87	128.92	123.14	135.19
8	Chontal	4 791	2 042	2 749	74.28	5 624	2 138	3 486	61.33	117.39	104.70	126.81
9	Huave	2 363	1 078	1 285	83.89							
10	Huasteco	21 003	9 195	11 808	77.27	25 628	10 478	15 150	69.16	122.02	113.95	128.30
11	Huichol	1 888	923	965	95.64	995	348	447	77.85	42.11	37.70	46.32
12	Kikapoo	129	48	81	59.25							
13	Mame	3 098	1 428	1 670	85.50							
14	Matlatzinca o pirinda	151	57	94	60.63	123	47	76	61.84	81.46	82.46	80.85
15	Maya	131 836	63 392	68 444	92.61	114 011	54 394	59 617	91.24	86.48	85.81	87.10
16	Mayo	6 164	2 884	3 280	87.92	6 667	3 020	3 647	82.81	108.16	104.72	111.19
17	Mazahua	29 268	9 997	19 271	51.87	39 587	15 294	24 293	62.96	135.26	152.99	126.06
18	Mazateco	45 254	21 049	24 195	87.03	55 743	25 798	29 945	86.15	123.18	122.50	123.77
19	Mexicano o náhuatl	355 295	160 980	194 315	82.84	360 071	164 646	195 425	84.25	101.34	102.28	100.57
20	Mixe	24 023	10 953	13 070	83.80	27 238	12 059	15 179	79.45	113.38	110.10	116.14
21	Mixteco	111 391	47 339	64 052	73.90	124 994	54 661	70 333	77.72	112.21	115.47	109.81
22	Otomí	94 693	40 133	54 560	74.55	87 404	36 458	50 946	71.56	92.30	90.84	93.38
23	Pápago	222	94	128	73.43	91	40	51	78.43	40.99	42.55	39.84
24	Popoloca	3 813	1 596	2 217	71.98	6 298	2 678	3 620	73.98	165.17	167.79	163.28
25	Tarahumar	14 290	6 934	7 356	94.26	11 717	5 715	6 002	95.22	81.99	82.42	81.59
26	Tarasco	15 243	6 071	9 172	66.19	19 637	8 739	10 898	80.19	128.83	143.95	118.82
27	Tepehua	2 232	967	1 265	76.44	1 561	550	1 011	54.40	69.94	56.88	79.92
28	Tepehuano	1 048	307	741	41.43	3 247	1 381	1 866	74.01	309.83	449.84	251.82
29	Tlapaneco	13 287	5 938	7 349	80.80	14 411	6 740	7 671	87.86	108.46	113.51	104.38
30	Tojolabal	4 771	1 902	2 869	66.29	6 882	3 221	3 661	87.98	144.25	169.35	127.61
31	Totonaco	58 561	25 676	32 885	78.07	59 242	27 262	31 980	85.25	101.16	106.18	97.25
32	Triqui	2 142	955	1 187	80.45							
33	Tzendal o tzeltal	32 359	15 892	16 467	96.50	34 502	17 944	16 558	108.37	106.62	112.91	100.55
34	Tzotzil	26 013	12 598	13 415	93.90	49 194	23 984	25 210	95.14	189.11	190.38	187.92
35	Yaqui	2 134	995	1 139	87.35	307	132	175	75.43	14.39	13.27	15.36
36	Zapoteco	111 660	46 781	64 878	72.10	104 661	43 399	61 262	70.84	93.73	92.77	94.42
37	Zoque	9 151	4 288	4 863	88.17	6 581	2 772	3 809	72.77	71.92	64.65	78.33
38	Otros dialectos indígenas	3 943	2 044	1 899	107.63	7 865	3 612	4 253	84.93	199.47	176.71	223.96

NOTAS: a).—Excluídos los mudos y los sordomudos. b).—El rubro "Otros dialectos indígenas" incluye: cucapá, cuitlateco, chocho, ocoroni, ópata, pame, seri, tepecano y los que no están catalogados.

Figure 1. "Population Five Years of Age or Older That Speaks Only an Indigenous Language, by Sex, in 1930 and 1940." (Emilio Alanís Patiño, "La población indígena de México," in Miguel Othón de Mendizábal, *Obras completas*, 6 vols. [Mexico City: Talleres Gráficos de la Nación, 1946–47], 1:96.)

to be found. That was Gamio's realization in a 1939 essay that was also an admission of how little synthesis or "integral"—cultural, biological, political, social, and economic—understanding had come from the socialist emphasis on empirically verifiable fact. In "Mexico's Social Reality," Gamio argued that Mexican social scientists knew little about the people they were trying to help. This was not just a Mexican problem, Gamio admitted, since "no country in the world" had specialists who fully knew that country's social reality. Yet in Mexico the problem was particularly acute because of Mexico's exceptionally heterogeneous social structure. Given that many groups "persisted in the same lifeways and forms of development as in remote times," Mexico's population would be "more confusing and difficult to analyze than that of other peoples." "Under no conditions," Gamio concluded, "are we authorized to generalize."[36]

The 1939 essay built on themes that Gamio had outlined in his Mezquital research, in a 1935 essay on "Mexico's Varied Markets," and even earlier, in an incipient form, in *Forjando patria*. The "Markets" essay mobilized an evolutionary taxonomy to establish a semblance of evolutionary order. In it, Gamio argued that modern countries had "general culture" and unified markets that sold standardized goods, but Mexico had three distinct, "multiple and dissimilar" markets, each of which sold distinct kinds of goods: a modern "universal" urban market comparable to markets in Sweden, Holland, and Belgium, a mixed market, and a primitive market that resembled its counterparts in primitive African or Asian villages. Participants in mixed and "antiquated" markets consumed products that were basic in both quality and quantity. Mexico's markets were arrayed hierarchically. Yet in the end Gamio had to admit that his categorization was limited since each type of market varied both in the scope of the geographic areas it served and in the goods it offered. That heterogeneity had to be documented and then analyzed, and for this, researchers would need to invent new social science tools: "What we must do is directly investigate that enormous and little known population group ... setting aside the exotic [foreign], doctrinaire unilateralism that so frequently leads us to force social phenomena into a preconceived framework in which it doesn't fit." Heterogeneity was not just a sign of backwardness but also an invitation to develop new distinctly Mexican social science tools.[37]

Gamio's protégé Lucio Mendieta y Núñez—at the time director of the Institute of Social Investigations of the Ministry of Agriculture and Development—echoed Gamio. Although generalizations were necessary, he wrote, they would be hard to reach, given "the enormous expanse of our territory and the heterogeneity of its population." In the short run, gathering more data was the more fruitful endeavor. Mendieta y Núñez therefore spurned theoretical and macroeconomic approaches to the economy and hoped for an applied approach based on data he called ethnographic: "humble, less extensive facts which have less apparent importance." Indeed, Mendieta y Núñez favored a "description of economic facts and of the customs that influence them," and he rejected other authors' globalizing methods for understanding "the evolutionary trajectory of the economy of humanity." Although Mexican researchers' assembling of facts admittedly might be "fragmentary and defective," Mendieta y Núñez directed his venom not at the ethnographers but at the armchair "pseudo-economists" who smiled with disdain at the "undoubtedly valuable data." By contrast, he praised the heroism of fieldworkers "who dirtied their suits with the dust of the pueblos."[38]

Mendieta y Núñez did not believe that ethnography should be the collection of stray facts. The kinds of facts collected, he noted, should reflect a priori decisions about what type of data mattered, and he applauded Manuel Basauri for investigating precisely those qualities of body and mind that might help determine a person's capacity for work. By focusing on one region, researchers like Basauri might, he said, come closer to a comprehensive and integrated analysis. Ethnographic facts like these would then need to be analyzed rigorously. Subsequent analysis would reveal patterns or identify the most crucial factors. Often this had not been the case in Mexican studies that relied simply on "statistics . . . reduced to a monotonous series of dry figures in large tomes and direct ethnographic and economic observation." But while Mendieta y Núñez, like Gamio, saw synthesis as necessary, neither believed that it was readily at hand.[39]

Methods like correlation and probability, which allowed generalizations to be reconciled with diversity, were not yet a part of the social science toolkit. The act of quantifying—counting, adding, measuring, tabulating—nevertheless allowed an empirical approach to Native lifeways that was compatible with evolutionary hierarchies. Indigenistas asked how many hectares of land different groups owned; how much corn, wheat, chili, or beans they produced; how many calories they consumed; how much wool they spun; how many sarapes they wove; how much money they earned; and how they spent that money. How many, they asked, were malnourished or sick? How many could read and write? Numbers, measures of efficiency and growth, allowed what might otherwise seem irremediably different or incongruent to be placed on the same scale.

CALCULO DE PRODUCCION POR KILOGRAMO DE FIBRA TORCIDA

Caso N°	Lugar de producción	Tipo de producción	Clase de fibra	Precio por Km. de fibra sin torcer Pesos	Minutos-trabajo	Valor minutos-trabajo Pesos	Gastos de producción Pesos	Utilidades Pesos	Valor por Km. de fibra torcida Pesos
1	Xuchitlán	Tallando la fibra (1)	Lechuguilla	....	640	0.57330	....	....	0.57330
2	Xuchitlán	Tallando la fibra (2)	Lechuguilla	....	768	0.65400	0.05000	....	0.70400
3	Maguey Blanco	Tallando la fibra (1)	Lechuguilla	....	420	0.81641	0.06929	....	0.88570
4	Maguey Blanco	Tallando la fibra (3)	Lechuguilla	....	360	0.71400	0.17160	....	0.88570
5	Xuchitlán	Tallando la fibra (3)	Guajá	....	360	0.57330	0.12670	....	0.70000
6	Maguey Blanco	Tallando la fibra (3)	Guajá	....	360	0.72996	0.21004	....	0.94000
7	Xuchitlán	Tallando la fibra (4)	Ixtle	....	540	0.46692	0.09558	....	0.56250
8	Xuchitlán	Comprando fibra	Lechuguilla	0.18	160	0.18000	0.18000	....	0.36000
9	Orizabita	Comprando fibra	Lechuguilla	0.18	140	0.12375	0.22175	0.13450	0.48000
10	Yolotepec	Comprando fibra	Lechuguilla	0.14	90	0.22640	0.14000	0.13450	0.36640

(1) Adquieren las pencas en terreno comunal.
(2) Comprando las pencas.
(3) Alquilan el terreno para sacar las pencas.
(4) Comprando las "cucharas" de las pencas de maguey.

TABLA COMPARATIVA DE VALORES JORNAL-HORA

Fibra de ixtle		Hilado-tejido del ayate		Fibra de lechuguilla		Torcido por kilo de lechuguilla	
Tipo de producción	Valor jornal-hora Pesos	Tipo de producción	Valor jornal-hora Pesos	Tipo de producción	Valor jornal-hora Pesos	Tipo de producción	Valor jornal-hora Pesos
Familiar	0.03700	Familiar	0.04000	Familiar	0.05000	Tallando la fibra	0.05375
A medias	0.02250	A salario	0.05000	Familiar	0.03950	Tallando la fibra	0.04720
A salario	0.03700	A destajo	0.05000	Familiar	0.11200	Tallando la fibra	0.11663
Familiar	0.02300	Familiar	0.05000	Familiar	0.10000	Tallando la fibra	0.11900
				A medias	0.10800	Tallando el guajá	0.09555
				A medias	0.10000	Tallando el guajá	0.12166
				A salario	0.08000	Comprando "cucharas"	0.05188
					0.04184	Comprando la fibra	0.07040
					0.06000	Comprando la fibra	0.05625
						Comprando la fibra	0.15125

Figure 2. "Calculation of Production per Kilogram of 'Twisted Twine'" and "Comparative Table of the Values of Hourly Wages." (Miguel Othón de Mendizábal, *Obras completas*, 6 vols. [Mexico City: Talleres Gráficos de la Nación, 1946–47], 6: n.p.)

Sarape-weaving could be compared to a hat-making by quantifying the hours spent in producing each item, the cost of wool versus the cost of fiber, and prices in various markets (figures 1 and 2). But not everything could be measured or counted. It is not that indigenista policymakers did not make judgments regarding art, spirituality, politics, or individual character. But those judgments could not be easily quantified and *integrated*.

Efficiency was a prime goal for Gamio and others. As early as 1924, Gamio had advocated the effective use of resources, telling a U.S. audience that Mexico's most urgent problem was "to arouse the latent energies and possibilities which in eight or ten millions of indigenes have lain dormant for several centuries." When Native peoples had acquired "the efficiency which characterizes modern action," he argued, they would be able to effectively use the natural resources of the country.[40] Along with Mendieta y Núñez, Gamio took inspiration from U.S. engineer Frederick Taylor's work on scientific management, calling for data that would help "multiply the fruits of labor, perfect them, and diminish fatigue." Scientific management would allow the work process and the biological condition of the worker to improve and would raise the economic level of the poor. Defective tools and backward techniques would have to be eradicated and indigenous and rural peoples educated regarding the rationalization of production. Their bodies would become healthier and therefore more productive once they had learned about diet and exercise and—as Gamio insisted repeatedly after taking a trip to Japan—the benefits of eating soy! Mendieta y Núñez, countering the argument that Taylorism aimed to secure profits to capital at the expense of labor, suggested that among ejido members and self-employed workers, efficiencies would benefit labor, not capital. Taylorist methods would allow the self-employed worker to achieve the same results with less effort.[41]

Criteria of efficiency, relying on measurement, allowed diversity to be ranked on a single scale. A complex problem such as the production and sale of ayate cloths, woven from agave fiber, could be reduced to numbers that could be compared: N skeins of yarn purchased for M pesos plus T hours of labor by X family members over Y days yielded Z ayates, which given a price of P for each ayate yielded a profit of W, which could purchase Q kilos of corn providing R calories per family member per day. Numbers promised ready conclusions not otherwise available given so much heterogeneity and a multifactorial social process.[42]

Increasing workers' productivity and consumption, Gamio wrote, would be good for the nation as well as the worker. The overriding agenda was without doubt based on a universal model of what it meant to be a modern nation. Gamio's and Mendieta y Núñez's ultimate goal in stimulating consumption was to kindle the national economy and advance the nation. Mexico's internal market was too small to provide a vibrant outlet for Mexican industry, according to Gamio, and Mexico's exports and imports seemed low given the country's population, vast territory, and natural resources. In "Mexico's Varied Markets," Gamio argued that too many Mexicans participated in restricted local or regional markets that sold limited varieties of unsophisticated goods. Because they were "lacking in needs," distant from urban influences, and lived in a "primitive cultural environment," providing these "semisavage" peoples with more income might be of secondary importance. If the state did not, as he put it in a report on the Mezquital's rural poor, "elevate their necessities," they would not consume more.[43]

In some cases, the modernization framework overpowered data collected under particularist pluralist paradigms. To sustain the conclusions generated by numerical aggregation and the evolutionary agenda, researchers and policymakers were often forced to push aside the very data they worked so hard to collect. For instance, lack of adequate nutrition was often cited by scholars as contributing to the ill health, proclivity toward disease, and degraded status of Native peoples. References to indígenas' "monotonous" diet of corn, chili, and salt were legion, and Gamio repeatedly decried the lack of meat and milk in Native diets and their "vegetarianism."[44] Nonetheless, data on Native diets did not document deficiency in any straightforward way. As researchers recorded the multiple factors that contributed to nutrition among a multiplicity of groups, they admitted how hard it was to reach any conclusions. Yet conclude they did. A presentation on nutrition at the 1940 Pátzcuaro conference argued that the "deficiencies" that characterized the diets of the "economically weak" were exacerbated among indigenous groups. Yet other conference presentations noted that Native peoples ate, on average, more calories than their non-Native rural counterparts. Native diets were, on average, deficient in proteins and some vitamins but not in calcium, phosphorus, and iron. As one presenter put it, some might even "conclude that the current diet is good." He disagreed.[45]

Similarly, when medical experts funded by the Mexican state and the Rockefeller Foundation actually studied the diet and nutritional status of the Otomí, they found "surprisingly little definite clinical nutritional deficiency," even though the Mezquital region was "one of the economically poorest in Mexico."[46] A similar study of nutrition carried out in the

Tarascan region around Cherán found the diet adequate in some ways but not in others. Minimum requirements for vitamins A and B1 were met, but total calorie intake and vitamin B2 were deficient. This mixed picture held even when looking only at the poorest families. This led the Cherán researchers to raise questions about the validity of the studies on which they based their conclusions. Were the data regarding what people ate accurate? Was the vitamin profile of the same food grown in different areas the same? How did processing methods affect nutrient availability? And did Tarascans have the same dietary requirements as populations from which the data on requirements were derived?[47] All these questions pointed to the difficulties occasioned by diversity. In the same journal issue in which researchers raised these questions, physical anthropologist Juan Comas cited a study by Mexican researcher José Gómez Robleda that indicated that Tarascans were deficient in muscular force and weight, a fact he attributed to "exploitation, misery, and a lack of culture." Existing studies, he averred, "make evident a clear biological (somatic and mental) deficiency." These conditions were, Comas hastened to add, transitory and therefore easily rectified.[48]

Epistemologies of Evolution: Compilation

Along with quantification and the use of hierarchical evolutionary categories, Mexican intellectuals turned to compilation as a way of recognizing heterogeneity while preserving an integral nation. During the 1930s and 1940s, Mexicans worked on a number of encyclopedias of Native peoples, which compiled information on forty- or fifty-odd Mexican ethnic groups, including Afro-Mexicans.[49] In the resulting books and exhibits, proximity presaged national unity. So did uniformity, but it was science, which collected, described, and classified, that created and ratified that national unity. Encyclopedias, exhibits, and compilations provided an illusion of homogeneity by consistently applying a regular set of categories across different peoples, even when the content of the categories did not necessarily match. Seeking uniformity, Mendieta y Núñez published a research outline that others might follow. But items had to be forced into categories that did not fully fit them.[50]

Despite the homogenizing goals, the messages these books and exhibits conveyed were far from unambiguous. The IIS, which Mendieta y Núñez directed beginning in 1939, organized a museum exhibit suggestively

Figure 3. "Ethnographic Map of the Mexican Republic." (Oscar S. Frías and Universidad Nacional Autónoma de México, "Mapa etnográfico de la República mexicana" [Mexico City: Instituto de Investigaciones Sociales, Universidad Nacional Autónoma de México, 1940].)

titled *México indígena*. Forty-eight indigenous races were on display, each represented in photographs, maps, charts, and typical objects and outfits. The photographs, most by noted photographers Raúl Estrada Discua and Enrique Hernández Morones, chronicled ethnographic characteristics; pathologies; expressions of material culture such as diet, clothing, housing, economy, and work instruments; expressions of social life such as ceremonies, funerary rituals, government, and festivities; and aspects of collective mental patrimony such as language, religion, folklore, art, history, and traditions. Besides the uniformity of categories, a sense of national unity was created by assembling them in the museum exhibit (and the related book published decades later). Data on each group were of interest as parts of a national whole. Describing the exhibit, however, Mendieta y Núñez had to note that each group also revealed "a different evolutionary picture" and that the exhibit as a whole attested "objectively and scientifically to the Mexican nation's social and cultural heterogeneity."[51]

At the same time as it conducted the research that led to the exhibit, the IIS created an "ethnographic map" of Mexico. The social sciences would make whole, or unify, Mexico's disparate peoples. They would

Figure 4. "Dr. Lucio Mendieta y Núñez, Director of the Instituto de Investigaciones Sociales, Universidad Nacional Autónoma de México, with Ethnographic Map." (Lucio Mendieta y Núñez, "Veinticinco años del Instituto de Investigaciones Sociales de la Universidad Nacional Autónoma de México," *Revista Mexicana de Sociología* 17, no. 2/3 [May–December 1955]: n.p.)

enumerate them (each ethnicity was numbered). But the map showed uneven, irregular splotches. The color-coded key at the bottom left neatly contrasted with the map. It was counterbalanced with the emblem of the National University placed on a diagonal to its upper right (figure 3). A photograph of Mendieta y Núñez in the *Revista Mexicana de Sociología* pictured the sociologist seated at a desk in the new IIS offices with the ethnographic map hanging centered on the wall behind him. This map was both the product of a Mexican social science and an expression of the power that authorized that science. At the same time, the map's irregular lines contrasted with the repetition of rectangles in the photo: the sociologist's desk, books and papers, and certificates on the wall, along with the wall panels and the frame of the map itself (figure 4).[52]

These aggregating efforts notwithstanding, the compilations that the SEP and IIS commissioned also aimed to provide readily accessible local knowledge to teachers, irrigation specialists, geologists, and medical personnel working in a given region. For each group studied, the compilations themselves relied on disparate investigations by a number of researchers. Readers or viewers who delved behind the categories and labels in books or exhibits would have noted a lack of uniformity: gaps in knowledge, lack of information, doubts. There might be data on housing for one group but not another. Data on music or folktales were available only in some cases. The book based on the 1946 *México indígena* exhibit, which was not published until 1986, made efforts to secure uniformity, including similarly framed shots of housing or clothing. Photographs of individuals were arranged in an identical manner, one ethnicity to a page, with three generations pictured for each ethnicity. Some people but not all were shown in profile, a presumably uniform pose that might help scientists determine facial characteristics. But the backdrops varied, and sometimes there was more than one person in the frame. Beneath the surface order, the heterogeneity that had characterized the fieldwork when the photographs were taken reemerged (figures 5 and 6).[53]

Mendieta y Núñez, attuned to theory and methodology, made of this diversity a virtue. To his data collection outline for economic ethnographers, he added that researchers should perfect and modify it "according to the object of study, the region, the particularities of the human groups among which the investigations take place."[54] He portrayed diversity not as a shortcoming—the inability to unite or even characterize the nation—but as a new epistemology. Mendieta y Núñez, Gamio, and others had begun to create distinct methodologies, perhaps even an alternative modernity and a Mexican science.

Indian as a Cultural and Economic Category

As Mexican investigators grasped for ways of knowing that reflected heterogeneity and indeterminacy, however, their participation in international discussions continually compelled them to specify the racial composition and evolutionary stage of the nation. Defining who was Indian remained a central task, one that justified the very existence of indigenismo, domestically and internationally. In 1936, Moisés Sáenz had sidestepped the taxonomic issue of deciding who was Indian by calling for a "practical" solution. The government should focus on places that were most "genuinely Indian."[55] Differences among Mexicans were not absolute for Sáenz. A group might be indigenous in some ways but not in others. His strategy was widely shared in indigenista circles. The inability

Figure 5. Facsimile of cropped photographs of Mazatecos
from Lucio Mendieta y Núñez's *México indígena*. (Courtesy of
Archivo Fotográfico "México Indígena" of the Instituto de
Investigaciones Sociales, Universidad Nacional Autónoma de
México.)

Figure 6. Uncropped photographs of Mazatecos
used in Lucio Mendieta y Núñez's *México indígena*.
(Courtesy of Archivo Fotográfico "México Indígena"
of the Instituto de Investigaciones Sociales,
Universidad Nacional Autónoma de México.)

CLASIFICACION DE ELEMENTOS DE CULTURA MATERIAL

EN PUEBLOS DEL VALLE DEL MEZQUITAL

Porcentaje de objetos materiales en función con su clasificación de
origen, tipo cultural, producción, resultado de consumo y uso.

Origen Cronologico.			Tipo Cultural			Origen de la produccion				Resultados del consumo.			USO	
Prehispánico.	Colonial.	Contemporáneo.	India.	Mixta.	Occidental.	Doméstica.	Regional.	Nacional.	Extranjera.	Eficiente.	Deficiente.	Perjudicial.	Continuo.	Esporádico.
43.80	13.50	2.70	37.40	25.70	36.90	17.00	40.60	28.90	13.50	80.10	14.60	5.30	93.90	6.70

Figure 7. Gamio's classification of elements of material culture in Mezquital Valley villages. (Folder 1, no. 4, Don Manuel Gamio: Proyecto Valle de Mezquital, Archivo Histórico del Instituto Indigenista Interamericano, Mexico City.)

to define or pinpoint difference seemed to fly in the face of the socialists' cultural pluralism, which demanded that differences be recognized and labeled—though not the socialist emphasis on class, a category that relied at least in part on a numerical ranking of efficiency and poverty. Fluid definitions of indigeneity were also associated with liberal policies based on notions of individual social mobility that might destroy indigeneity itself, as Sáenz had recognized.[56]

Indigenistas had been facing the challenge of defining indigeneity for some time. Gamio confronted it first in his Teotihuacán research and then again in the Mezquital. In line with the reigning materialist agenda of the 1930s, he developed a typology that included biological-somatic and geographical criteria. He also insisted on the importance of tangible, quantifiable material culture. Intellectual (or spiritual) culture—by which Gamio meant science, religion, ethics, folklore, and the arts—was, Gamio averred, "abstract" and therefore hard to classify, especially since foreign scientific principles did not provide useful guidelines. Numbers, which could be easily transposed from one context to another and compared, helped create universal standards. When it came to intellectual culture, quantification and numerical specification was not always possible.[57]

SAMPLE GROUP OF ITEMS OF MATERIAL CULTURE	Chronological Origin			Cultural Type				Origin and Character of Production						Character of Use and Consumption					Classification of Intercultural Processes					
	Pre-Spanish	Colonial	Contemporary	Native	European	American	Mixed	Domestic	Regional	National	Foreign	Manual	Mechanical	Efficient	Defective	Harmful	Continuous	Sporadic	Adaptation	Adoption	Survival	Displacement	Replacement	Fusion
Metate (corn grinding stone)	x			x				x		x				x		x					x			
Phonograph			x			x					x	x	x								x			
Cowboy saddle		x		x				x		x		x					x	x						
Machete		x		x						x		x	x			x								x
Huaraches (sandals)	x			x				x		x				x		x					x			
Peyote (a cactus drug)	x			x				x								x	x				x			

Figure 8. Gamio's methods of classification of material culture. (Manuel Gamio, "Cultural Patterns in Modern Mexico," *Quarterly Journal of Inter-American Relations* 1, no. 2 [April 1939]: 52.)

The objects people used were for Gamio the best measure of civilization. In contrast to ways of thinking or even physical features, which could be diffuse, "any [census] enumerator knows at first sight if the dress, the house, the domestic utensils and industries, and even the general ideas of the individual being recorded are of the backward indigenous type or of the modern culture type."[58] Based on this proposition, Gamio established a method for classifying material culture based on four parallel categorizations: chronological origin (pre-Columbian, colonial, contemporary); cultural type (indigenous, mixed, Western); geographic origin (domestic, regional, national, foreign); and nature of consumption (efficient, deficient, harmful). He also added a fifth criterion aimed at characterizing the importance of an object: whether it was used continuously or sporadically. For each criterion, he calculated the percentage of items in each category, down to two decimal points (figure 7).

In a version of this taxonomy Gamio published in the United States and titled "Cultural Patterns in Modern Mexico," he included a chart similar to the one used by fieldworkers in the Mezquital. Gamio sought to show the convergence of the four axes he had defined based on an integral analysis of a number of factors: the cultural pattern referred to in the title of the essay. (The title alluded to the cultural typologies developed by Ruth Benedict in her book *Patterns of Culture*.) Yet there was a problem. Readers might readily read Gamio's chart as showing heterogeneity and dispersion.

In fact, a reader might, based on the format of the chart, conclude that the different factors could combine in different ways: that someone might wear sandals (*huaraches*) and listen to music on a phonograph when in town or that in some families the husband used a modern plow and the wife ground corn on a *metate* (figure 8).[59]

No doubt recognizing the limitations of this approach, in his Mezquital research Gamio tallied each item. The goal here was to gain a better picture of the overall evolutionary stage of the Otomí and their nonindigenous neighbors based on an index indicating the proportion of more advanced goods they used. But here again the chart did not seem to yield a clear message because the numbers for each classification did not match up. In the text of an English-language exposition of his method, Gamio in fact put forth a twofold procedure of analysis. First, the proportion of objects of indigenous or European origin had to be determined in order to gauge "the degree of evolutionary backwardness or progress of certain groups in comparison with others."[60] Then the objects themselves had to be analyzed to see whether they were harmful or slightly useful. The state would aim its assistance at the most backward groups, attacking their most harmful, least efficient practices (and in the process bringing Native peoples into broader national and international markets).[61] Sáenz's sliding scale of indigeneity reappeared.

An approach based on material culture was implemented nationally by the agricultural engineer and statistician Emilio Alanís Patiño, who headed Mexico's census office from 1933 to 1938 and went on to become the director of Mexico's Dirección General de Estadística (General Department of Statistics). Alanís Patiño had studied with Corrado Gini in Rome and worked with Gini's team on their pilot study in Ixmiquilpan, in the Mezquital Valley, in 1933. As the census bureau's director, he tested statistical measures of material culture through a study of death certificates.[62] These measures became part of the 1940 Mexican census, which queried indicators of material culture (footwear, sleeping arrangements, housing materials, and type of house), food (tortillas versus bread), tools (possession of sewing machines), and language.[63]

In analyzing the 1940 census, Alanís Patiño revealed the difficulties of categorization, even based on elements of material culture that could be counted. For instance, given that people might eat different amounts of tortillas or bread, how to define who was indigenous? Alanís Patiño chose to include only those persons who never ate bread, since the consumption of even small amounts of bread, he said, signified the "abandonment of indigenous habits." He here presumably equated indigeneity with untainted pre-Columbian custom and associated change with mestizaje and a movement away from indigeneity. But perhaps suspecting that eating bread was not a foolproof measure, he hastened to add that in Yucatán all but 6 percent of the population ate bread, "despite its large indigenous population and the fact that Yucatán does not produce wheat."[64] In a report to the 1940 Pátzcuaro conference on family budgets, he enunciated the same definitional problem: could methods used to study urban proletarian families be used to study indigenous economies? He thought not, given differences in "evolutionary state, composition [of families] and customs and necessities." But there was more: "The word 'indígena' does not at present correspond to a unique and well-defined idea. A person, family, or social group may be classified as indigenous because of their geographical origins (aboriginal), because of their biological (anthropomorphic or serological) characteristics, because of their language, because of their economic characteristics or because of cultural forms. They may be indigenous along all these criteria simultaneously, but that is not necessarily the case and often their indigeneity may be more or less according to which scale is being used to classify them." Alanís Patiño then chose to use "conventional" (that is, nonscientific) criteria, classifying as indigenous those individuals, families, and groups that differed from "populations of a European type" in language and culture. This was an overly capacious definition, he admitted, but he would use it for now.[65]

Seeing that the combination of more than one characteristic might yield a more definitive definition of indigeneity, Alanís Patiño and the census cross-tabulated different measures, assaying a more integral analysis, albeit one limited to material culture. For instance, how many people wore shoes and Western clothing, went barefoot and wore Western clothing, or went barefoot and wore indigenous clothing? Pointing to a correlation that might signal indigeneity, he wrote that "sleeping on the floor or *tapexco* [bedroll] is an indigenous habit that is associated with the lack of consumption of bread." Here, too, a qualification was in order: "Nevertheless, there are more than a million individuals who eat bread but keep sleeping in the Native fashion." Was this, he wondered, because they had not been exposed to modern culture and rejected it or because they could not afford to buy both a bed and bread?[66]

The answer to this question would determine what types of policies were necessary. Did Native peoples need more cash or more exposure to modern culture, including schools and radios? But the difficulty of answering the question not only showed Alanís Patiño how difficult it was to define who was Indian but also revealed the extent to which the material and the cultural were, in fact, intertwined. Things like bread and beds, Alanís Patiño noted, were associated with both "old ethnic divisions" and "current economic classes." What a person ate seemed a crucial indicator, since eating a particular food implied certain ways of cooking and particular tools needed to grow and prepare it. If indigenous foodways persisted, there would be material consequences. By contrast, whether people wore shoes or not seemed to be more a direct function of their income. And, then, people who had a "more evolved material culture" would also acquire new ideas and new emotions. Economic changes had cultural consequences. It was also hard to separate out "indigenous habit" and economic "deficiency" because almost all Native people were poor. Returning to the Yucatán, he noted that more than sixty thousand people were bilingual but wore shoes and Western clothing. They could afford these items. In Oaxaca, which had proportionately fewer speakers of Native languages, more people wore indigenous clothing and went barefoot because they were poorer. Alanís Patiño thus argued that that income shaped material culture, a fact confirmed by the many urban poor who were modern but lacked shoes. Yet not just economics but emotions, geography, and history also influenced people's decisions about consumption.[67] Each of these explanations would imply a different state strategy of reform and assistance. Culture might shape economics, economics might shape culture, or they might evolve or persist in tandem.

Gamio similarly raised the issue of Native peoples who possessed wealth but because of their attachment to tradition failed to live at a more advanced cultural level. In some ways this was not surprising, given that Gamio viewed biological race or heritage, material culture, and intellectual culture as separable—hence the need to separate out and define different combinations. But he insisted that generally cultural advances could not be made without improving economic conditions. They were a necessary if not sufficient condition.[68]

By the 1940s indigenistas had forged a novel strategy for addressing the multiple dilemmas they faced. Increasingly, they split off distinct elements of indigenous lifeways as a way of reconciling cultural pluralism—whether it was desired or simply inevitable—with their certainty regarding the benefit of certain modern scientific advances. They privileged economic criteria and those aspects of material culture that could easily be counted and ranked: objects owned or consumed, tools used. At the same time, they defined differences as primarily cultural (by which indigenistas meant intellectual and spiritual culture) and portrayed these cultural differences as less consequential. Economics and science led to progress; culture was relatively immaterial. This viewpoint jibed with view that evolution was not unilateral and that there might therefore be divergent but equally efficient cultures. It mitigated concerns that Western medicine and agricultural techniques or Spanish language instruction and literacy would necessarily erase what made the Otomí or the Tarascans distinct cultures. This allowed indigenistas also to embrace cultural pluralism. Gamio now argued that if the goal of government was to stimulate human happiness, then categorizations and hierarchies might not pertain when it came to ethics, law, religion, or art—ambits of life that not only varied greatly from place to place but also advanced and receded over time. For instance, applying a Western morality to "nudist" or "semi-nudist" Native peoples might lead researchers to see them as indecent. But unless their lack of clothing was the result of poverty (which could be objectively measured and situated in evolutionary terms), it would be wrong to condemn scant clothing automatically since such attire might be a useful adjustment to the local climate. Moreover, the path to overall well-being would not be a "continuously ascending curve."[69]

This unstable solution jibed with the conditions spawned by World War II. Although Nazi racism no doubt counseled against intolerance, social and economic engineering gathered force as Mexico and Latin America as well as the United States sought to manage the demands of war. The U.S. demand for Mexican products pushed the Mexican government, which was already augmenting its ability to direct and coordinate economic development, to enact national-level policies aimed at stimulating economic efficiencies and growth. In this context, indigenistas embraced cultural difference but insisted on economic modernization.

Conclusion

Throughout the 1930s and 1940s Mexican indigenistas articulated a twofold agenda. First, they sought to integrate the nation, to create a semblance of accord and portray its totality. This they achieved less by homogenizing than by displaying and describing, then aggregating and compiling. Homogeneity was not totally cast aside, but it was rendered as a future goal. The present involved Mexicans on different rungs of the evolutionary ladder. Yet just as Mexico's Native peoples had evolved before the conquest, so they would continue to evolve. And it was this fact that led indigenistas to frame modernizing alternatives that made spaces for the heterogeneous present.

Increasingly in the 1940s, indigenistas characterized intellectual and spiritual culture as the site of heterogeneity while seeing material culture and economy as the site of necessary evolution. Economic efficiencies became more important as the revolution veered rightward. Yet these were haphazard trends. Culture could at times be ranked on an evolutionary scale, and economies continued at times to be appreciated ethnographically and locally. Recognizing that culture and economy did not march in lockstep—indeed, that elements of each could change at different paces and in divergent directions—indigenistas also suggested that there could be more than one modernity and that "integral" analyses were, perhaps, not possible. The unevenness of Mexico's modernization did not necessarily mark it as a failure or indicate the inferiority of its social science. Both modernity and science could be plural. Still, indigenistas also felt that they needed to develop racial as well cultural and economic taxonomies that transcended the local and allowed them to participate in national and global dialogues. In so doing, they facilitated not just comparisons based on hierarchical categories but also a degree of connection and commensurability that re-created inequality.

In the end, those efforts at dialogue across borders ended up entangled in the discourses of culture and economy they mobilized. In Mexico, economic modernization won out as a goal and primary category of analysis, and with it class analysis, which was present already in Cárdenas's speech at Pátzcuaro. Ethnicity was relegated to the local sidelines. Yet culture and race were never absent for long. They popped up incessantly when economic hierarchies were discussed. As Mexicans so often pointed out, there were many non-Indian poor. But then it turned out that Indians were poor because they were Indian, economically and culturally.

Conclusion

Race, Culture, and Class

During 1942–45, Mexican debates regarding how to define, and address, indigeneity were reprised in dialogue with U.S. scholars. Writing in the IAII journal *América Indígena*, Mexicans offered, once again, a *practical* or tactical definition of indigeneity aimed at guiding social policies, especially economic policies. Rejecting overly general theories, they split culture from economy and comfortably accepted the resulting taxonomic incongruities. By contrast, U.S. scholars articulated a functionalist approach that stressed connections between culture and economy and suggested that indigenous lifeways might easily become disorganized and ultimately disappear.

Manuel Gamio provided the prelude to this debate in a series of three essays published in *América Indígena*. Policymakers, he asserted, needed "to know for sure something of capital importance . . . , which is the number of individuals in the continental population that can be correctly classified with the generic term of Indian." Without that knowledge, he declared, Native peoples could not receive the "special treatment for social betterment" that they deserved. A true racial categorization would require working out a number of technical difficulties and a great deal of time and money, Gamio noted, and it might stimulate "harmful racial concepts." But it was necessary.[1]

The goal of such a classification, according to Gamio, was not to split hairs over who was indigenous and who was mestizo but rather to address the needs of everyone having or using those culturally indigenous attributes that were deemed most harmful and to raise the cultural level of citizens who remained "at the lowest evolutionary stages." This was an evolutionary but nontaxonomic perspective. Biological race did not matter, according to Gamio, who labeled the population of interest to indigenistas as "Indo-mestizo." Harmful indigenous attributes should receive the attention of indigenistas whether the people possessing them were racially "pure Indian," white, or mestizo. In fact, indigenistas would attend to whites who were culturally indigenous as well as blacks and mulattoes because all had a "biological development . . . and economic-cultural characteristics that correspond to anachronistic and inferior evolutionary stages." In contrast, neither Indians who were culturally white nor poor whites living in the mountains of the southern United States who were physically deficient or ill were of interest. Both had adopted Western culture. Indigenistas' attention would be proportional to the prevalence of indigenous cultural elements among any given group.[2] Here Gamio repeated the sliding-scale formula that Sáenz suggested in his 1936 blueprint for the DAI.[3]

Scholars in the United States challenged the Mexican viewpoint on two fronts. The first had to do with whether culture and economics functioned autonomously. Scholars steeped in functionalism worried that material improvements might provoke greater, and harmful, disorganizing changes. This view would have been familiar to most Mexican anthropologists, but their experiences—as well as their statistics—told them that this was not the only possible outcome. For anthropologist Julian Steward of the Bureau of American Ethnology, the Mexicans as well as their followers in the United States were, quite simply, too romantic, too fixated on cultural persistence. In what was no doubt an overly Manichean formulation, Steward, who edited the *Handbook of South American Indians*, contrasted sentimental "Indianists," who sought to preserve differences, to "anthropologists," who saw modernization and assimilation as inevitable. The Indianists either froze Indians in a pre-Columbian past or posited a cultural core of values that would persist despite the adoption of Western technologies and other Western attributes. The anthropologists were influenced by functionalism and viewed cultures as organic wholes that would be thoroughly disturbed even by small changes. As a result, the anthropologists could not fathom how Native cultures persisted. But neither anthropologists nor Indianists adequately understood how social change came about, according to Steward. Changes, he believed, would normally and inevitably lead to a degree of disorganization, but Native cultures, like all cultures, could respond by reintegrating themselves. Still, Steward believed that in the end indigeneity might lose its distinctive qualities. "Any nation will always have differences between localities, and between urban and rural areas. Some of those differences can still be called Indian," he wrote. But in the end, "readjustments will someday lead Indians so far from their aboriginal beginnings that any distinctiveness will be comparable to that of other local variations found within a larger culture area, to which their lives will be increasingly interrelated. Then we shall see Indians not as set off racially and culturally from surrounding peoples but as cultural variants, which, though distinctive in various ways, participate in a stream of social change that seems destined for all mankind." This point of view was not far from what Indianist-anthropologists like Gamio and Moisés Sáenz had been suggesting. But in contrast to Gamio, who believed that science should determine which attributes of indigeneity were helpful and which were noxious and should be jettisoned, Steward suggested that anthropologists lacked the knowledge necessary to judge. Drawing from the functionalist toolkit, he maintained that changes in one part of the culture could lead to unforeseeable changes in another. "How far," he asked, "can one go teaching the scientific facts of meteorology, soil properties, seed germination, plant fertilization and growth, proper cultivation, and food values without affecting Native ritual?"[4]

This discussion regarding the nature of acculturation and change over time intersected with a second debate regarding the nature of racial distinctions. The issue of racial distinctions emerged in 1942 when Sol Tax, a student of Robert Redfield, published an essay on the Guatemalan Highlands in which he argued that because social mobility presumed cultural fluidity, Native assimilation was inevitable. Drawing on ideas that reflected mainstream U.S. views regarding race, Tax claimed that Guatemala's Highland Native peoples did not suffer racial discrimination. Their problems were instead related to economic, health, and educational status. Associating racial discrimination with Jim Crow segregation, Tax suggested that because perceived differences between Guatemala's Indians and ladinos (nonindigenous people) were based on language and culture, which could be easily modified, rather than on hard racial distinctions grounded in biological inheritance, those differences were class distinctions. Indians could therefore become ladinos if they learned to speak Spanish and acquired ladino lifeways. Different languages and cultures, he further argued, would tend to disappear as Western education, medicine, and technologies were introduced into Native communities. "Sentimental" Indianists—this was a term Sáenz had used in 1936—might want to preserve Native cultures, but although some aspects of Native cultures might become part of national culture, the cultures as such would inevitably die out: "Indian culture as such would be as defunct in all of the country as it is today in large parts." In this context, sentimental indigenismo might, as Gamio had hinted, actually create hostility where it had not previously existed.[5]

The argument that policies might hasten separation and hostility would have been familiar to Mexicans who had contrasted their liberal social order to U.S. segregation. It would also have been familiar to an older generation in the United States that had heard the argument that allotment was necessary in order to free Native peoples to become citizens. But the idea that culture and language were related to class rather than "race" or that culture was fluid and distinct from a hard biological inheritance would not have resonated strongly among Mexican indigenistas.

The first, and quite forceful, public response to Tax came from John Collier. Associating Tax's argument with the liberal views of social mobility that had driven allotment, he insisted that racism was not caused by indigenismo. Moreover, education would not necessarily dilute Indianness. From there, the crux of Collier's argument followed Gamio's analysis, which Collier characterized as "the thesis for which the Inter-American Indian Institute stands . . . and the total experience of countries like Mexico and the United States, and not of those countries alone." According to Collier, "To insist that the Indian does not exist or, as an Indian, should be ignored, unless his biological, linguistic, social, legal and economic identifications are exactly coterminal would be to confuse the subject hopelessly." Those who were culturally Indian, Collier pointed out, were generally those with "the highest concentration of Indian blood . . . who call themselves Indians, whom Guatemala calls Indians, and who speak their pre-Columbian languages." This was an assertion that Gamio, Emilio Alanís Patiño, and Sáenz would have approved of, and one they had tried— without much success—to prove with numbers. It was what Alanís Patiño had called a conventional, common-sense approach.[6]

Redfield defended Tax by pointing to differences between the United States and Latin America. In the United States, he wrote, white views toward Indians were influenced by "the strength of race prejudice as between Negroes and whites." In Guatemala, the cultural differences between ladinos and Indians were, by contrast, similar to "class differences." Racial differences were rigid and based on notions of biology; class differences permitted mobility. Redfield also suggested that the assimilation of Guatemala's Indians into white culture through education was likely, if not inevitable. The gist of Collier's own policies, he reminded the commissioner, was to "mitigate the disorganizing effects of this trend and to help the Native peoples retain something of their old life." Redfield also counseled Collier that although Tax rejected the characterization of ladino/Indian differences as *racial*, Tax's rejection did not imply that they should not be characterized as *Indian*. However, Redfield did feel that in places like Guatemala where, in contrast to the United States, Indians constituted a majority, the problems faced by Native peoples might best be addressed through general social policies that were presumably directed toward improving education, health care, and economic conditions linked to social status and class.[7] Mexicans had been debating this issue—and flip-flopping among generalized class-based policies, ethnographically based policies, and the adaptation of general policies to specific situations—for some twenty years.

Collier and Emil Sady, the U.S. representative to the IAII from 1941 to 1942, reiterated the need for state policies that counteracted, and helped Native peoples counteract, forces of assimilation. Inevitably, a specific government agency was needed, even if it was—in contrast to the U.S. Indian Service—merely an advisory agency that counseled other state institutions not concerned chiefly with Native peoples. This agency would take the preservation of culture and cultural tolerance as its main goals.[8] The split between material and nonmaterial culture articulated by Gamio reappeared.

This conflict was reprised in a slightly different way in 1945, when Collier responded to an essay by anthropologist Beate Salz in which she noted a tension in indigenismo between its homogenizing nationalism and its economic platform, on the one hand, and its insistence on difference and special treatment toward Native peoples, on the other. Indigenistas made the two compatible by characterizing modern cooperatives like the ejido with pre-Hispanic forms, blending modernity and tradition, economic and cultural. But in Latin America, where Native cultures constituted majorities, demands for land reform, labor rights, education, and health care could all be based on notions of citizenship or universal human rights. With the specter of World War II haunting, Salz argued that to do otherwise would be to stimulate conflict and perhaps violence. Like Tax, Salz suggested that Indianists' assertion of special protections for Native peoples could spur racism.[9]

Collier, siding with indigenistas like Gamio and Luis Chávez Orozco, disagreed. Difference did not inevitably lead to conflict, he said. Native peoples had long been democratic. *Their* forms of difference would contribute to a harmonious pluralism. Sady articulated a slightly different solution, arguing that "native administration" would serve a number of groups "of whatever race" that possessed material, intellectual, and spiritual cultures that required specific policies. But some Native peoples—those politically, educationally, legally, economically, medically, and/or religiously furthest from mainstream modern culture—needed an integral program that only specialized administrators and, in certain cases, special legal provisions could deliver. These peoples were culturally, but not racially, distinct. Censuses should tabulate the specific liabilities that governments could and should address.[10]

In a historical analysis of past Mexican policies, Lucio Mendieta y Núñez reached a more classically liberal conclusion. He identified five regimes through which the West had dealt with Native peoples: (1) extermination (as in the United States); (2) segregation (also practiced by the United States); (3) exploitation (European colonialism in Africa or privately by wealthy Latin American landowners); (4) paternalist protection (as in the Laws of the Indies); and (5) indifference. This last option was the one employed by Latin American nations following independence. They allowed Native institutions—local governments, legal practices—to persist without giving them legal status. But Native peoples who came into contact with whites were subject to the dominant laws, and they suffered under legal regimes that did not in reality protect their individual rights as workers or landholders. The Mexican Revolution had changed that by creating a legal regime that took into consideration collective landholding. But that regime did not discriminate racially. This was, he insinuated, the right path. If the revolution had failed in its programs toward Native peoples, it was not because its programs had not been culturally specific enough but because not enough "energy" and money had been put toward the effort. Paternalism, which annulled individual initiative, was not the answer.[11]

This squabble came to a close with a salvo from anthropologist Oscar Lewis, who had replaced Sady as the U.S. representative to the IAII. In a paper Lewis cowrote with Ernest Maes of the U.S. National Indian Institute, Lewis sought to create forms of measurement that, local differences notwithstanding, could be consistently applied across the Americas. Reiterating the difficulties of defining who was indigenous, the authors noted that existing calculations counted "predominantly indigenous" people as those who were of "pure race." Given the prevalence of racial mixing, racial and legal definitions of who counted as Native—the latter often enshrining racial characterizations or other conventional forms of distinction—were not adequate. Maes and Lewis argued for using cultural criteria. But which? Rather than foreground historical factors relating to origins or describe agglomerations of traits, they wrote, scholars should focus on those traits that were of the greatest *practical* importance. Gamio's emphasis on material culture moved in that direction, but Lewis and Maes pointed to problems with his scheme. First, not all items of pre-Hispanic origin were inefficient. In other words, the criteria did not align neatly. Moreover, given climatic and other forms of variation, it was often difficult to rank items definitively, limiting their usefulness as universal measures. They proposed a four-point scheme that sidestepped the issue of definition. Beginning with "so-called Indian groups," administrators should determine what the most pressing needs and deficiencies were and figure out the extent to which different groups presented those needs and deficiencies. In some cases, universal policies of land distribution, road-building, provision of health care, or schooling in Spanish would need to be adapted. In still other cases, those policies simply would not work, and state officials would need to develop special techniques. They promoted a process of graded localization and specification of peoples and problems, but they insisted that by aggregating these data they would get a picture of a national reality. Experts might also use numerical criteria to define as indigenous those peoples that had the greatest number of problems in the largest proportion, they suggested. What those deficiencies were might vary from country to country, but each nation could strive to develop criteria that more conclusively determined, for itself, who was indigenous and who was not. These criteria would serve as a kind of index of indigeneity, allowing indigenousness to be, in essence, means tested. These criteria might or might not align with conventional ideas, they added. They also noted that colonial oppression or exploitation, a history of four hundred years of misery, should be taken into consideration. From this perspective, poor whites in Uruguay could not be considered indigenous, but Caribbean blacks, who had in any case adopted indigenous characteristics, should be.[12] In essence, Lewis and Maes recapitulated aspects of the Mexican debate while calling for a more rigorous quantification that took into account multiple factors. Their goal was not a single evolutionary ranking based on deficiencies but one that allowed for variations in the importance of different deficiencies, a pluralist evolutionary view.

INDIGENISMO AS A hemispheric intellectual and political movement was mostly led and financed by Mexicans. Influence flowed from South to North, as the *América Indígena* debate showed. In the 1920s and 1930s, U.S. scholars and policymakers looked to Mexico as an example that might help the United States learn to effectively govern its own racial differences. The National Research Council first considered Mexico and Latin America in the context of immigration reform. Redfield traveled to Tepoztlán to better understand Chicago's Mexican community. And Stuart Chase contrasted mestizo Tepoztlán to Middletown, Indiana, and asked what lessons a more traditional, less neurotic Mexico might offer. Chase also raised questions about what was "American." Collier used his experiences among immigrants, alongside knowledge he gained in Mexico, to craft an Indian New Deal that preserved difference but also sought to integrate Native peoples into the United States. He looked to Mexico to help the IS fashion policies that might allow Native peoples to choose when and how to adapt to modernity. Along with Laura Thompson, he applied lessons derived from Mexico's Native policies to U.S. African Americans, Spanish Americans, and Guamanians and to other "dependencies" abroad. Collier and Thompson also used what they learned in the more coercive context of the Poston prison camp.

Mexican social scientists, like their Euro-U.S. counterparts, strove to be scientific. Gamio equated science with an irreversible upward trajectory. But he and his Mexican collaborators were well aware that science was associated with the Euro-U.S. "West" and directed by North Atlantic institutions, and they therefore struggled to find ways to be both scientific and Mexican. The process required them to "Indianize" themselves at least a bit. Still, Mexicans could not dislodge the locus of science. Their efforts at Mexicanization were at best contradictory. They adapted a science premised on the trajectory of the West, but they could not fully develop an alternative science that did not disparage Native Mexico to some degree. They did not succeed in reconciling difference within liberalism. But their haphazard efforts to contest norms of nationhood that presumed, even if mythically, a shared history and ancestry led to creative efforts. Those efforts deserve serious and sustained historical attention. Their racism must be criticized, but we cannot stop there.

Running parallel to the epistemological dilemma Mexican intellectuals faced were the dilemmas posed by liberal politics. Mexico sought to become a proper nation-state in a context in which the interrelated demographic, economic, and racial characteristics of nationhood were forcefully shaped by Euro-U.S. models. The United States in particular helped make immigration and immigrants into an "issue." In the context of Good Neighbor policies, U.S. participants in Pan-American forums and international eugenic circles did not always have their way, however. Latin Americans bent the debates and countered the United States by participating in a Latin eugenics that viewed diversity as a resource rather than a liability. Notions of Nordic superiority and racial purity that originated in the United States and Europe nevertheless shaped the terms of debate, forcing Mexicans to consider how to talk back to Madison Grant and his ilk. As Mexicans tried to write against this narrative without fully rejecting it, progressive U.S. intellectuals took note. The United States could not, after all, claim to be pure Anglo-Saxon. Perhaps Mexico had lessons to offer. Certainly Franz Boas believed that was the case when, in the immediate aftermath of his work on immigrants, he initiated research in Mexico on cultural contacts and the diffusion of cultures. Boas's students would dominate U.S. anthropological study of Native peoples of the United States and Mexico. They rejected determinist theories of biology and unilateral views of assimilation, adopting theories of acculturation in their stead.

Domestically, Mexican indigenistas faced the dilemma of how to govern a diverse citizenry with laws and programs that presumed an abstract equality—and sameness—among citizens. They debated whether Native peoples should have distinct forms of representation and whether they should be governed by separate institutions or separate laws. Should they receive different kinds of education? Should they be integrated into national markets premised on ideas about interchangeable consumers who ate and drank and dressed alike? If so, how would that economic integration into the marketplace occur? On these questions, Mexican governments wavered. Institutionally, their indecision manifested itself as the repeated creation and dissolution of agencies aimed at studying Native issues. Although at times agencies dealing with Native issues developed distinct policies along pluralist lines, more often they simply applied broader national policies in ways consistent with the practices of particular communities or regions. Often indígenas were treated simply as campesinos and addressed in class terms. The debates in the journal *América Indígena* contrasted nations with indigenous majorities to those in which Native peoples were minorities. But at least in Mexico, the existence of a Native (or "Indo-mestizo") majority was largely a convenient fiction that perpetuated universal and class-based economic policies—not the other way around.

Intellectually, Mexican indigenistas tried out a number of strategies as they sought to reconcile racial and cultural differences within a liberal democratic political order. Gamio suggested, at times, that differences could be accepted in the short run but would dissolve in the long run. Native peoples, the Conference of Philologists and Linguists proclaimed, would be taught in Native languages so that they might (later) learn Spanish. The sociologist Mendieta y Núñez proposed the continuation of what he claimed was a Mexican historical precedent: laissez faire. National policymakers might simply ignore political and legal forms that contradicted liberal forms of governance but were not evidently harmful. These strategies were compatible with assimilationist theories of whitening that sought to improve backward peoples. In practice, they allowed differences to be tolerated and even encouraged.[13]

Another strategy indigenistas deployed was to accept some but not all aspects of Native lifeways and to suggest that Native cultures would combine with a modern national culture. The Otomí might speak their Native language but make hats and rugs that would be sold in Mexico City. They might eat corn tortillas that included soybeans. Indigenistas criticized practices they saw as less evolved, especially those that distanced Native peoples from national markets. They sought to make those presumably backward practices disappear. Yet at times they documented without judgment the heterogeneity they witnessed, and at times they praised aspects of Native lifeways. It was not just, as previous scholarship has pointed out, Native peoples' artistry and craftsmanship that indigenistas lauded. They also praised Native peoples' allegiances to family and community, their political traditions and democratic spirit, their knowledge of the land, their physical strength, and their willingness to do hard work. Indigenistas, inspired by what they saw as they toured pockets of the country previously unknown to national policymakers, tried to understand the existing, if changing, lifeways of Mexicans. Native peoples did not in fact reject all "modern" customs. They might cling to certain ways of thinking and doing but not others. If this was inevitable—as indigenistas had no doubt it was—then how best to channel it? Too often, indigenistas heeded the desires of national policymakers over those of the peoples they met. They served as imperfect mediators.

Indigenistas ordered diversity as they documented it, categorizing phenomena based on a hierarchical evolutionary scale that ranked organized religion over superstition, machines over hand tools, germ theory over knowledge of herbs, meat over corn. Yet as censuses revealed, different categories did not always correlate. Some Native people ate corn tortillas and wore shoes. Some spoke Spanish and Maya. Some got vaccinated and visited the *curandera*. Some went to school but used a digging stick rather than a plow. Often enough, indigenistas manifested an inability to synthesize the data they collected in ways that offered the overarching conclusions policymakers needed to create global modernizing policies toward indigenous peoples. Rather than ignore diversities and divergences, indigenistas noted them. Occasionally, they championed them. They made policy ethnographically.

Mexicans often argued that evolution might proceed along different lines, a view that jibed with the scientific belief in universal laws of development, whereby cultures evolved toward greater complexity, efficiency, and sophistication. But there might be multiple evolutionary trajectories. From within this paradigm, outside acculturating factors, including the force of capitalist modernity, were of secondary but not inconsequential importance. Change would respond to local conditions. In the postwar era, U.S. scholars adopted this indigenista strategy and termed it "plural evolution."[14]

In the United States, Collier, and even more so Laura Thompson, believed that outside influences, including state policy, could exert a positive modernizing influence if government agents could nativize themselves at least a bit. They, too, believed in ethnography. Collier and Thompson emphasized pluralism and cultural integrity, holding up the example of the Hopi, among whom autonomy, the evolving persistence of traditional forms, and a groupness based on democratic leadership prevailed. Collier argued that this preservation of difference actually allowed the Hopi to choose when and how to adapt to modernity, to pour modern contents into unbreakable traditional molds. In making these arguments, Collier drew selectively on a number of disciplines and perspectives that sought to preserve local differences within a broader social order, including anarchist doctrines of self-help that he had first tested while working with immigrants on the Lower East Side of Manhattan. Later, he took as a model Mexicans' recuperation of the ethnographically informed policies set in place by the Spanish Empire and British indirect rule. In line with these precedents, Collier and Thompson investigated culture within geographically bounded, face-to-face groups. Their interest in small-scale communities was compatible with a U.S. legal system that defined indigeneity as tribal membership and made the reservation a geographical expression of that "tribe," creating a local sovereignty.

Collier and his collaborators also drew increasingly on the functionalist perspectives that took shape during the 1930s and 1940s. Dorothea and Alexander Leighton and Thompson moved in circles influenced by Bronislaw Malinowski. The anthropologist A. R. Radcliffe-Brown taught at the University of Chicago. The functionalism of Malinowski and Radcliffe-Brown conceptualized cultures as bounded and integrated. Changes in economic organization might therefore spur new forms of community life, new ways of working and traveling and speaking, even new psychic dispositions. From this perspective, the divergent paths of change and exchange that Collier and his collaborators envisioned became harder to see.[15]

Collier and his U.S. collaborators looked to social psychology to understand processes of acculturation in general and its face-to-face dimensions in particular. Collier and Thompson, along with the Leightons and others, hoped that relations between white administrators and Natives—and between both and other intermediaries such as researchers and more Westernized Natives—could be based on sympathy and a back and forth influence. They knew that this was more aspiration than reality: "We are woefully ignorant, and yet so cock-sure," Collier and Thompson wrote in 1944.[16] Yet they held onto the hope that fuller knowledge and better communication would help them act more democratically. Alexander Leighton, who worked on Native issues and ran the Bureau of Social Research at the Poston internment camp, was more pessimistic regarding the barriers of "'caste and class'" that he recognized as part of "the very nature of administrative hierarchy." In a book penned shortly after the end of World War II, he lamented that "in spite of our democratic philosophy, when we Americans have attempted to administer other peoples our performance has often been far from either admirable or practicable. From Alaska to Guam, from the Philippines to the Indian reservations we have been guilty of being authoritarian democrats. It is little wonder that some Native people feel that they would rather have out-and-out imperialism than this business of being led up to a feast and jerked back as soon as they attempt to partake."[17] Leighton had learned from Poston residents that effective self-government could not be simply engineered from above.

In characterizing democracy as built on local and face-to-face interactions, Collier and his collaborators had minimized the coercive institutional and political contexts in which they tried to create democratic governance. First Collier and the IS downplayed the coercion involved in IS-mandated tribal constitutions. Later, their myopic focus on the local led to the tragic irony of trying to build democratic "self-government" in a prison camp. Collier was no doubt aware of how Congress, state policies and appropriations, the character of the IS bureaucracy, and IS interactions with Native peoples shaped politics on the reservations. They were daily frustrations. Yet Collier as well as Thompson and the Leightons often failed to address adequately how the realities of liberal democratic governance and norms of Americanness encroached on their hoped-for forms of local democratic self-government.

Overall, by emphasizing the local, U.S. policymakers and functionalist scholars sought to provide a roadmap for postwar liberal democratic governance of non-white groups at home and abroad. But their map could not lead them toward reconciling local democracy with the social, political, and economic forces that brought distinct places and diverse groups operating on different scales into conversation with one another. In this, their pluralism replicated orthogenetic models of cultural evolution that could not account for the diffusion and interactions of cultures.

The epistemological strategy of positing universality and generating universal laws was not unrelated to the tremendous magnitude and scope of U.S. power, actual and desired. The United States was both the seat of knowledge production and a norm for development. As the nation entered World War II and projected its power abroad, theories of race, culture, and indirect colonial rule helped scholars move from domestic to foreign contexts. At home, Collier and Thompson argued for preserving difference. Abroad they rejected a bland "undifferentiated internationalism" and advocated an "ordered heterogeneity," cautioning leaders not to try to impose U.S. forms of representative government.[18] The Indian Service's governance of Native peoples nevertheless became a model for governing dependencies and other domestic minorities. At Poston, Collier and Leighton sought to provide a roadmap for governing occupied Japan. Even as Collier and Alexander Leighton looked for techniques and frameworks that could account for difference within liberal polities premised on ideas of equality and homogeneity, they sought to generate universal laws—one of the goals of Radcliffe-Brown's structural functionalism. They believed in creating those laws by amassing separate case studies. Those laws would then help generate policies that might be applied in different contexts. Modernization theories built on these bases. The field of comparative politics that took shape in the postwar era sought to understand the various factors and combinations of factors that shaped modernization, conceived of as a movement toward already known modern ideals but one that started from different points and traveled along different paths.

With increasing clarity during the postwar years, Mexicans understood that their assigned role within a global scientific endeavor was not to elaborate universal models. Instead, they were to provide the empirical materials out of which U.S. scholars might construct social theories.[19] As part of this shift and perhaps contributing to it, race began to take a backseat to class. Economics and sociology displaced anthropology, with numbers helping to create equivalence among disparate cases and at least potential equality among citizens. Correlations accounted for diversity while helping to generate universal laws. And where legal distinctions separated Native peoples from non-Native U.S. citizens, or blacks from whites, numbers made gradual social improvement seem possible. Evolutionary concepts persisted.

These themes and the North-South conflicts they would generate were evident already in 1942, when Gamio and Collier debated Tax and Redfield in the pages of *América Indígena* regarding how to develop transnational criteria for determining who was indigenous. Gamio and his allies advocated a "practical" definition based on who might benefit most from modernizing state policies. This was a relative measure unlike the legal categories used in the United States. Particular people, even whites, might be more or less indigenous in their culture. To address the presumed deficiencies of those cultures required a combination of targeted differential policies and universal policies. Numerical descriptors and policies based on them helped resolve some of the more intractable difficulties generated by the need to name, define, and rank cultures and races. Yet scholars kept circling back to the twinned debates regarding universal human rights and difference, on the one hand, and how to sustain ideas about cultural integrity in the face of inevitable change and inevitable power, on the other. The war did not just remind them of the difficulties posed by racism. For some, it sounded a caution regarding all cultural and racial distinctions.

As the discussion in *América Indígena* presaged, these debates were beginning to be staged more clearly in terms of North-South differences: romantic and presumably unscientific indigenistas versus expert anthropologists; sentimental pluralists versus functionalist assimilationists; fluid, cultural indigeneity premised on economic factors versus stark, legal racial divisions; indigenous-mestizo Mexico and white-black United States. Still, Collier, Lewis, Sady, and Maes had spent a good deal of time in Mexico and with Mexicans (as well as with other Latin Americans). Their viewpoints were shaped by these experiences. Their science and their politics straddled the North-South divide but did so within a context of rising U.S. hegemony that was dissolving the middle ground on which they stood.

Notes

Abbreviations

A & P	National Research Council, Division of Anthropology and Psychology, 1919–1939, Division Collections, National Academy of Sciences, Washington, D.C.
CIW	Carnegie Institution of Washington, Washington, D.C.
IAII	Archivo Histórico del Instituto Indigenista Interamericano, Mexico City
IAII-JC	John Collier Papers, Archivo Histórico del Instituto Indigenista Interamericano, Mexico City
IAII-EJS	Estados Unidos en el Archivo Histórico: Emil J. Sady, 1943–1945, 1946–1960, Archivo Histórico del Instituto Indigenista Interamericano, Mexico City
IAII-PCII	*Primer Congreso Indigenista Interamericano: Acta final, asistentes, ponencias*, Archivo Histórico del Instituto Indigenista Interamericano, Mexico City
IAII-PVM	Don Manuel Gamio: Proyecto Valle del Mezquital, Archivo Histórico del Instituto Indigenista Interamericano, Mexico City
JARC	Japanese-American Relocation Centers Records #3830, Division of Rare and Manuscript Collections, Cornell University Library, Ithaca, N.Y.
JCP	John Collier Papers, Sanford, N.C.: Microfilming Corp. of America, 1980
LTP	Laura Thompson Papers, 1905–1997, National Anthropological Archives, Suitland, Md.
LSRM	Laura Spelman Rockefeller Memorial, Rockefeller Archive Center, Sleepy Hollow, N.Y.
NRC	National Research Council, National Academy of Sciences, Washington, D.C.
OFCJC	Office Files of Commissioner John Collier, 1933–1945, Record Group 75, Records of the Bureau of Indian Affairs, 1793–1999, U.S. National Archives, Washington, D.C.
RRP	Robert Redfield Papers, Special Collections Research Center, University of Chicago Library
RFCJC	Reference Files of Commissioner John Collier, 1933–1945, Record Group 75, Records of the Bureau of Indian Affairs, 1793–1999, U.S. National Archives, Washington, D.C.

Introduction

1. Chase, *Mexico*; Chase, *Men and Machines*; Chase, *Prosperity*; Chase, *New Deal*. Silber, "Chase, Stuart." Lynd and Lynd, *Middletown*. On U.S. intellectuals' enchantment with Mexico as a preindustrial idyll, see Delpar, *Enormous Vogue*.

2. Chase, *Mexico*, 14–17; Redfield, *Tepoztlan*. Wilcox, *Robert Redfield*, chaps. 1, 2; Stocking, "Ethnographic Sensibility of the 1920s and the Dualism of the Anthropological Tradition," in *Ethnographer's Magic*, 301–7.

3. Chase, *Mexico*, chap. 1. Igo, *Averaged American*, 54–59, notes that the Lynds' book largely ignored the "African" population of Muncie.

4. On academic disciplines, see Ross, *Origins of American Social Science*; Porter and Ross, *Cambridge History of Science*; Cravens, "History of the Social Sciences"; Olvera Serrano, *Economía y sociología*; Olvera Serrano, "Institucionalización"; Rutsch, *Entre el campo y el gabinete*; and García Mora and Krotz, *Antropología en México*. On the development of applied anthropology in the United States, see Spicer, "Early Applications."

5. A nuanced example of a book focused on nation and modernity is Chatterjee, *Nation and Its Fragments*. As Coronil, "Beyond Occidentalism," 52–54, notes, the West may be a metaphor rather than a real geographical place, but it has acquired a tangible quality.

6. On race as chameleonlike, see Holt, *Problem of Race*.

7. On nation and modernity, see Chatterjee, *Nation and Its Fragments*; Chakrabarty, "Postcoloniality"; Prakash, "Writing Post-Orientalist Histories"; Appelbaum, Macpherson, and Rosenblatt, "Introduction: Racial Nations," in *Race and Nation*; and Lomnitz-Adler, *Deep Mexico, Silent Mexico*.

8. Especially useful to my thinking on liberalism have been Chakrabarty, "Postcoloniality"; Mehta, "Liberal Strategies"; Pateman, *Sexual Contract*; and Mallon, *Peasant and Nation*.

9. On the African diaspora, see Hanchard, *Racial Politics*; Bourdieu and Wacquant, "Cunning of Imperialist Reason"; Seigel, *Uneven Encounters*; Guridy, *Forging Diaspora*; Putnam, *Radical Moves*; and Andrews, *Afro-Latin America*. On immigration, see FitzGerald and Cook-Martin, *Culling the Masses*; Young, *Alien Nation*; and Chang, "Towards a Hemispheric Asian American History."

10. Works that focus on race as a concept that bridges groups include Molina, *Fit to Be Citizens?*; Baker, *Anthropology and the Racial Politics*; Cohen, "In Black and Brown"; Chang, *Color of the Land*; and Wade, *Race and Ethnicity*. Compare also studies of Latin America that have focused on African-descended populations (primarily in the Caribbean and Brazil) or Native populations (primarily in Mesoamerica and the Andes): Bronfman, *Measures of Equality*; Alberto, *Terms of Inclusion*; Romo, *Brazil's Living Museum*; Gotkowitz, *Histories of Race and Racism*; and Larson, *Trials of Nation Making*. On the division between studies of African-descendant and indigenous populations, see Weinstein, "Erecting and Erasing Boundaries."

11. See Giraudo, *Ambivalente historia*; Saldaña-Portillo, *Indian Given*; and the literature on settler colonialism, but the focus of that literature on white settlement makes it less appropriate for the study of Latin America. See Goldstein, *Formations of United States Colonialism*.

12. Moreton-Robinson, *Critical Indigenous Studies*; Simpson and Smith, *Theorizing Native Studies*; Mallon, *Decolonizing Native Histories*.

13. Historians and other scholars now agree on the shifting, malleable nature of racial categorization. See Appelbaum, Macpherson, and Rosemblatt, "Introduction: Racial Nations," in *Race and Nation*; de la Cadena, *Indigenous Mestizos*; Jacobson, *Whiteness of a Different Color*; Stoler, *Race and the Education of Desire*; Wade, *Race, Nature, Culture*; Appelbaum, *Muddied Waters*; Weinstein, *Color of Modernity*; Telles and Project on Ethnicity and Race in Latin America, *Pigmentocracies*; and Stocking, *Race, Culture, and Evolution*.

14. Destabilizing U.S. exceptionalism has been a goal of postnationalist American studies. See McCoy and Scarano, *Colonial Crucible*; Rowe, *Post-Nationalist American Studies*; Kramer, "Power and Connection"; Calhoun, Cooper, and Moore, *Lessons of Empire*; Kaplan and Pease, *Cultures of United States Imperialism*; Joseph, Legrand, and Salvatore, *Close Encounters of Empire*; Skukhla and Tinsman, *Imagining Our Americas*; and Briggs, *Reproducing Empire*.

15. I thereby challenge prior work on the origins of Latin American studies. Drake and Hilbink, "Latin American Studies"; Merkx, "Editor's Foreword" (1994); Merkx, "Editor's Foreword" (1995). Compare Berger, *Under Northern Eyes*, which does not, however, focus on anthropology or race.

16. My argument regarding nationalism and conversations across borders is shaped by Joseph and Nugent, *Everyday Forms of State Formation*; Lomnitz-Adler, *Deep Mexico, Silent Mexico*; Lomnitz-Adler, *Exits from the Labyrinth*; Tenorio Trillo, "Stereophonic Scientific Modernisms"; and de la Peña, "Nacionales y extranjeros."

17. Seigel, "Beyond Compare"; Cooper, "Race, Ideology, and the Perils of Comparative History"; Stoler, "Tense and Tender Ties."

18. The debate has a long history. It is played out in Bourdieu and Wacquant, "Cunning of Imperialist Reason"; French, "Missteps of Anti-Imperialist Reason"; and Costa, "Myth of Racial Democracy," in *Brazilian Empire*.

19. Stoler, "Tense and Tender Ties."

20. Likewise, as Coronil, "Beyond Occidentalism," argues, in recognizing certain connections but not others, scholarly accounts may reassert the influence and dominance of imperial and colonial powers, especially when those accounts fail to foreground the agency of the colonized or the diversity of colonizers.

21. Chakrabarty, "Postcoloniality," 3. To be sure, Chakrabarty also emphasizes the violence that instantiated this knowledge project and continues to support it. Epistemology is only one facet of power, and it often functions within coercive contexts.

22. Shapin, "Placing the View from Nowhere." Latour, *We Have Never Been Modern*, questions the temporal divide between premodern and modern. Rodriguez, "Beyond Prejudice and Pride," reviews Latin Americanist interventions in this debate.

23. Engerman, "Social Science in the Cold War"; Isaac, *Working Knowledge*; Kuklick, "Personal Equations"; Linstrum, "Politics of Psychology."

24. Selcer, "View from Everywhere," 326. The history of science, history of ideas, and history of anthropology literatures have increasingly focused on the North-South circulation of ideas and on the role of fieldwork. See Engerman

et al., *Staging Growth*; Tilley, *Africa as a Living Laboratory*; L'Estoile, Neiburg, and Siguad, *Empires, Nations, and Natives*; Krotz, "Anthropologies of the South"; Steinmetz, *Sociology and Empire*; Neiburg and Plotkin, *Intelectuales y expertos*; and Zimmerman, *Alabama in Africa*.

25. Chakrabarty, "Postcoloniality," 23. For postcolonial approaches, see Harding, *Sciences from Below*; Anderson, "Subjugated Knowledge"; and Haraway, *Primate Visions*.

26. On translation, see Verran, *Science and an African Logic*; and Verran, "Postcolonial Moment."

27. For Gamio's trajectory, see Archivero 12, IAII; Comas, "Vida y obra"; González Gamio, *Manuel Gamio*; Brading, "Manuel Gamio"; Walsh, "Eugenic Acculturation"; and Nahmad Sitton and Weaver, "Manuel Gamio."

28. On Sáenz, see Britton, "Moisés Sáenz"; and Mejía Zúñiga, *Moisés Sáenz*. On Sáenz and Dewey, see Flores, *Backroads Pragmatists*; Bruno-Jofré and Martínez Valle, "Ruralizando a Dewey"; and John Dewey, "Mexico's Educational Renaissance," *New Republic*, Sept. 22, 1926, 116–18. On Chávez Orozco, see the introduction to Wilkie and Wilkie, *Frente a la Revolución*. On Mendieta y Núñez, see Olvera Serrano, "Primera socialización."

29. Isaac, *Working Knowledge*.

30. Yurchenco, *Around the World*, 132–44.

31. The principal sources on Collier include Collier, *From Every Zenith*; Kelly, *Assault on Assimilation*; Rusco, *Fateful Time*; Philp, *John Collier's Crusade*; and Kunitz, "Social Philosophy of John Collier."

Part I

1. For the global context, see Stocking, *Ethnographer's Magic*; and Conklin, *In the Museum of Man*.

2. Vaughan, *Cultural Politics in Revolution*, 29, 197.

3. The literature on the Revolution is vast. A recent review can be found in the introduction to Gillingham and Smith, *Dictablanda*. For a succinct account of events, see Joseph and Buchenau, *Mexico's Once and Future Revolution*.

4. Joseph, *Revolution from Without*. Gamio, *Forjando patria*, 168, notes that the Revolution was not primarily indigenous.

5. Key sources on Mexican indigenismo include Brading, "Manuel Gamio"; Dawson, *Indian and Nation*; Knight, "Racism, Revolution, and Indigenismo"; Hewitt de Alcántara, *Anthropological Perspectives*; Lewis, *Ambivalent Revolution*; Palacios, *Pluma*; Vaughan, *Cultural Politics in Revolution*; Giraudo and Lewis, "Rethinking Indigenismo"; and de la Peña, "Nacionales y extranjeros." Indigenismo also extended to the arts, though that is not a focus of this book. On this aspect, see Vaughan and Lewis, *Eagle and the Virgin*; and López, *Crafting Mexico*.

6. Ngai, *Impossible Subjects*; Gerstle, *American Crucible*; Jacobson, *Whiteness of a Different Color*.

7. "Scientific News and Notes," *Science* 45, no. 1188 (Oct. 5, 1917): 335–36; American Anthropological Association, "Uncensoring Franz Boas"; Price, "'Shameful Business.'"

8. Kelly, *Assault on Assimilation*; Collier, *From Every Zenith*; Walch, "Terminating the Indian Termination Policy"; Philp, *John Collier's Crusade*. On efforts to minimize federal control over reservations and devolve power to Native authorities, see also the presentation by the assistant commissioner of Indian affairs: Joseph McCaskill, "La terminación del control monopolizador de la Oficina de Asuntos Indígenas sobre los Indios," IAII-PCII, vol. 4, no. 7. On nineteenth-century Mexican liberalism, which played itself out in diverse ways in different regions, see Mallon, *Peasant and Nation*; Purnell, *Popular Movements and State Formation*; Caplan, *Indigenous Citizens*; and McNamara, *Sons of the Sierra*.

9. Kourí, "Interpreting the Expropriation"; Kourí, "Invención del ejido"; Simpson, *Ejido*.

10. On these shifts in different contexts, see Appelbaum, Macpherson, and Rosemblatt, *Race and Nation*.

11. Institute for Government Research, *Problem of Indian Administration*; Kelly, *Assault on Assimilation*, chaps. 6, 7; Philp, *John Collier's Crusade*, chaps. 2–5.

12. Bowler, *Evolution*, provides the best synthesis of debates in Europe and the United States. See also Numbers and Stenhouse, *Disseminating Darwinism*, and, on the United States, Cravens, *Triumph of Evolution*; and Bowler, *Eclipse of Darwinism*. Eugenics and demography dovetailed with feminist concerns regarding reproduction. See Kline, *Building a Better Race*; and Gordon, *Woman's Body, Woman's Right*.

There is a growing literature on studies of evolution by scholars outside of Europe and the United States. See Glick, Puig-Samper, and Ruiz, *Reception of Darwinism*; Hale, "Political and Social Ideas"; Suárez y López Guazo, "Evolucionismo, mejoramiento racial y medicina legal"; Miranda and Vallejo, "Sociodarwinismo y psicología"; and Miranda and Vallejo, *Derivas de Darwin*. For a global perspective, consult Bashford and Levine, *Oxford Handbook of the History of Eugenics*, which also covers the evolutionary theories that preceded eugenics.

13. Redfield, *Tepoztlan*, 80, 134; Redfield and Villa Rojas, *Chan Kom*.

14. Gamio uses the term "unilateral" to describe isolated research efforts but draws a parallel between those efforts and the diverse strata of the population. See, e.g., Gamio, *Forjando patria*, 134. See also Gamio and Pan American Union, *Present State*, 9; and Gamio, *México nuevo*, 12.

15. See note 12 above. For Latin America, the most complete source remains Stepan, "*Hour of Eugenics*." Bowler, *Evolution*, and Hale, *Political Descent*, both argue that Darwin himself embraced Lamarckian mechanisms, which he saw as complementing natural selection. The divisions between Lamarckian and Darwinian theories became pronounced only after August Weismann postulated the existence of the germ cell.

16. Although this focus could be interpreted as implying that individual free will or culture could shape the evolutionary process, human action was interpreted as guided by God. In a similar vein, Herbert Spencer followed Auguste Comte in seeing the ascendant movement of humanity as a universal natural law. Spencer stressed parallel developments in different times and places. Casini, "Evolutionary Theory," 56, 60; Bowler, *Eclipse of Darwinism*, chap. 6; Bowler, *Evolution*; Cravens,

Triumph of Evolution, 34–41; Paul, "Eugenics and the Left"; Paul, "Selection"; Paul, "'In the Interests.'"

17. Gabino Barreda, perhaps the most influential intellectual of the mid-nineteenth century, drew from Comte as well as Spencer and promoted "moral gymnastics," exercise of the faculties along Lamarckian lines to inculcate altruistic tendencies. Stehn, "From Positivism to 'Anti-Positivism'"; Hale, "Political and Social Ideas." Hale, *Political Descent*, chap. 4, describes English socialists as espousing similar views. Spencer himself believed that the state hindered self-help, moral benefit, and mutual cooperation.

18. This tendency can be evidenced in Gamio and Pan American Union, *Present State*, and in the socialist approaches discussed in Chapter 4, below.

19. Cravens, *Triumph of Evolution*, 34–45; Bowler, *Eclipse of Darwinism*, chap. 8.

20. Cravens, *Triumph of Evolution*; Stern, *Eugenic Nation*.

21. Robert H. Lowie, "Reminiscences of Anthropological Currents in America Half a Century Ago," *American Anthropologist* 58, no. 6 (December 1956): 995–1016. See also Stocking, *Race, Culture, and Evolution*; Stocking, *Ethnographer's Magic*; Kuklick, "Theory of Evolution," 87–88; and, on diffusion from one society to another versus internal orthogenetic development, Blaut, "Diffusionism." Innovations might also begin in one area and spread to other less developed areas.

22. Stocking, *Ethnographer's Magic*, esp. chap. 4.

23. Chase, *Mexico*, chap. 1; Vasconcelos, "Mestizaje," 71, in Stavans, *José Vasconcelos*; Gamio, "Revisión de las constituciones latinoamericanas," in Pan American Scientific Congress, *Proceedings of the Second Pan American Congress*, 374; Gamio, *Forjando patria*, 127–30; Melville J. Herskovits, "The Negro in the New World: The Statement of a Problem," *American Anthropologist* 23, no. 1 (January–March 1930): 145–55; Gershenhorn, *Melville J. Herskovits*.

24. Degeneration had long been a fear of European and Latin American elites. See Pick, *Faces of Degeneration*; Zimmerman, "Racial Ideas and Social Reform"; Armus, *Ailing City*; Borges, "'Puffy, Ugly, Slothful and Inert'"; and Rodriguez, *Civilizing Argentina*.

25. Key works on eugenics include Nye, "Rise and Fall"; Stern, *Eugenic Nation*; Stepan, *"Hour of Eugenics"*; López y Suárez Guazo, *Eugenesia y racismo*; Walsh, "Reason and Faith"; Paul, *Controlling Human Heredity*; Bashford and Levine, *Oxford Handbook of the History of Eugenics*; Kevles, *In the Name*; and Miranda and Vallejos, *Darwinismo social*.

26. On the relation between eugenics and demography—and efforts to distance population studies from the presumably less scientific and more racist eugenics—see Ramsden, "Carving Up Population Science"; Ramsden, "Social Demography and Eugenics"; and Ramsden, "Eugenics from the New Deal." See also Cassata, *Building the New Man*.

27. On feminism and puericulture, see Birn, "Child Health"; Stern, "Responsible Mothers"; and Guy, "Politics of Pan-American Cooperation." The intersection of Latin American feminism and eugenic concerns and the Pan-American context is explored in Lavrin, *Women, Feminism*; and Ehrick, *Shield of the Weak*.

28. Stern, *Eugenic Nation*; Stepan, *"Hour of Eugenics"*; Fairchild, *Science at the Borders*.

29. On Gini and the IUSIPP, see Cassata, *Building a New Man*, 141. On the NRC, see Barkan, *Retreat of Scientific Racism*, 113. See also Ramsden, "Eugenics from the New Deal," 393.

30. FitzGerald and Cook-Martin, *Culling the Masses*; Stepan, "*Hour of Eugenics*."

31. Stepan, "*Hour of Eugenics*"; Ramsden, "Carving Up Population Science."

32. Stern, "'Hour of Eugenics' in Veracruz." More hardline Mexican positions are underscored in Urías Horcasitas, *Historias secretas*.

33. Fairchild, *Science at the Borders*.

34. Divisions in the population movement are skillfully analyzed by Ramsden in "Carving Up Population Science," "Eugenics from the New Deal," and "Social Demography and Eugenics." On the NRC and SSRC, see chapter 2, below.

Chapter 1

1. Gamio and Pan American Union, *Present State*, 1–2. Compare Manuel Gamio, "Trade and Culture in Latin America," *Nation*, Jan. 16, 1929. For similar earlier formulations, see Manuel Gamio, "El Instituto Antropológico Central de México," in Pan American Scientific Congress, *Proceedings of the Second Pan American Congress*, 375–77; and Gamio, *Forjando patria*, 288.

2. Gamio and Pan American Union, *Present State*, quotation on 7; Manuel Gamio to John C. Merriam, Nov. 7, 1923, record group: Archaeology, folder: Gamio, Manuel Dr. Lecture, 1923–1924, CIW; Gónzalez Gamio, *Manuel Gamio*, 67.

3. A. V. Kidder, Memorandum for Dr. Merriam re: Gamio Project, ca. 1931, record group: Archaeology, folder: Gamio Correspondence, 1925–1927, 1931, CIW.

4. Gamio, *Minima and Electron*; Gamio, *De vidas dolientes*.

5. Earle, *Return of the Native*, chap. 1.

6. Evans, *Romancing the Maya*; Bueno, "Forjando Patrimonio"; Rutsch, *Entre el campo*, 60–70; Kourí, "Interpreting the Expropriation"; Villoro, *Grandes momentos*.

7. "Edward Herbert Thompson," http://www.newworldencyclopedia.org/entry/Edward_Herbert_Thompson. Harvard had helped sponsor Thompson's explorations. This issue is also discussed in the Archaeology record group, CIW.

8. *Boletín del Museo Nacional*, 3rd ser., 1, no. 12 (June 1912): 254, cited in Fernando González Dávila, "El doctor Nicolás León frente al evolucionismo," in Rutsch and Wacher, *Alarifes, amanuenses y evangelistas*, 162; Rutsch, "Sobre historia de la antropología mexicana, 1900–1920," in ibid., 275–92; Rutsch, *Entre el campo*, 103–83.

9. Rutsch, *Entre el campo*, 222–24; Franz Boas to R. S. Woodward, Mar. 23, 1905, record group: Administration, folder: Boas, Franz, 1902–1908 (2 of 2), CIW; Godoy, "Franz Boas and His Plans," 228–29.

10. Godoy, "Franz Boas and His Plans," 228–29. Gamio also studied with Marshall Saville and Adolf Bandelier. Manuel Gamio, "Franz Boas en México," *Boletín Bibliográfico de Antropología Americana (1937–1948)* 6, no. 1/3 (January–December 1942): 35–42.

11. George Grant MacCurdy, "Seventeenth International Congress of Americanists Second Session-City of Mexico," *American Anthropologist* 12, no. 4 (October–December 1910): 600–605.

12. On this story regarding Leopoldo Batres, see Rutsch, *Entre el campo*, 261.

13. Nicolás León, "Historia de antropología física en México," *American Journal of Physical Anthropology* 2, no. 3 (July–September 1919): 233–44; Boas, *Mind of Primitive Man*; González Gamio, *Manuel Gamio*, 26, 27, 31; Gamio, "Franz Boas en México," 36.

14. "Inauguración de las Escuela de Etnología," *El País*, Jan. 21, 1911.

15. "La 'Escuela Internacional de Arqueología y Etnología Americanas' continuará sus investigaciones," *Ethnos* 1, no. 2 (May 1920): 50; Franz Boas, "Summary of the Work of the International School of American Archeology and Ethnology in Mexico," *American Anthropologist* 17, no. 2 (April–June 1915): 384–95, quotation on 385; Godoy, "Franz Boas and His Plans," 228–42. Seler had cataloged Mexican antiquities at the Museo Nacional. See Rutsch, *Entre el campo*.

16. These arguments are succinctly summarized in Franz Boas, "The Methods of Ethnology," *American Anthropologist* 22, no. 4 (October–December 1920): 312, 317. For an earlier version of the same argument, see Boas, *Mind of Primitive Man*.

17. Rutsch, *Entre el campo*; Kourí, "Invención del ejido."

18. Justo Sierra, *The Political Evolution of the Mexican People*, trans. Charles Ramsdell (Austin: University of Texas Press, 1969), cited in Stehn, "From Positivism to 'Anti-Positivism,'" 56; Gamio, "Franz Boas en México."

19. Kourí, "Interpreting the Expropriation."

20. Andrés Molina Enríquez, "El verdadero concepto de la etnología: La ciencia de gobernar," mentioned in MacCurdy, "Seventeenth International Congress"; Gamio, "Instituto Antropológico Central," 377; González Gamio, *Manuel Gamio*, 48.

21. Gamio, "Instituto Antropológico Central"; Manuel Gamio, "Revisión de las constituciones latinoamericanas," in Pan American Scientific Congress, *Proceedings of the Second Pan American Congress*, 374–75.

22. González Gamio, *Manuel Gamio*, 48; Gamio, "Instituto Antropológico Central," 377; Gamio and Pan American Union, *Present State*, 29.

23. Gamio, "Revisión de las constituciones latinoamericanas," 374–75; Lucio Mendieta y Núñez, "Situación de las poblaciones indígenas de América ante el derecho actual: Ensayo presentado al Tercer Congreso Científico Panamericano," *Boletín de la Secretaría de Educación Pública* 3, no. 10 (March 1925): 103–11, quotations on 111, 104–5. This presentation was given in October 1924. See also Gamio, *Forjando patria*, 127–130, 314; and Alfonso Toro, "Importancia de los antecedentes históricos en la cuestión agraria," *Ethnos* 1, no. 5 (August 1920): 107–8. Innovations in political forms are discussed in Lomawaima, "Federalism: Native, Federal, and State Sovereignty."

24. Gamio, "Instituto Antropológico Central."

25. Mendieta y Núñez, "Situación de las poblaciones indígenas," quotations on 111, 104–5.

26. Gamio, *Forjando patria*, 314.

27. Ibid., 4, 13.

28. Ibid., 3–6.

29. Ibid., 9–14.

30. Ibid., 172.

31. Ibid., 18–19.

32. Ibid., 316, ellipses and emphases in original.

33. Ibid., 308–10.

34. This is one of the central insights of the literature on settler colonialism. Goldstein, *Formations of United States Colonialism*; Wolfe, *Settler Colonialism*.

35. Gamio, *Forjando patria*, 38–39.

36. Sáenz, *México íntegro*, ix–x, 207–8; Sáenz, *Carapan*, 32. The terms were used inconsistently, but Mexicans often referred to "incorporation" as assimilation to a dominant culture and counterposed it to "integration," which they characterized as the nonhomogenizing recognition of Native peoples as citizens. On these terms, see Pedro Gerardo Rodríguez, "Presentación," in Sáenz, *Carapan*. The term "interculturation," akin to transculturation and also counterposed to "integration," is used by Daniel Rubín de la Borbolla, "Prólogo," in Luis Chávez Orozco, *Memoria*, ix.

Scholars counterpose Sáenz's integrationist approach with prior incorporationist approaches, viewing the former as less assimilationist. They also characterize Sáenz as being more pluralist than Gamio. See Palacios, "Postrevolutionary Intellectuals"; and Dawson, *Indian and Nation*. I view the two indigenistas' approaches as strikingly similar. As Loyo Bravo argues in *Gobiernos revolucionarios y educación popular*, Sáenz was a staunch assimilationist early in his career. Unlike Gamio, he did not live through the modernizing approaches of the post-Cárdenas era.

37. On the new department, see Sáenz, *Carapan*, 211–32. On the reference to Nordic races, see Sáenz, *México íntegro*, 207. See also Orosco, "José Vasconcelos"; Sáenz, *Antología*, 25, 38, 141–42.

38. Sáenz, *México íntegro*, 127.

39. Ibid., 128–29; see also x–xi.

40. Gamio, *Forjando patria*, 172. Sierra had noted in 1900 that "science, converted into an amazingly complex and efficient tool, has accelerated a hundredfold the evolution of certain peoples." Cited in Stehn, "From Positivism to 'Anti-Positivism,'" 56.

41. Gamio, *Forjando patria*, 188–89.

42. Manuel Gamio, "Investigaciones arqueológicas en México, 1914–1915," in Pan American Scientific Congress, *Proceedings of the Second Pan American Scientific Congress*, 373.

43. Manuel Gamio, "Nacionalismo e internacionalismo," *Ethnos*, 2nd ser., 1, no. 2 (February–April 1923): 1–3; Gamio, *Forjando patria*, 189.

44. Gamio, "Nacionalismo e internacionalismo."

45. Ibid.; Gamio, *México nuevo*, 1–3.

46. Gamio, *México nuevo*, 11, 173, 177.

47. On Zangwill and other authors responsible for the idea of the United States as the land of self-invention, see Gerstle, "Liberty, Coercion." Zangwill himself may have been more ambivalent about the loss of traditions than many recognize. See Shumsky, "Zangwill's 'The Melting Pot.'"

48. Gamio, *Forjando patria*, 59, 188–89, 134.

49. Ibid., 185, 187.

50. Fell, *José Vasconcelos*, 206, 217; Loyo Bravo, *Gobiernos revolucionarios y educación popular*, 167–94, 292–301; Dawson, *Indian and Nation*, 21–29. Later, to ensure that its charges remained committed to teaching Native populations, the Casa del Estudiante Indígena educated its charges directly, but in 1932, officials shuttered the boarding school.

51. Fell, *José Vasconcelos*, 216, argues that Gamio with his more ethnographic approach battled Vasconcelos for control of Native affairs. On the pamphlets, see "Informe del Departamento de Educación y Cultura Indígena," *Boletín de la Secretaría de Educación Pública* 1, no. 2 (Sept. 1, 1922): 261–66. Sáenz, *México íntegro*, 252.

52. Gamio and Pan American Union, *Present State*, 4.

53. For questionnaires filled out by teachers, see folder 26, IAII-PVM; Fell, *José Vasconcelos*, 227; "Primera universidad indígena en la República," *El Universal*, Feb. 23, 1922, cited in *Boletín de la Secretaría de Educación Pública* 1, no. 4 (1923): 576–77; and Lauro Caloca, "Departamento de Cultura Indígena: Informe del jefe del departamento," cited in ibid., 573–74.

54. Vasconcelos cited in Fell, *José Vasconcelos*, 206.

55. Stavans, *José Vasconcelos*.

56. Ibid., 71.

57. Ibid., 59, 65.

58. Ibid., 72.

59. Sáenz, *México íntegro*, 207–8.

60. Ibid., x–xi.

61. Ibid., 5, 48–49.

62. Orosco, "José Vasconcelos"; José Vasconcelos, "The Latin American Basis of Mexican Civilization," in Vasconcelos and Gamio, *Aspects of Mexican Civilization*, 20. In "Segundo Congreso Mexicano del Niño: Convocatoria y temas oficiales," *El Imparcial*, ca. June 1922, a congress participant likewise refers to "mestizos of Mexican and of other races."

63. Sáenz, *Antología*, 154–55, 229.

64. Mexico, Dirección General de Estadística, *Censo general de la República*; Mexico, *Tercer censo de población*; Manuel Gamio, "El censo de la población Mexicana desde el punto de vista antropológico," *Ethnos* 1, no. 2 (May 1920): 44–45; Gamio and Pan American Union, *Present State*, 8, 12–14; Sáenz, *Antología*, 122; Sáenz, *Carapan*, 32. On the treatment of racial categories in Latin America, see Loveman, *National Colors*; Telles and Project on Ethnicity and Race in Latin America, *Pigmentocracies*; Clark, "Race, 'Culture,' and Mestizaje"; Nobles, *Shades of Citizenship*; and Saldívar and Walsh, "Racial and Ethnic Identities."

65. Sáenz, *Antología*, 135.

66. Loyo Bravo, *Gobiernos revolucionarios y educación popular*, 292–301; Dawson, *Indian and Nation*, chap. 2.

67. Sáenz, *Carapan*, 113.

68. The list of participants suggests that there were no Latin American participants in the 1912 conference. See Eugenics Education Society, *Problems in Eugenics*.

69. Birn, "Child Health," 691; Instituto Interamericano del Niño, la Niña y Adolescentes, "Congreso Panamericano," http://iin.oea.org/congreso-panamericano.html; Nunes, "Infancia latinoamericana."

70. Víctor Fernández Manero and Rafael Santamarina, "Lo que es el Departamento de Psicopedagogía e Higiene de la Secretaría de Educación Pública y Bellas Artes de México y la labor que ha realizado hasta ahora," paper presented at the First International Mental Hygiene Conference, Mar. 31, 1930, in Depto. de Psicopedagogía e Higiene, Primer Congreso Internacional de Higiene Mental, Ciudad de Washington, U.S.A., folder 18, box 147, SEP.

71. Rafael Santamarina, "La cuestión de los anormales"; and "Informe de la clasificación de alumnos hecha en la Escuela Primaria 'Alberto Correa' Número 120," both in *Boletín de la Secretaría de Educación Pública* 6, no. 9 (September 1927): 125–33. Alberto Lozano Garza, "Algunas palabras en favor de los niños anormales," in *Memoria del Primer Congreso Mexicano del Niño*, 267–69.

72. Santamarina, "Cuestión de los anormales," 130.

73. Rafael Santamarina, "Conocimiento actual del niño mexicano desde el punto de vista médico-pedagógico," in *Memoria del Primer Congreso Mexicano del Niño*, 264–66. "Informe del Señor Doctor Don Rafael Santamarina, jefe del Departamento de Psicopedagogía e Higiene Escolar de la Secretaría de Educación Pública, en la inauguración de los Cursos de médico-escolar," *Boletín de la Secretaría de Educación Pública* 4, no. 6 (1925): 161–65.

74. Gamio, *Mexican Immigration*, 71–72.

75. Hastings, *Clasificación*, 27–28, 151–80, quotation on 32.

76. Víctor Fernández Manero and Rafael Santamarina, "Lo que es el Departamento de Psicopedagogía e Higiene de la Secretaría de Educación Pública y Bellas Artes de México y la labor que ha realizado hasta ahora," paper presented at the First International Mental Hygiene Conference, Mar. 31, 1930, in Depto. de Psicopedagogía e Higiene, Primer Congreso Internacional de Higiene Mental, Ciudad de Washington, U.S.A, folder 18, box 147, SEP.

77. Informe de Labores, Dirección de Higiene Escolar, 1926, pp. 2–13, ref. 137, folder 25, box 5114, SEP. These school inspections had begun in the Porfiriato.

78. Conferencia "El papel del maestro en la realización de los fines de la higiene escolar," trasmitida por radio por el C. Dr. Carlos S. Jiménez, el día 12 de febrero de 1925, pp. 2–6, ref. 134, folder 1, box 5111, SEP.

79. "Segundo Congreso Mexicano del Niño: Convocatoria y temas oficiales," *El Imparcial*, ca. June 1922. Compare "Acta final de la Primera Conferencia Panamericana de Eugenesia y Homicultura," Dec. 21, 1927, in Depto. de Psicopedagogía e Higiene, folder 1, box 138, SEP. See also *Memoria del Primer Congreso Mexicano del Niño*, 8.

80. *Memoria del Primer Congreso Mexicano del Niño*, 8, 17. The more strident racism of Antonio F. Alonso may have been prompted by his extensive contact with the United States. See American Public Health Association, *Public Health Papers*, 314; and American Ophthalmological Society, *International Congress*.

Mexico's position regarding immigration, prompted by a virulent anti-Chinese campaign, is detailed in FitzGerald and Cook-Martin, *Culling the Masses*. See also Young, *Alien Nation*; and Schiavone Camacho, *Chinese Mexicans*.

81. "Acta final de la Primera Conferencia Panamericana de Eugenesia y. Homicultura"; United States, *Report of the Delegates*, 270–73. Stepan, "*Hour of Eugenics*," 178–82. On measures of fitness and health, see Fairchild, *Science at the Borders*.

82. Gamio, "Estéril," in *De vidas dolientes*, 77–115; "El celibato y el desarrollo de la población en México," *Ethnos*, 2nd ser., 1, no. 2 (February–April 1923): 66–70, republished in Gamio, *México nuevo*, 173–77.

83. Gamio, "Estéril."

84. Gamio, "Celibato."

85. "El Segundo Congreso Internacional de Eugenesia," *Ethnos* 1, no. 5 (August 1920): 128–30.

86. Ibid. On the Universal Races Congress, see *Ethnos* 1, no. 4 (July 1920): 76; and *Ethnos* 1, nos. 6–7 (September–October 1920): 140–42. On the two aspects, see *Ethnos* 1, nos. 8–12 (November 1920–March 1921): 251–52; and "Airoso papel de México en el Segundo Congreso de Eugenesia," *Excélsior*, Nov. 28, 1921, 5.

Gamio's perspective on the conference may have been influenced by his mentor Boas, although Boas shared with both Gamio and eugenicists the view that certain lesser peoples should be uplifted. Gamio had taken the opportunity during his visit to New York to deliver some lectures on his Teotihuacán work and defend a shortened version of that study as his Ph.D. dissertation, so there is no doubt that he saw Boas on the trip. Franz Boas, "Eugenics," *Scientific Monthly* 3, no. 5 (November 1916): 471–78.

87. On Italian eugenics, see Cassata, *Building the New Man*; and Gini, "Address to the Third International Congress of Eugenics." On French pronatalism, see Camiscioli, *Reproducing the French Race*.

88. Alexandra Minna Stern, "From Mestizophilia to Biotypology: Racialization and Science in Mexico, 1920–1960," in Appelbaum, Macpherson, and Rosemblatt, *Race and Nation*, 194.

89. Biographical information on Emilio Alanís Patiño can be found in desde Abreu, Ermilo, hasta Biblioteca Nacional, 1940–1959, México en el Archivo Histórico del Instituto Indigenista Interamericano, IAII.

90. Maria Sophia Quine, "The First-Wave Eugenic Revolution in Southern Europe: Science sans *Frontières*," in Bashford and Levine, *Oxford Handbook of the History of Eugenics*, 377–97, esp. 390; Corrado Gini, "Premiers résultats d'une expédition italo-mexicaine parmi les populations indigènes et métisses du Mexique," *Genus* 1, nos. 1–2 (June 1934): 147–76.

91. Vasconcelos is mentioned in Gini, "Premiers résultats," 148. Corrado Gini, "Response to the President's Address," in International Eugenics Conference, *Decade of Progress*, 25–28.

92. Cassata, *Building the New Man*, 148 and ff.; Quine, "First-Wave Eugenic Revolution,"; Gini, "Premiers résultats."

93. Manuel Gamio, "Comentarios sobre la evolución de los pueblos latinoamericanos," reprinted in *México nuevo*, 9–20, originally published in 1932, based on a 1931 presentation. On the presentation, see "The International Congress for Studies Regarding Population," *Science* 73, no. 1902 (June 12, 1931): 635.

94. Gamio, "El desarrollo anormal de nuestra población," in *México nuevo*, 21.

Chapter 2

1. Redfield and Villa Rojas, *Chan Kom*; Redfield, *Village That Chose Progress*, 153, cited in Quetzil E. Castañeda, "Stocking's Historiography of Influence." See also Castañeda, *In the Museum*.

2. The Mexicans in Chicago, journal, folder 2, box 59, RRP. B. F. Coen, who was working on the "Spanish" in Colorado, wrote to Robert Redfield: "I noticed a few days ago in the *Journal of the American Sociological Society*, a statement to the effect that you are taking up a study of the Mexican communities with the idea of showing the background for the Mexican and Spanish-American as we find them in the United States." Coen to Redfield, Oct. 19, 1926, folder 4, box 1, RRP. Wilcox, *Robert Redfield.*

3. On Redfield's studies, see Courses Offered for the Degree of Doctor of Philosophy, Department of Sociology and Anthropology, Candidate: Robert Redfield, Date of examination, Aug. 15, 1928, folder 4, box 1, RRP; The Mexicans in Chicago, journal.

4. Especially relevant are the trajectories of Lloyd Warner, Evon Vogt, Sol Tax, and Oscar Lewis.

5. Stocking, *Ethnographer's Magic*, 304.

6. Calderón Mólgora, "Historias rurales"; Stocking, *Ethnographer's Magic*, 302; Clifford, *Robert Redfield*, 14–15, 30–31; Gamio, *Mexican Immigration*, xi; Report of the Joint Committee of the Committee on Problems and Policies of the SSRC Meeting with Other Representatives of the Social Sciences in Attendance upon the Dartmouth Conference of Social Scientists and Allied Groups, July 31–Sept. 3, 1925, folder 569, box 53, series 3, LSRM.

7. The Americanists' conferences were an earlier instance of foreign interest in Latin America in which concern with race figured prominently.

8. Godoy, "Franz Boas and His Plans," 230; Manuel Gamio, "Trade and Culture in Latin America," *Nation*, Jan. 16, 1929.

9. On the postwar period, see Rosemblatt, "Modernization, Dependency."

10. Ngai, *Impossible Subjects*; Fairchild, *Science at the Borders*; Cravens, *Triumph of Evolution.*

11. "Organization of the Research Council," *Proceedings of the National Academy of Sciences of the United States of America* 2, no. 10 (Oct. 15, 1916): 607–8. The NRC is discussed at length in Cravens, *Triumph of Evolution.*

12. R. M. Yerkes, "Psychology and National Service," *Science* 46, no. 1179 (Aug. 3, 1917): 101–3; "The Psychological Examination of Recruits," *Science* 46, no. 1189 (Oct. 12, 1917): 355–56; Carson, "Army Alpha, Army Brass," 278–309.

13. "Report of the Meeting of the Executive Committee," *Proceedings of the National Academy of Sciences of the United States of America* 2, no. 12 (Dec. 15, 1916): 740; "Suggestions Relating to the New National Army by the Anthropology Committee of the National Research Council," *Proceedings of the National Academy of Sciences of the United States of America* 3, no. 8 (Aug. 15, 1917): 527. On the anthropology committee, see "The Work of the National Research Council," *Science* 46, no. 1179 (Aug. 3, 1917): 99–101; and "The Physique of Recruits," *Science* 46, no. 1193 (Nov. 9, 1917): 460–61, quotation on 461.

14. W. H. Holmes and Aleš Hrdlička, "Report of the Committee on Anthropology," *Proceedings of the National Academy of Sciences of the United States of America* 4, no. 2 (Feb. 15, 1918): 52–54; National Research Council, *Fifth Annual Report*, 19, 53.

15. General C. E. McClung (Chairman of the Division of Biology and Agriculture of the NRC), Memorandum for Dr. Angell, Oct. 27, 1919, International Congresses Eugenics, Second Organizing Committee, Foreign Relations Record Group: 1919–1921, the NRC; "Official Correspondence, National Research Council," *American Anthropologist* 21, no. 3 (July–September 1919): 338–42; "Anthropological Notes," ibid., 343–46.

16. W. V. Bingham to Members of the Division of Anthropology and Psychology, Dec. 18, 1919, Early Projects of the Division: General, 1919–1920, A & P.

17. Ibid. On tropical research, see NRC, *Sixth Annual Report*, 53. This report covers the period January 1–June 30, 1921.

18. Division of Anthropology and Psychology, Project Budget, Jan. 15, 1920, Early Projects of the Division: General, 1919–1920, A & P. See also NRC, *Fifth Annual Report*, 53–55, 78. This Committee on the Study of the People of the United States seems to have been transformed into the Committee on Race Characters. The two are listed separately on the NRC website: http://www.nasonline.org/about-nas/history/archives/collections/dap-1919-1939.html. But material referring to the Committee on Race Characters is filed with the papers of the Committee for the Study of the People of the United States in the NRC A & P archive. On Wissler, see Freed and Freed, *Clark Wissler*; and George Peter Murdock, "Clark Wissler, 1870–1947," *American Anthropologist* 50, no. 2 (April–June 1948): 292–304.

19. Clark Wissler to J. R. Angell, Nov. 20, 1919, Psychological Study of People of the U.S., Beginning of Program, A & P.

20. Benton-Cohen, "Other Immigrants"; Fairchild, *Science at the Borders*; Stern, "Buildings, Boundaries, and Blood."

21. NRC, *Sixth Annual Report*, 45–46.

22. W. V. Bingham for the Committee on the Study of the People of the United States, *Study of the American People*; and Clark Wissler, "Memorandum on Investigation of People of the United States," both in Psychological Study of People of the U.S.: General, 1920–1921, A & P.

23. Clark Wissler, "Opportunities for Coordination in Anthropological and Psychological Research," *American Anthropologist* 22, no. 1. (January–March 1920): 1–12, quotations on 7, 9–11.

24. A. E. Jenks to Robert Yerkes, Oct. 23, 1923, with attached document by Paul Popenoe; and "Research Outline from the Division of Anthropology and Psychology, Dec. 10, 1923," both in Committee on Race Characters, 1923–1926, A & P.

25. For reports of lack of agreement within the committee, see G. E. Seashore to Vernon Kellogg, Sept. 30, 1921, Committee on Race Characters, 1921–1922; and Report of the Committee on Race Characters, 1921–1922, both in A & P. NRC, *Sixth Annual Report*, 48.

26. Robert Yerkes, "Suggestions for Committee on Scientific Problems of Human Migration," Jan. 25, 1923, p. 2, folder 629, box 58, series 3, LSRM; Wissler, *Final Report*, 2–4. "Pittsburgh Station: Statement of Dec. 30, 1923"; and "Report on the

Analysis and Measurement of Personality by W. V. Bingham and C. S. Yoakum," both in folder 625, box 59, series 3, LSRM.

27. Franz Boas, "Changes in the Bodily Form of Descendants of Immigrants," *American Anthropologist* 14, no. 3 (July–September 1912): 530–62; Franz Boas, "Race and Progress" (1931), in *Race, Language, and Culture* (New York: Free Press, 1966 [1940]), 3–17; Boas, *Mind of Primitive Man.*

28. Yerkes, "Suggestions for Committee."

29. Robert DeC. Ward to Jenks, Nov. 5, 1923; and Jenks to Yerkes, Oct. 23, 1923, both in Committee on Race Characters, 1923–1926, A & P. Wissler to C. Seashore, 7 Nov. 1921, Psychological Study of People of the United States: General, 1920–1921, A & P.

30. Yerkes, "Suggestions for Committee"; Cravens, *Triumph of Evolution,* 38–39; Clark Wissler, "Report of Progress on the Study of Physical Inheritance and Environmental Changes among the Offspring of Mixed Marriages," Feb. 1, 1924, folder 635, box 59, series 3, LSRM.

31. Dr. Williams, "Intellectual and Other Mental Problems of Immigration," Proceedings of the Conference on Human Migrations, Nov. 18, 1922, folder 629, box 58, series 3, LSRM.

32. Wissler, "Report of Progress," argued that "anatomical characters can segregate in a population."

33. W. V. Bingham and C. S. Yoakum, "The Analysis and Measurement of Personality," Dec. 30, 1924, folder 635, box 59, series 3, LSRM.

34. [Henry] Laughlin, "The Measure of Specific Degeneracies in Immigrant and Native Populative [*sic*] Groups of the United States"; and Kate H. Claghorn, "Problems of Research in Immigration Suggested in Social Work," both in National Research Council, Proceedings of the Conference on Human Migrations, Nov. 18, 1922, folder 629, box 58, series 3, LSRM, 10–13, 23–30. Claghorn's publications include Kate Holladay Claghorn, "The Protection and Distribution of Immigrants," *Proceedings of the Academy of Political Science in the City of New York* 2, no. 4 (July 1912): 199–206; "Crime and Immigration"; and "The Limitations of Statistics," *Publications of the American Statistical Association* 11, no. 81 (1908): 97–104.

35. [W. V.] Bingham, "Intellectual Status and Race," in National Research Council, Proceedings of the Conference on Human Migrations, Nov. 18, 1922, pp. 10–14, folder 629, box 58, series 3, LSRM, 39–40. Yoakum and Yerkes, *Army Mental Tests,* 218.

36. Claghorn, "Problems of Research in Immigration."

37. "Research Outline from the Division of Anthropology and Psychology, Dec. 10, 1923," Committee on Race Characters, 1923–1926, A & P. On fundamental researches, see Wissler to Jenks, Sept. 17, 1923, A & P.

38. "An American Anthropological Research Institution," in "Research Outline from the Division of Anthropology and Psychology, Dec. 10, 1923"; Jenks to Robert Ward, Nov. 7, 1923; and Jenks to Wissler, Sept. 17, 1923, all in Committee on Race Characters, 1923–1926, A & P.

39. National Social Science Research Council, Memorandum Outline of the General Fields of Inquiry Sent on May 21, 1924, to the Members of the Committee on Human Migrations, Committee on Scientific Problem of Human Migration

Liaison with the SSRC, 1923–1925, A & P; Harold C. Bingham, "Suggestions for Migrations Research," folder 635, box 59, series 3, LSRM; Memorandum of Interview G. S. Ford with Dr. Robert Yerkes, Subject, Human Migration Projects under the National Research Council, Mar. 25, 1925, folder 631, box 59, series 3, LSRM. On the SSRC, see Robert T. Crane et al., "The Social Science Research Council," *American Political Science Review* 18, no. 3 (August 1924): 594–600.

40. Memorandum to the Committee on Scientific Problems of Human Migration, May 28, 1925; Yerkes to Mary Van Kleeck, Jan. 29, 1925; and R. S. Woodworth to Raymond Dodge, June 24, 1925, all in Committee on Scientific Problem of Human Migration Liaison with the SSRC, 1923–1925, A & P.

Committee members Dodge and Yerkes, along with Wissler, moved to a new Institute of Psychology at Yale University created by President James Angell. Angell was a psychologist who had previously headed the NRC and the Carnegie Corporation, and Yale received an injection of funding from the LSRM Foundation, led by Beardsley Ruml, a former student of both Angell and Bingham. On the connections of LSRM's Ruml, see Lemov, *World as Laboratory*, 55. On the creation and funding of the Institute of Psychology, see Miles, "Raymond Dodge," 109.

41. National Social Science Research Council, Memorandum Outline of the General Fields of Inquiry Sent on May 21, 1924, to the Members of the Committee on Human Migrations; and Minutes of the First Meeting of the Committee on the Social Aspects of Human Migration Appointed by the Social Science Research Council, n.d. [ca. May 1924], both in Committee on Scientific Problem of Human Migration Liaison with the SSRC, 1923–1925, A & P.

42. Report of the Joint Committee of the Committee on Problems and Policies of the SSRC Meeting with Other Representatives of the Social Sciences in Attendance upon the Dartmouth Conference of Social Scientists and Allied Groups, July 31–Sept. 3, 1925, folder 569, box 53, series 3, LSRM. My account is based on this document. Redfield, *Tepoztlan*, vi–vii.

43. Report of the Committee on the Scientific Aspects of Human Migration, app. 4, Dec. 15, 1925, folder 811, box 68, subseries 6, series 3, LSRM; "Human Migration as a Field of Research," *Social Service Review* 1, no. 2 (June 1927): 258–69.

44. Report of the Committee on the Scientific Aspects of Human Migration, app. 3.

45. Ibid.

46. Gamio, *Mexican Immigration*, chap. 4.

47. Ibid., app. 1, 197–203.

48. Redfield in Gamio, *Mexican Immigrant*, vi–vii, 140.

49. NRC, Division Collections, Division of Anthropology and Psychology, 1919–1939, http://www.nasonline.org/about-nas/history/archives/collections/dap-1919-1939.html; Social Science Research Council, *Consolidated List of Council Committees, 1924–1997*.

50. Report of Progress, Committee on the American Negro, 1926–1927; and Committee on the Negro, Preliminary Report, ca. Nov. 1926, both in Committee on the Study of American Negro: General, 1926–1929, A & P; Herskovits, *American Negro*.

51. Division of Anthropology and Psychology, Conference on Racial Differences, Washington, D.C., Feb. 25, 26, 1928, Feb. Conference on Racial Differences, 1928, A & P; Minutes of the Meeting of the Advisory Committee on Interracial Relations of the Committee on Politics and Policies of the Social Science Research Council, Held in Washington, Jan. 22, 1927, folder 711, box 68, subseries 5, series 3, LSRM.

52. Conference on Racial Differences; Minutes of the Meeting of the Advisory Committee on Interracial Relations.

53. Conference on Racial Differences.

54. Goddard, *Kallikak Family*; Dugdale, *Jukes*. The Jukes were restudied in Estabrook, *Jukes in 1915*.

55. Franz Boas, "Changes in the Bodily Form of Descendants of Immigrants," *American Anthropologist* 14, no. 3 (July–September 1912): 530–62.

56. Conference on Racial Differences, 16–19.

57. Ibid., 79. Lewis, "Boas, Darwin." These were the sorts of questions that would guide the emerging field of culture and personality studies, a field closely tied to many of Boas's students.

58. Conference on Racial Differences, 79, 29–34.

59. On discourses of originary purity, see Wade, "Rethinking *Mestizaje*."

60. Conference on Racial Differences.

61. Joint Committee on Racial Matters of the Social Science Research Council and the National Research Council, Minutes of Meeting at the Merrill-Palmer School, Detroit, May 25, 1928; Fay-Cooper Cole to Knight Dunlap, Sept. 17, 1928; and Franz Boas to Dunlap, Apr. 1, 1929, all in Committee on Race Problems Joint with SSRC: Institutionalization of Infants from Controlled Data Accumulation, 1928–1931, A & P.

62. Minutes of Meeting at the Merrill-Palmer School; Report Made to the SSRC Committee on Problems and Policy, August 1930; and R. S. Woodworth, Joint Committee on Racial Matters of the Social Science Research Council and the National Research Council, Final Report, all in Committee on Race Problems Joint with SSRC: Institutionalization of Infants from Controlled Data Accumulation, 1928–1931, A & P.

63. Proceedings of the Conference on Preparation and Publication of a Handbook of South American Indians, Philadelphia, Jan. 6, 1934, Conference on Publication of Handbook of South American Indians, January 1934, A & P.

64. Ibid.

65. Cole to Redfield, Nov. 19, 1926, folder 4, box 1, RRP.

66. Robert Redfield, Ralph Linton, and Melville J. Herskovits, "A Memorandum for the Study of Acculturation," *Man* 35 (October 1935): 145–48.

67. Ibid.; Stocking, *Ethnographer's Magic*, 143–44. Stocking, 133, notes that "acculturation studies may thus be viewed as the outgrowth of a practical interest in problems of race contact."

68. Redfield to Robert Ezra Park, Tepoztlán, Morelos, Mexico, Feb. 16, 1927, folder 2, box 1, RRP.

69. Letter, Tepoztlán, El Parque, Morelos, Mexico, Dec. 4, 1926, folder 2, box 1, RRP. This appears to be from Clara Park, or "Mom," to her husband, Robert Ezra Park.

70. Redfield to Park, Feb. 16, 1927.

Part II

1. John Collier, "A Birdseye View of Indian Policy Historic and Contemporary" (Washington, D.C.: Bureau of Indian Affairs), Dec. 30, 1935, box 26, OFCJC.

2. The postrevisionist perspective on Mexico is outlined and debated in Joseph and Nugent, *Everyday Forms*; McCormick, *Logic of Compromise*, Introduction; and Gillingham and Smith, *Dictablanda*, Introduction. Scholarship on Collier and the Indian New Deal is summarized in Schwartz, "Red Atlantis Revisited." See also Barsh, "Progressive-Era Bureaucrats," and the ensuing debate on pp. 18–64 in the same issue.

3. Works on the give-and-take of fieldwork include Kuklick, "Personal Equations"; Gieryn, "City as Truth-Spot"; and Linstrum, "Politics of Psychology."

4. Miguel O. de Mendizábal, "Monografías de pueblos indígenas: Condiciones económicas, sociales y políticas del municipio de Santa María Tepeji," in *Obras completas*, 6:199–223.

5. Copy of letter from Juanito Medina to Day School Teachers, Zia Pueblo, Dec. 29, 1942, folder: Project Correspondence and Committee Reports, 1942–1944 (1 of 2), box 10, LTP; Laura Thompson to John Collier, Dec. 16, 1942, reel 17, JCP. Also on Zia, see Thompson to Collier, Confidential memorandum, Dec. 22, 1942, reel 17, JCP. Oscar Lewis, "Medicine and Politics in a Mexican Village," in *Anthropological Essays*, 300–310.

6. On this period, see Joseph and Nugent, *Everyday Forms*; Fallaw, *Cárdenas Compromised*; Lewis, *Ambivalent Revolution*; and Boyer, *Becoming Campesinos*. Historians debate how radical the Cárdenas administration was. Knight, "Cardenismo."

7. See Joseph and Buchenau, *Mexico's Once and Future Revolution*, for a succinct narrative.

8. Dawson, *Indian and Nation*, chap. 3, esp. 75–76. Emilio Alanís Pantiño, "La población indígena de México," in Mendizábal, *Obras completas*, 1:45, asserts that the DAI budget rose from $367,000 pesos in 1936 to $4,084,000 pesos in 1945, with a big jump in 1938, when the Native boarding schools were transferred from the SEP to the DAI. See also Cecilia Greaves, "La política y el proyecto de educación indígena del avilacamachismo," in Bertely Busquets, *Historias, saberes*, 95–120.

9. Miguel O. de Mendizábal, "El problema de las nacionalidades oprimidas y su resolución en la URSS," in *Obras completas*, 4:389–99; Lombardo Toledano, "El problema de las minorías oprimidas," in Lombardo Toledano, *Problema del indio*, 101–8. On Lombardo Toledano, see also Spenser, "Viaje"; and Aguirre Beltrán, *Aportación*.

10. Mendizábal, "Problema de las nacionalidades oprimidas"; Mendizábal, "La etnología," *Obras completas*, 4:151–52, argued that local mestizos did not have economic power but controlled politics, saying, "Politics is now their economic base."

The only way to combat this was through indigenous organization but "without creating miniature nationalities as the North Americans are doing." The latter type of organization, which was being followed by the United States and the Soviet Union, was not viable "because the indigenous communities are so far along in their process of disorganization that it would be impossible to reconstitute them." He also argued that Mexico aimed to incorporate Native peoples into "the economic life of the country."

11. Both McCormick, *Logic of Compromise*, and Vaughan, *Cultural Politics in Revolution*, argue that the rightward turn began in 1938.

12. Leighton and Kluckhohn, *Children of the People*, 194–95. On functionalism, see Stocking, *After Tylor*, chaps. 6–8; and Adam Kuper, "Anthropology," 354–78.

13. For an early discussion of the Indian New Deal, see Scudder Mekeel, "An Appraisal of the Indian Reorganization Act," *American Anthropologist* 46, no. 2, part 1 (April–June 1944): 209–17; and John Collier, "Collier Replies to Mekeel," *American Anthropologist* 46, no. 3 (July–September 1944): 422–26. Postrevisionist accounts include Vaughan, *Cultural Politics in Revolution*; Lewis, *Ambivalent Revolution*; Fallaw, *Cárdenas Compromised*; Boyer, *Becoming Campesinos*; and McCormick, *Logic of Compromise*. On the self-mythologizing of postrevolutionary governments, see Kourí, "Invención del ejido."

14. Barsh, "Progressive-Era Bureaucrats," and the ensuing debate on pp. 18–64 in the same issue.

15. On stock reduction, see Parman, *Navajos*. Revisionists have also challenged the periodization of reforms, portraying the Indian New Deal and Cardenista programs as less novel, in intent and in effect, than their creators claimed. Post-1968 accounts pointed to continuities between Porfirian and postrevolutionary indigenous policies, noting that critiques of disentailment emerged at the turn of the twentieth century. Cardenismo, others insisted, simply grafted itself onto existing local politics. On the ground, little changed. Similarly, Barsh has suggested that the roots of Collier's Indian New Deal lie in the 1920s. After all, the federal government granted citizenship to Native people in 1924 and in 1926 created the Meriam Commission on Indian Administration, which criticized allotment in its report.

16. Rosier, "Real Indians"; Rosier, "'Old System.'"

17. Vaughan, *Cultural Politics in Revolution*; Dillingham, "*Indigenismo* and its Discontents." Rus, "La comunidad revolucionaria institucional," in Joseph and Nugent, *Everyday Forms*, also focuses on divisions within communities.

18. But they were not conscious of their own role. Compare Verran, "Postcolonial Moment."

19. Pan American Union, *Eighth International Conference of American States*, 98–103; Giraudo, "'No hay propiamente todavía Instituto,'" 6. Collier to Sophie Aberle, Jan. 17, 26, 1940; and Collier to Aberle, telegram, Jan. 26, 1940, all in reel 24, JCP.

20. John Collier, "Memorandum Regarding the Division of Inter-American Cooperation," May 28, 1941, reel 46, JCP. The U.S. Congress mandated funding for the IAII, required by the Pátzcuaro Convention for all member states, soon afterward but directed that funding come from the State Department: G. G. Smith to Harold D. Smith, Aug. 3, 1942, folder: U.S. Inter-American Indian Institute

(1942), box 410, record group 229, Records of the Office of Inter-American Affairs, 1937–1951, U.S. National Archives.

21. Acta de la sesión inaugural del Consejo Directivo del Instituto Indigenista Interamericano, celebrado en la Ciudad de México el 25 de marzo de 1942, Archivero 12, doc. 47, IAII; on Gamio's trajectory, see Comas, "Vida y obra."

22. Indeed, Alexander Leighton, whom Collier tapped to direct research within the camp, ended up working with a group of college-educated prisoners he had trained at Poston for the Office of War Information. In December 1945, Leighton traveled to Hiroshima as part of the U.S. strategic bombing survey. Rosemblatt and Benmergui, "Science of Democracy."

23. See chapter 2 above on an NRC initiative proposed by Jenks. The collection and organization of empirical cases was a hallmark of wartime activity. Two such endeavors were the Cross-Cultural Survey at the Yale University Institute for Human Relations, created in 1937, and the Ethnogeographic Board of the Smithsonian Institution. Lemov, *World as Laboratory*; Farish, "Archiving Areas"; Bennett, *Ethnogeographic Board*.

24. Sandeen, *Picturing an Exhibition*.

Chapter 3

1. Molina, *How Race Is Made*; Kelly, *Assault on Assimilation*, chaps. 6, 7; Philp, *John Collier's Crusade*, chaps. 2–5.

2. My thinking here draws from Calhoun, Cooper, and Moore, *Lessons of Empire*, esp. Stoler, "Imperial Formations"; McCoy and Scarano, *Colonial Crucible*; Kramer, "Power and Connection"; and Goldstein, *Formations of United States Colonialism*.

3. Boas found Collier too emotional: Franz Boas to Robert Gessner, Apr. 17, 1933, reel 13, JCP; on Brill, see John Collier to Laura Thompson, Dec. 17, 1941, reel 25, JCP; on Collier's divorce, see finding aid, Yale University Library, Manuscripts and Archives, "Guide to the John Collier Papers."

4. "Tenement Dwellers to Give Pageant of the Peoples," *New York Times*, May 24, 1914, 11; Philp, *John Collier's Crusade*, 16–17.

5. See Philp, *John Collier's Crusade*, 10, on Collier's reading of Kropotkin.

6. "Tenement Dwellers"; John Collier, "Neighborhood Clubs," *New York Times*, Apr. 11, 1913, 8, cited in Schwartz, "Red Atlantis Revisited," 511; "Bureau to Heal Community Woes: Clearing House to Co-Operate between City Government and Immigrant Population," *New York Times*, June 4, 1917, 11; "Wants City to Run Movies and Dance Halls for Poor," *New York Times*, Apr. 27, 1913, SM-7.

7. At least that is how Collier remembered things. John Collier, Leadership as the Controlling Need for Democracies, Washington, D.C., Oct. 15, 1937; and Collier, "The Camp Fire Girls and Their Debt to the First Americans," Jan. 1, 1936, both in box 26, OFCJC. See also Philp, *John Collier's Crusade*, 21.

8. Collier, *From Every Zenith*, 124. Collier retired to Taos and asked to be buried on Pueblo land, but for reasons that remain unclear, his request was not honored. Philp, *John Collier's Crusade*, 236.

9. John Collier, "Red Atlantis," *Survey* 49 (October 1922): 15, 26.

10. Ibid., 18.

11. Kelly, *Assault on Assimilation*, chaps. 6, 7; Philp, *John Collier's Crusade*, chaps. 2–5; John Collier, "Amerindians," *Pacific Affairs* 2, no. 3 (March 1929): 116–22, quotation on 118.

12. On Lummis, see Collier, "Red Atlantis," 63. Lummis studied with Latin American expert Adolf Bandelier and wrote *The Awakening of a Nation: Mexico of To-Day* (1898). On Collier's visits to Mexico, see Collier, *From Every Zenith*, 354–56. John Collier, "Mexico: A Challenge," *Progressive Education* 9, no. 2 (February 1932): 95, 96. See also John Collier, Address at the National Conference of Social Work, Detroit, Michigan, June 13, 1933, box 26, OFCJC.

13. John Collier, "Indians Come Alive," *Atlantic Monthly*, September 1942, 75–81.

14. Hauptman, "Africa View," esp. 362–63; John Collier, "Africa View—and Indian," *American Indian Life* 18 (July 1931): 31–40, emphasis in original. Huxley later became the first secretary general of UNESCO and in that role took an active position against racism. F. M. Keesing, "The Maoris of New Zealand: An Experiment in Racial Adaptation," *Pacific Affairs* 1, no. 5 (October 1928): 1–5; Collier, "Amerindians."

15. John Collier, Address of Mr. John Collier, Commissioner of Indian Affairs, at Annual Meetings of Home Missions Council and Council of Women for Home Missions, January 1936, New York City: Joint Committee on Indian Work of the Home Missions Councils, Feb. 29, 1936; and Meeting of John Collier with the Indians of Western Oklahoma at Anadarko, Oklahoma, for the purpose of discussing and explaining the Wheeler-Howard Bill, Mar. 20, 1934, both in box 26, OFCJC.

16. John Collier, "The Coming of Dr. Saenz," *Indians at Work* 1, no. 6 (November 1933): 1–3. On IS personnel's visit to Mexico, see "Mexican Rural Schools and Our Indian Program," *Indians at Work* 1, no. 8 (December 1933): 10–15.

17. On Native IS personnel, see Collier, *From Every Zenith*, 227; Address by John Collier at the National Conference of Social Work, Detroit, Mich., June 13, 1933, box 26, OFCJC.

18. Meeting of John Collier with the Indians of Western Oklahoma.

19. Ibid.

20. Charles W. Collier to Carlos Girón Cerna, Nov. 4, 1941, IAII-JC.

21. John Collier to Alida C. Bowler, Jan. 17, 1940, reel 24, JCP. It is possible that Collier's view of the Mexicans also changed over the years and that the earlier invocation at least was not a calculated misrepresentation.

22. John Collier, "New Policies in Indian Education," *New Mexico Quarterly* 3, no. 4 (November 1933): 202–5.

23. Address by John Collier to the Returned Students of the Navajos at Program of the Returned Students, Fort Wingate, N. Mex., July 7, 1933, box 26, OFCJC.

24. John Collier, "Aspects of the Personnel Problem of the Indian Service in the U.S.; of Possible Interest to Other American Countries," Mar. 1, 1940, reel 32, JCP. John Collier, Talk Given by Commissioner Collier at Bacone College, Muskogee, Okla., Feb. 6, 1937, on the Occasion of the Dedication of the New Boys' Dormitory, Named in Honor of Isaac McCoy, Feb. 6, 1937, box 26, OFCJC.

25. Kelly, "Anthropology and Anthropologists," 11–12. Mekeel to Collier, memorandum, May 20, 1936; and F. H. Daiker to Collier, memorandum, May 29, 1936, both in box 26, OFCJC. Scudder Mekeel, "An Appraisal of the Indian Reorganization Act," *American Anthropologist* 46, no. 2, part 1 (April–June 1944): 209–17; John Collier, "Collier Replies to Mekeel," *American Anthropologist* 46, no. 3 (July–September 1944): 422–26; "Anthropologists and the Federal Indian Program," *Science* 81, no. 2094 (Feb. 15, 1935): 170–71.

AAU personnel included Julian Steward, who would work on projects in Mexico and elsewhere in Latin America for the Institute of Social Anthropology of the Smithsonian Institution's Bureau of American Ethnology, and Charles Wisdom, who had written a Ph.D. dissertation on Guatemala's Chorti Indians. Scudder Mekeel, an anthropologist who had studied Sioux acculturation for his Yale University doctoral dissertation, headed the AAU. Less than a year after Collier took office, he read Redfield's study of the Maya of Yucatán and looked into the possibility of using Redfield's methods for an IS study of acculturation. Memorandum of Conversation with Mr. John Collier, Jan. 27, 1934, record group: Administration, folder: Bureau of Indian Affairs, 1934, CIW. Reinhardt, "Crude Replacement."

26. John Collier, "The United States Indian Administration as a Laboratory of Ethnic Relations," *Social Research* 12, no. 3 (September 1945): 265–303, quotation on 285.

27. Collier to Aberle, Feb. 8, 1941, reel 25, JCP.

28. Laura Thompson, "Action Research among American Indians," *Scientific Monthly* 70, no. 1 (January 1950): 34–40.

29. John Collier, "Editorial," *Indians at Work* 8, no. 12 (August 1941): 1–9. Keesing, *South Seas*, vi; Thompson, *Beyond the Dream*, 80; Stanford University, Faculty Senate, "Memorial Resolution."

30. Collier, "Editorial." John Collier, "Emerging Concepts of Indian Unity," draft of essay for *América Indígena*, Oct. 10, 1941; and, in Spanish, John Collier, "Nuevos conceptos sobre la unidad indígena," *América Indígena* 1, no. 1 (October 1941): 11–15, both in IAII-JC.

31. Collier, "Editorial."

32. Thompson, *Beyond the Dream*, 9–12, 35.

33. Ibid., chaps. 4, 5, 8.

34. Ibid., 102.

35. Ibid., 100–103.

36. Keesing, *South Seas*, 69; Bronislaw Malinowski, introduction to Thompson, *Fijian Frontier*, xxi.

37. Keesing, *South Seas*, 68.

38. Ibid., 175.

39. Ibid., 176–77.

40. Ibid., 81–83.

41. Ibid., 89–90.

42. Melville J. Herskovits, "Applied Anthropology and the American Anthropologists," *Science* 83, no. 2149 (Mar. 6, 1936): 221.

43. John Collier, Memorandum Regarding the Division of Inter-American Cooperation, May 28, 1941, reel 46, JCP. On Native participation in the Civilian Conservation Corps, see Morgan, "'Working' from the Margins: Documenting American Indian Participation in the New Deal Era," in Sleeper-Smith et al., *Why You Can't Teach United States History*, 181–96.

44. Collier, "Emerging Concepts"; Collier, "Nuevos conceptos." At Pátzcuaro, Father John Cooper of Catholic University had read a paper in which he equated Dutch and British colonial administration and the current, "experimental" uses of anthropology by government Indian bureaus in Canada, the United States, and Mexico. John M. Cooper, "Antropología y los problemas indígenas de las Américas," ponencia Pátzcuaro, IAII-PCII. Chávez Orozco, "Manifestations of Democracy," published in Spanish as *Las instituciones democráticas*.

45. John Collier, "A Civilization Knows Itself," Speech on Pan-American Day at University of Chicago, Apr. 14, 1941; and John Collier, "We Ourselves in Relation to the World Struggle," Sept. 10, 1941, both in box 26, OFCJC.

46. Collier referenced social psychology in Collier, Talk Given by Commissioner Collier at Bacone College. On Cooley and Collier, see Kunitz, "Social Philosophy of John Collier." Collier to J. L. Moreno, Apr. 7, 1942, reel 25, JCP; Collier to Laura Thompson, Oct. 28, 1941, folder 4: Indian Office, October 1941–February 1942, box 10, LTP.

47. Jacob L. Moreno, "How Kurt Lewin's 'Research Center for Group Dynamics' Started," *Sociometry* 16, no. 1 (February 1953): 101–4; Kurt Lewin and Ronald Lippitt, "An Experimental Approach to the Study of Autocracy and Democracy: A Preliminary Note," *Sociometry* 1, no. 3–4 (January–April 1938): 292–300. On Lewin, see Cravens, *Before Head Start*, 158–69, 188–91.

48. [Thompson?] to Collier, Nov. 28, 1941, folder 4: Indian Office, October 1941–February 1942, box 10, LTP; Thompson, "Action Research," 34.

49. Hsueh, "Hawthorne Experiments"; Gillespie, *Manufacturing Knowledge*, 85–86; Lee, "'Most Important Technique.'"

50. J. C. McCaskill, Memorandum for the Commissioner, Mar. 2, 1942; Memorandum of Understanding between the Director of the WRA and the Secretary of the Interior, Apr. 14, 1942; and Collier to Harold L. Ickes, memorandum, Mar. 4, 1942, all in box 21, OFCJC. Milton S. Eisenhower to Ickes, May 18, 1942, box 22, OFCJC.

51. Dillon S. Myer, "The Truth about Relocation," Aug. 6, 1943, folder 4, box 1, JARC.

52. John Collier, "Fellow Citizens," June 27, 1942; and Milton S. Eisenhower to Collier, memorandum, May 29, 1942, both in box 21, OFCJC. Hayashi, *Democratizing the Enemy*, 106.

53. Collier to Thompson, Apr. 16, 1942, folder: Correspondence, Coordinator, Committee on Human Development, University of Chicago, April–December 1942 (2 of 2), box 10, LTP.

54. Details of this research are in Karin Alejandra Rosemblatt and Leandro Benmergui, "Japanese-American Confinement and Scientific Democracy: Colonialism, Social Engineering, and Government Administration," unpublished ms. (2013).

55. McCaskill, Memorandum for John Collier.

56. The term "colony" is used, e.g., in Collier to Eisenhower, Apr. 15, 1942, reel 25, JCP; Leighton, *Governing of Men*, 376–77.

57. Leighton, *Governing of Men*, 379, 382; Head Personality–Circumstances of Study, index card, box 31, JARC. Alexander H. Leighton, "Assessing Public Opinion in a Dislocated Community," *Public Opinion Quarterly* 7, no. 4 (Winter 1943): 656.

58. On pragmatism's failure to address racial disparities, see Fallace, *Dewey and the Dilemma of Race*.

59. Conrad M. Arensberg, "Report on a Developing Community: Poston, Arizona," *Applied Anthropology* 2, no. 1 (October–December 1942): 1–21, quotation on 11. Guerrier, "Applying Anthropology," claims, based on researchers' use of the Hawthorne studies, that the BSR aimed to make confinees productive and efficient workers. I see this as an overly mechanistic reading that fails to recognize the Hawthorne lessons regarding communication. On public opinion and communications research, see Igo, *Averaged American*.

60. Quotation from Collier, "Fellow Citizens."

61. Collier to Eisenhower, Apr. 15, 1942, box 22, OFCJC. See also Alexander H. Leighton, "Training Social Scientists for Post-War Conditions," *Applied Anthropology* 1, no. 4 (1942): 25–30.

62. Laura Thompson, draft of "An Attempt to Study Indian Personality," for *América Indígena*, September 1942, folder: Coordinator, Committee on Human Development, University of Chicago, April–December 1942 (2 of 2), box 10, LTP.

63. Thompson to Collier, Dec. 16, 1942; and Laura Thompson, "Some Essentials for a Democratic Colonial Program," n.d., both in reel 17, JCP. That this work was for the State Department is mentioned in Felix Keesing, Some Notes Taken at New York Meeting, Dec. 30, 1942, reel 32, JCP.

64. Thompson, "Some Essentials."

65. John Collier, "What the American Indians Will Do in the Future for Themselves and for Us," *Predictions: Forecasts by Experts of Things to Come* 1, no. 2 (Summer 1943): 92–97, box 26, OFCJC Minutes of Meeting of Jan. 30, 1943, Conference Room Department of the Interior, reel 32, JCP.

66. On Sady, see Emil J. Sady to Manuel Gamio and Institute Personnel, Jan. 30, 1943; and Sady to Gamio and Juan Comas, Feb. 24, 1946, both in IAII-EJS. Keesing, Some Notes Taken.

67. Keesing, Some Notes Taken; John Collier and Laura Thompson, "A Declaration of Interdependence: A Creed for Americans as World-Citizens," Feb. 4, 1944, RFCJC.

68. Ward Shepard to John Collier, memorandum, Mar. 19, 1943, reel 17, JCP; John Collier and Saul K. Padover, "An Institute of Ethnic Democracy," *Common Ground* 4, no. 1 (Autumn 1943): 3–7. Criticisms of the proposal for government action can be found in "Are Race Relations the Business of the Federal Government? A Symposium," *Common Ground* 4, no. 2 (December 1944): 3–21. Opponents felt that it was not the role of the government to intervene in such matters.

69. Cogan, *We Fought the Navy*, 36, 46, app. 2; John Collier, Advance copy of the Nov. News Letter of the Institute of Ethnic Affairs, Oct. 22, 1946, IAII-JC.

70. Collier, Advance copy of the Nov. News Letter.

71. Cogan, *We Fought the Navy.*

72. Collier, *America's Colonial Record.*

73. John Collier, A project for a preliminary outline study of the political, social, economic, and psychological factors in the underdeveloped countries as they affect American consideration of the Point Four Program, Nov. 14, 1949, reel 41, JCP.

74. On the building, see Gamio to Cogan, Feb. 2, 1950, IAII-JC. On payments, see National Indian Institute, "Proceedings of the meeting of the Policy Board," Mar. 21–22, 1950, reel 46, JCP.

75. Truman, Executive Order 9710; Jane W. Pijoan, "The Spanish Speaking People of the United States," reel 40, JCP.

76. Collier to Lucy W. Adams, Apr. 16, 1942, box 21, OFCJC. On uniformity, see also Collier to Thompson, Apr. 16, 1942, ibid.

77. Leighton, "Training Social Scientists," 29.

78. Leighton, "Assessing Public Opinion," 652–53.

79. Leighton, *Governing of Men,* 246.

80. Ibid., 249, 345–46. Leighton, "Morale," n.d., folder 21, subseries correspondence–L (Unit I/2299), Leighton, Alexander H., series I–Correspondence with individuals and related material, Adolf Meyer Collection, 1890–1940, Medical Archives of the Johns Hopkins Medical Institutions.

Chapter 4

1. Cárdenas, "Discurso."

2. On the need to recognize how fieldworkers responded to local conditions, see Saldívar, "Everyday Practices of Indigenismo."

3. Cárdenas, "Discurso."

4. Past scholarship on indigenismo has focused on indigenistas' evolutionary views and linked those evolutionary viewpoints to racist thinking and policy. Some scholarship has also pointed to the pluralism of certain indigenistas. Dawson, *Indian and Nation*; Knight, "Racism, Revolution, and Indigenismo"; Brading, "Manuel Gamio"; Saldívar, "'It's Not Race, It's Culture.'"

5. Mendizábal, "Ética indígena." Socialists shared the evolutionary views of Lewis Henry Morgan, who had influenced Friedrich Engels. Morgan, "Ethnical Periods," in *Ancient Society.*

6. Its placement there also reflected a number of pragmatic considerations. The minister of agriculture had been Gamio's classmate. See Gómez Gamio, *Manuel Gamio,* 48.

7. Gamio and Pan American Union, *Present State,* 19–28.

8. Loyo Bravo, *Gobiernos revolucionarios y educación popular,* 258–60, 286.

9. "Informe del Departamento de Educación y Cultura Indígena," *Boletín de la Secretaría de Educación Pública* 1, no. 2 (Sept. 1, 1922): 261–66, quotation on 268. It is unclear whether this is part of the essay on the previous page, published in the daily *El Universal.*

10. Fell, *José Vasconcelos,* 218.

11. On Bassols, see Britton, *Educación y radicalismo.* See also Palacios, "Postrevolutionary Intellectuals"; and Vaughan, *Cultural Politics in Revolution.*

12. Narciso Bassols, "El programa educativo de México," in *Obras*, 177–78. On the unscientific nature of past approaches, see Basauri, *Población indígena*. Loyo Bravo, "¿Escuelas o empresas?," 78. Sáenz had an exceedingly strained relationship with the Marxist Bassols but believed that the SEP had been implementing facets of socialist education long before it became official policy. Sáenz, *Carapan*, 19.

13. Palacios, "Postrevolutionary Intellectuals," 315, 333, 336–37.

14. Manuel Mesa A., "Organización y funcionamiento de las Misiones Culturales," Feb. 14, 1933, folder 13, no. 2, IAII-PVM.

15. Vargas Lozano, "Polémica Caso-Lombardo."

16. Citations from "La posición ideológica de la Universidad frente a los problemas del momento. Importancia social de la Universidad en el mundo actual," and *Excélsior* and *El Universal* newspapers, August 1933, in Hernández Luna, "Polémica," 89, 91; Vicente Lombardo, "El reculamiento del espíritu," in *Idealismo vs materialismo dialéctico* (Mexico City: Universidad Obrera de México, 1963), 64, cited in Vargas Lozano, "Polémica Caso-Lombardo," 15.

17. Hernández Luna, "Polémica"; Vargas Lozano, "Polémica Caso-Lombardo," 15.

18. Cotter, *Troubled Harvest*; Olvera Serrano, "Institucionalización." In 1942, the Anthropology Department moved to the Instituto Nacional de Antropología e Historia (INAH), and it later became the freestanding Escuela Nacional de Antropología e Historia (ENAH). Pinet, "Conmemoración," 15–16.

19. Mesa A., "Organización y funcionamiento." On Actopan, see Manuel Gamio, "Comentarios y sugestiones relativos a la educación y el conocimiento de la población," ca. 1932, folder 7, no. 2, pp. 42–43, IAII-PVM. Loyo Bravo, "¿Escuelas o empresas?," 78; Loyo Bravo, "El conocimiento del indio: Nuevo camino para su asimilación (1930–1940)," in Bertely Busquets, *Historias, saberes*, 69–94. Fábila, *Valle de El Mezquital*, 9, gives the dates of Gamio's stay as February to May 1933, but documents in the IAII archive show Gamio active in late 1932. See Manuel Gamio to Secretario de Educación Pública, Oct. 10, 1932, folder 4, no. 2, IAII-PVM.

20. Manuel Mesa A. to Director del Instituto de Investigaciones Sociales de la Escuela Regional Campesina El Mexe, Jan. 27, 1933, folder 13, no. 1, IAII-PVM.

21. Manuel Gamio, "Ante-programa de trabajos del Instituto de Investigaciones," ca. 1932, folder 4, no. 4, p. 1, IAII-PVM. Gamio drew on the example of his previous work in Teotihuacán, which had sought to provide a utilitarian education. See Gamio and Pan American Union, *Present State*, 19–28.

22. Manuel Gamio, "Comentarios y sugestiones relativos a educación en el medio mexicano," ca. 1932, folder 7, p. 3, IAII-PVM. See also Manuel Gamio, "Las características culturales y los censos indígenas," *América Indígena* 2, no. 3 (July 1942): 15–19.

23. Manuel Gamio, "Bosquejo para el trabajo del investigación de instituto a cargo del Dr. D. Manuel Gamio en la Región de la Escuela Campesina de El Mexe, Hgo.," ca. 1932, folder 4, no. 3, p. 4, IAII-PVM.

24. Ibid.; Gamio, *Mexican Immigration*.

25. Basauri, *Monografía de los tarahumaras*.

26. Fábila, *Valle de El Mezquital*, 32. For other taxonomies that followed the same logic see Basauri, *Monografía de los tarahumaras*; Basauri, *Población indígena de México*, 1:8–9; and Mendieta y Núñez, "La etnografía económica," *El Trimestre Económico* 2, no. 6 (1935): 142–44.

27. Letters from schoolteachers can be found in folder 26, no. 3, IAII-PVM. Manuel Basauri, "Proyecto para el estudio médico que efectuará el Instituto de Investigación de la Escuela Regional del Campesino de El Mexe," Dec. 28, 1932, folder 4, no. 6 IAII-PVM.

28. Manuel Gamio, "Investigaciones y sugestiones sobre las necesidades educativas que tiene que satisfacer la Escuela Regional Campesina de 'El Mexe,' en el Valle del Mezquital, Edo. de Hgo," ca. 1932, folder 10, pp. 45–99, IAII-PVM. The final chapter of this document can be found in folder 2, no. 2. Fábila, *Valle de El Mezquital*, 32; Miguel O. de Mendizábal, "Evolución histórica y social del Valle del Mezquital," in *Obras completas*, 6:7–258.

29. Palacios, "Postrevolutionary Intellectuals."

30. Bassols, "Programa educativo de México," in *Obras*, 178–79.

31. Carlos Basauri, "El problema del bilingüismo y la educación indígena: Ponencia del profesor Carlos Basauri, Jefe del Departamento de Educación Indígena ante la III Conferencia Interamericana de Educación" (1937), in *Población indígena de México*, 1:117–19.

32. Basauri, *Población indígena de México*, 1:118.

33. Spenser, "Viaje"; Vicente Lombardo Toledano, "Cómo resolvió el régimen soviético el problema de las nacionalidades oprimidas" (1936), in *Problema del indio*, 106; Aguirre Beltrán, *Aportación*, 18–25. The nationalities policy was discarded at the PCM meeting in 1941.

Emilio Alanís Patiño, in Mendizabal, *Obras completas*, 1:37–39, rejected the nationalities policy: "In truth the Soviet Union has defended the vernacular languages of its peoples out of respect and in the pursuit of justice for its national minorities, but also because the Soviets' goals can be better served by using autochthonous languages rather than imposing the Russian language."

34. "Introducción," in Chávez Orozco, *Memoria*, 17–18, 7–10.

35. Cárdenas, "Discurso."

36. Manuel Gamio, "El concepto de la realidad social de México," *Revista Mexicana de Sociología* 1, no. 2 (May–June 1939): 11–17.

37. Manuel Gamio, [Draft of "La educación y el conocimiento de la población,"] ca. 1935, folder 10, pp. 15–29, IAII-PVM. For a similar formulation, see Gamio, "Características culturales," 15–19. The quotation is from Manuel Gamio, "Los varios mercados mexicanos," *El Trimestre Económico* 2, no. 5 (1935): 5.

38. Mendieta y Núñez, "Etnografía económica," 152, 133, 153. See also Gómez Robleda and México, Secretaría de Educación Pública, *Pescadores y campesinos*, Prologue by Lucio Mendieta y Núñez, p. xiii.

39. Mendieta y Núñez, "Etnografía económica," 152.

40. Gamio and Pan American Union, *Present State*, 14. Gamio, "Factores adversos," 182.

41. Gamio, "Factores adversos," 179; Mendieta y Núñez, "Etnografía económica," 151. Having traveled to Japan, Gamio became obsessed with the introduction of the nutritious soybean. Omura, "Manuel Gamio y Japón"; Manuel Gamio, Sánchez E. Fuentes, and Maya Morrison, *Recetas para derivados alimenticios del frijol soya* (Mexico City: Instituto Lingüístico de Verano, 1951).

42. Miguel O. de Mendizábal, "Industrias de los otomíes contemporáneos," and "Monografías de pueblos indígenas," in *Obras completas*, 6:151–258.

43. Gamio, "Factores adversos"; Gamio, "Varios mercados mexicanos"; Gamio, "Ante-programa de trabajos."

44. Gamio, "Factores adversos," 186–87; Gamio, folder 1, IAII-PVM. See also IAII-PCII, vol. 2, sección: Biológica; Sáenz, *Antología*, 134.

45. Emmanuel Palacios Ramírez, "Algunas consideraciones sobre cómo lograr la elevación del estado cultural de la población indígena en materia de alimentación," April 1940, vol. 2, sección: Biológica, no. 5, IAII-PCII; Dr. Jesús Díaz Barriga, "Los problemas de la alimentación de los indígenas mexicanos," vol. 2, sección: Biológica, no. 3, IAII-PCII; Dr. José Quintín Olascoaga, "Lo que México se propone realizar por medio de la Comisión Nacional de Alimentación para mejorar el estado de nutrición de los indígenas de la República," vol. 2, sección: Biológica, no. 6, IAII-PCII.

46. Anderson et al., "Study of Nutritional Status," 899.

47. Ralph L. Beals and Evelyn Hatcher, "The Diet of a Tarascan Village," *América Indígena* 3, no. 4 (October 1943): 295–304.

48. Juan Comas, "La Asistencia Pública y el desarrollo biológico del indígena," *América Indígena* 3, no. 4 (October 1943): 339.

49. Basauri, *Población indígena de México;* Rojas González et al., *Etnografía de México;* Mendieta y Núñez, *México indígena.*

50. Mendieta y Núñez, "Etnografía económica," 142–44.

51. Lucio Mendieta y Núñez, "Veinticinco años del Instituto de Investigaciones Sociales de la Universidad Nacional Autónoma de México," *Revista Mexicana de Sociología* 17, no. 2/3 (May–December 1955): 251–55, quotation on 253.

52. Ibid., 248, n.p.

53. Mendieta y Núñez, *México indígena.* The project is explored in Dorotinsky Alperstein, "Puesta en escena."

54. Mendieta y Núñez, "Etnografía económica."

55. When, after stepping down as subsecretary of education, Sáenz began looking for a place to set up his experimental station cum school, he explicitly searched for places that were remote but accessible—home to Native peoples who could easily be on their way to becoming Mexican but were stuck on the path. Sáenz, *Carapan*, 31, 223, 229.

56. Saldívar, "'It's Not Race, It's Culture,'" rightly insists that scholarship must take into account power rather than simply difference. However, she misses the polysemy of the term "race" and its overlap with the term "culture." My argument here and below is also in dialogue with Bourdieu and Wacquant, "Cunning of Imperialist Reason."

57. Gamio, [Draft of "Educación"].

58. Gamio and Pan American Union, *Present State*, 13

59. Manuel Gamio, "Cultural Patterns in Modern Mexico," *Quarterly Journal of Inter-American Relations* 1, no. 2 (April 1939): 52.

60. Ibid., 50. Index: Gamio, [Draft of "Educación"].

61. Gamio, "Características culturales," 17.

62. Emilio Alanís Patiño, Sept. 30, 1914, Alanís Patiño folder, desde Abreu, Ermilo, hasta Biblioteca Nacional, 1940–1959, México en el Archivo Histórico del Instituto Indigenista Interamericano, IAII. Alanís Patiño, "Población indígena"; "Ing. Emilio Alanís Patiño (1905–1998)," http://www.anech-chapingo.org.mx/Docs/PDF/Semblanzas/Emilio_Alanis_Patino.pdf.

63. Dirección General de Estadística, *Sexto censo*, 34–35; Gamio, "Características culturales"; Alanís Patiño, "Población indígena," 77.

64. Alanís Patiño, "Población indígena," 78.

65. Emilio Alanís Patiño, "Las estadísticas sobre los presupuestos familiares en los grupos indígenas," IAII-PCII, vol. 4, sección: Socio Económica, no. 26.

66. Alanís Patiño, "Población indígena,"78.

67. Ibid., 78–79.

68. Gamio, "Características culturales," 15–19.

69. Gamio, [Draft of "Educación"].

Conclusion

1. Manuel Gamio, "Consideraciones sobre el problema indígena en América," *América Indígena* 2, no. 2 (April 1942): 17–23. See also "Las características culturales y los censos indígenas," ibid. 2, no. 3 (July 1942): 15–19; "Calificación de características culturales de los grupos indígenas," ibid. 2, no. 4 (October 1942): 17–22.

2. Gamio, "Características culturales."

3. Sáenz, *Antología*, 154–55.

4. Julian H. Steward, "Acculturation and the Indian Problem," *América Indígena* 2, no. 4 (October 1942): 323–28.

5. Sáenz, *Carapan*, 215; Sol Tax, "Ethnic Relations in Guatemala," *América Indígena* 2, no. 4 (October 1942): 43–48.

6. Collier's response is appended to Tax, "Ethnic Relations."

7. Robert Redfield in "Comments on Dr. Tax's Article by R. Redfield, J. Collier, E. J. Sady and C. C. Presnall," *América Indígena* 3 no. 1 (January 1943): 83–86.

8. Ibid., 86–89.

9. Beate Salz, "Indianismo," *Social Research* 11, no. 4 (November 1944): 441–69, and "Some Considerations on Mr. Collier's Article," *América Indígena* 5, no. 3 (July 1945): 247–54. Historian Frank Tannenbaum also saw conflict as likely. Noting that incorporation had not worked, he wrote that there was an "implicit contradiction inherent in Indianismo and Nacionalismo. The wisdom which might lead to an accommodation between them—a cultural and linguistic autonomy within a common political unity—is probably not to be expected." Frank Tannenbaum, "Agrarismo, Indianismo, y Nacionalismo," *Hispanic American Historical Review* 23, no. 3 (August 1943): 394–423, quotation on 421.

10. John Collier, "¿Indianismo o racismo?," *América Indígena* 5, no. 3 (1945): 241–46. Emil J. Sady, "Native Administration in America," *América Indígena* 2, no. 4 (October 1942): 23–28.

11. Lucio Mendieta y Núñez, "El tratamiento del indio," *América Indígena* 4, no. 2 (April 1944): 112–22.

12. Oscar Lewis and Ernest E. Maes, "Base para una nueva definición práctica del indio," *América Indígena* 5, no. 2 (April 1945): 107–18.

13. Mendieta y Núñez, "Tratamiento del indio."

14. Steward, *People of Puerto Rico*.

15. Stocking, *After Tylor*, 352–66.

16. Collier and Thompson, "Declaration of Interdependence."

17. Leighton, *Governing of Men*, 249, 345–46. Leighton, "Morale," n.d., folder 21, subseries correspondence—L (Unit I/2299), Leighton, Alexander H., series I—Correspondence with individuals and related material, Adolf Meyer Collection, 1890–1940, Medical Archives of the Johns Hopkins Medical Institutions.

18. Collier and Thompson, "Declaration of Interdependence."

19. Rosemblatt, "Modernization, Dependency."

Bibliography

Manuscript Collections

Mexico City
  Archivo Histórico de la Secretaría de Educación Pública
    Departamento de Psicopedagogía e Higiene
  Archivo Histórico de la Secretaría de Salubridad y Asistencia
    Colección Salubridad Pública
  Archivo Histórico del Instituto Indigenista Interamericano
    Archivero 12
    Don Manuel Gamio: Proyecto Valle del Mezquital, 1932–1956
    Estados Unidos en el Archivo Histórico: Emil J. Sady, 1943–1945, 1946–1960
    John Collier, 1940–1963
    México en el Archivo Histórico, 1940–1959
    Primer Congreso Indigenista Interamericano: Acta final, asistentes, ponencias,
      vols. 1–5
United States
  Carnegie Institution of Washington
  Cornell University Library, Division of Rare and Manuscript Collections
    Japanese-American Relocation Centers Records #3830
  John Collier Papers, 1922–1968, Sanford, N.C.: Microfilming Corp. of
    America, 1980
  Medical Archives of the Johns Hopkins Medical Institutions
    Adolf Meyer Collection, 1890–1940, Series I—Correspondence with
      individuals and related material, Subseries—Correspondence—L, Unit
      I/2299—Leighton, Alexander H.
  National Anthropological Archives, Suitland, Md.
    Laura Thompson Papers, 1905–1997
  National Academy of Sciences, National Research Council, Washington, D.C.
    Division of Anthropology and Psychology, 1919–1939, Division Collections
    Division of Foreign Relations, 1919–1939, Division Collections
  Rockefeller Archive Center, Sleepy Hollow, N.Y.
    Laura Spelman Rockefeller Memorial
    Social Science Research Council
  University of Chicago Library, Special Collections Research Center
    Robert Redfield Papers
  U.S. National Archives, College Park, Md.
    Record Group 229, Records of the Office of Inter-American Affairs,
      1937–1951
  U.S. National Archives, Washington, D.C.

Record Group 75, Records of the Bureau of Indian Affairs, 1793–1999
Office Files of Commissioner John Collier, 1933–1945
Reference Files of Commissioner John Collier, 1919–1945

Periodicals

América Indígena,
1941–80
American Anthropologist,
1910–56
American Indian Life, 1931
American Journal of
Physical Anthropology,
1919
American Political Science
Review, 1924
Applied Anthropology, 1942
Boletín Bibliográfico
de Antropología
Americana, 1942
Boletín de la Secretaría
de Educación Pública,
1922–25
Bulletin of the Pan
American Union,
1924–25
Common Ground, 1943

El País, 1911
El Trimestre Económico,
1935–39
Ethnos, 1920–23
Excélsior, 1921
Genus, 1934, 1936
Indians at Work, 1933
Man, 1935
The Nation, 1929
New Republic, 1926
New York Times, 1913–17
Pacific Affairs, 1928–29
Proceedings of the
Academy of Political
Science in the City of
New York, 1912
Proceedings of the
National Academy of
Sciences of the United
States of America,
1916–18

Progressive Education,
1932
Publications of the
American Statistical
Association, 1908
Public Opinion Quarterly,
1943
Quarterly Journal of
Inter-American
Relations, 1939
Revista Mexicana de
Sociología, 1939–55
Science, 1917–36
Scientific Monthly,
1916–50
Social Research, 1944–45
Social Service Review,
1927
Sociometry, 1938, 1953
The Survey, 1922

Published Primary Sources

American Ophthalmological Society. *An International Congress of Ophthalmology:*
Proceedings, Washington D.C., April 25, 26, 27, 28, 1922. Washington, D.C.: n.p.,
1922.
American Public Health Association. *Public Health Papers and Reports.* Vol. 19.
Concord, N.H.: Republican Press Association, 1894.
Anderson, Richmond K., Jose Calvo, Gloria Serrano, and George C. Payne.
"A Study of the Nutritional Status and Food Habits of Otomi Indians in
the Mezquital Valley of Mexico." *American Journal of Public Health* 36, no. 8
(August 1946): 883–903.
Basauri, Carlos. *Monografía de los tarahumaras.* Mexico City: Talleres Gráficos de
la Nación, 1929.
———. *La población indígena de México: Etnografía.* 3 vols. Mexico City: Secretaría
de Educación Pública, Oficina Editora Popular, 1940.
Bassols, Narciso. *Obras.* Edited by Jesús Silva Herzog and Alonso Aguilar
Monteverde. Mexico City: Fondo Cultural Económica, 1964.

Bennett, Wendell Clark. *The Ethnogeographic Board*. Washington, D.C.: Smithsonian Institution, 1947.

Boas, Franz. *The Mind of Primitive Man*. 1911. New York: Macmillan, 1938.

———. *Race, Language, and Culture*. 1940. New York: Free Press, 1966.

Boas, Franz, and Manuel Gamio. *Álbum de colecciones arqueológicas*. Publicaciones de la Escuela Internacional de Arqueología y Etnología Americanas. Mexico City: Imprenta del Museo Nacional de Arqueología, Historia y Etnografía, 1921.

Cárdenas, Lázaro. "Discurso del presidente de la república en el Primer Congreso Indigenista Interamericano," April 14, 1940. Memoria política de México website. http://memoriapoliticademexico.org/Textos/6Revolucion/1940PCM.html.

Chase, Stuart. *Men and Machines*. New York: Macmillan, 1929.

———. *Mexico: A Study of Two Americas*. In collaboration with Marian Tyler. New York: Macmillan, 1931.

———. *A New Deal*. New York: Macmillan, 1933.

———. *Prosperity: Factor or Myth*. New York: Charles Boni, 1929.

Chávez Orozco, Luis. *Las instituciones democráticas de los indígenas mexicanos en la época colonial*. Mexico City: Ediciones del Instituto Indigenista Interamericano, 1943.

Chávez Orozco, Luis, and United States National Indian Institute. *Manifestations of Democracy among Mexican Indians during the Colonial Period*. Washington, D.C.: National Indian Institute, Department of the Interior, 1944.

Claghorn, Kate Holladay. "Crime and Immigration: A Clinical Study of Two Hundred and Thirteen Immigrants Admitted to Sing Sing Prison within a Period of Nine Months." In *Report of Committee of the Institute*. N.p.: n.p., 1910.

Collier, John. *America's Colonial Record*. London: Fabian Publications and Victor Gollancz, 1947.

———. *From Every Zenith: A Memoir; and Some Essays on Life and Thought*. Denver, Colo.: Sage Books, 1963.

Comas, Juan. *Bosquejo histórico de la antropología en México*. Mexico City, 1950.

———. *Los Congresos Internacionales de Americanistas: Síntesis histórica e índice bibliográfico general, 1875–1952*. Mexico City: Instituto Indigenista Interamericano, 1954.

———. *Ensayos sobre indigenismo*. Mexico City: Instituto Indigenista Interamericano, 1953.

———. "La vida y la obra de Manuel Gamio." In *Estudios antropológicos publicados en homenaje al doctor Manuel Gamio*, 1–26. Mexico City: Universidad Nacional Autónoma de México, 1956.

Cuarto Congreso Panamericano del Niño. *Boletín*. Santiago: La Ilustración, 1923.

Dugdale, R. L. *The Jukes*. 1910. New York: Arno, 1970.

Estabrook, Arthur H. *The Jukes in 1915*. Washington, D.C.: Carnegie Institution, 1916.

Eugenics Education Society. *Problems in Eugenics: Papers Communicated to the First International Eugenics Congress Held at the University of London, July 24th to 30th, 1912*. London: Eugenics Education Society, 1912.

Fábila, Alfonso. *Valle de El Mezquital*. Mexico City: Editorial Cultura, 1938.

Foster, George McClelland, ed. *A Cross-Cultural Anthropological Analysis of a Technical Aid Program*. Washington, D.C.: Smithsonian Institution, 1951.

Gamio, Manuel. *Comentarios sobre la evolución de los pueblos latino-americanos*. Rome: Istituto Poligrafico dello Stato, Librería, 1932.

———. *De vidas dolientes*. Mexico City: Ediciones Botas, 1937.

———. *Forjando patria (pro nacionalismo)*. Mexico City: Porrúa Hermanos, 1916.

———. *Hacia un México nuevo: Problemas sociales*. Mexico City: N.p., 1935.

———. *The Mexican Immigrant: His Life-Story: Autobiographic Documents*. Chicago: University of Chicago Press, 1931.

———. *Mexican Immigration to the United States: A Study of Human Migration and Adjustment*. Chicago: University of Chicago Press, 1930.

———. *Mexican Immigration to the United States: A Study of Human Migration and Adjustment*. Reprint ed. New York: Dover, 1971.

———. *The Minima and the Electron (Conjectures of an Amateur)*. Mexico City: N.p., 1932.

———. *Programa de la Dirección de Estudios Arqueológicos y Etnográficos*. Mexico City: Oficina Impresora de la Secretaría de Hacienda, Departamento de Fomento, 1918.

Gamio, Manuel, and Pan American Union. *The Present State of Anthropological Research in Mexico*. Washington, D.C.: Government Printing Office, 1925.

Gini, Corrado. "Address to the Third International Congress of Eugenics Held in the American Museum of Natural History, New York City, 22–23 August 1932." http://www-history.mcs.st-and.ac.uk/Extras/Gini_Eugenics.html.

Goddard, Henry A. *The Kallikak Family: A Study in the Heredity of Feeble-Mindedness*. New York: Macmillan, 1912.

Harper, Allan G., Josefina de Román, and United States National Indian Institute. *Los indios de los Estados Unidos*. Washington, D.C.: National Indian Institute, Department of the Interior, 1942.

Hastings, Montana Lucia. *Clasificación y estudio estadístico de 3,719 alumnos: La mayoría de primer año de enseñanza secundaria de la Ciudad de México*. Mexico City: Editorial Cultura, 1929.

Herskovits, Melville J. *Acculturation: The Study of Culture Contact*. New York City: J. J. Augustin, 1938.

Institute for Government Research. *The Problem of Indian Administration: Report of a Survey Made at the Request of Hubert Work, Secretary of the Interior, and Submitted to Him, February 21, 1928*. Baltimore: Johns Hopkins Press, 1928.

International Eugenics Conference. *A Decade of Progress in Eugenics: Scientific Papers of the Third International Congress of Eugenics Held at American Museum of Natural History, New York, August 21–23, 1932*. Baltimore: Williams and Wilkins, 1934. https://ia600402.us.archive.org/2/items/decadeofprogress00inte/decadeofprogress00inte_bw.pdf.

Keesing, Felix M. *The South Seas in the Modern World*. New York: John Day, 1941.

Kelly, William H., ed. *Indian Affairs and the Indian Reorganization Act: The Twenty Year Record*. Tucson: University of Arizona, 1954.

Leighton, Alexander H. *The Governing of Men: General Principles and Recommendations Based on Experience at a Japanese Relocation Camp.* Princeton, N.J.: Princeton University Press, 1945.

Leighton, Dorothea, and Clyde Kluckhohn. *Children of the People: The Navaho Individual and His Development.* Cambridge, Mass.: Harvard University Press, 1947.

Lewis, Oscar. *Anthropological Essays.* New York: Random House, 1970.

———. *Life in a Mexican Village: Tepoztlán Restudied.* Urbana: University of Illinois Press, 1951.

Lombardo Toledano, Vicente. *El problema del indio.* Mexico City: Secretaría de Educación Pública, Dirección General de Educación Audiovisual y Divulgación, 1973.

Lummis, Charles Fletcher. *The Awakening of a Nation: Mexico of To-Day.* New York: Harper, 1898.

Lynd, Robert S., and Helen M. Lynd. *Middletown: A Study in Contemporary American Culture.* New York: Harcourt, Brace, 1929.

Memoria del Primer Congreso Mexicano del Niño. Mexico City: El Universal, 1921.

Mendieta y Núñez, Lucio. *México indígena.* Mexico City: Editorial Porrúa, 1986.

Mendizábal, Miguel O. de. *La ética indígena: Conferencia pronunciada la noche del 27 de septiembre de 1923 en el Salón de Actos del Museo Nacional.* Mexico City: Imprenta del Museo Nacional de Arqueología, 1923.

———. *Obras completas.* 6 vols. Mexico City: Talleres Gráficos de la Nación, 1946–47.

Mexico, Departamento Autónomo de Asuntos Indígenas. *Memoria de la Primera Asamblea de Filólogos y Lingüistas.* Mexico City: Antigua Imprenta de E. Murguía, 1940.

Mexico, Dirección General de Estadística. *Censo general de la República Mexicana verificado el 20 de octubre de 1895.* Mexico City: Oficina Tipográfica de la Secretaría de Fomento, 1897.

Mexico, Secretaría de Agricultura y Fomento, Dirección de Estadística. *Tercer censo de población de los Estados Unidos Mexicanos verificado el 27 de octubre de 1910.* Mexico City: Secretaría de Hacienda, Departamento de Fomento, 1918.

Mexico, Secretaría de la Economía Nacional, Dirección General de Estadística. *Sexto censo de población 1940, resumen general.* Mexico City: Dirección General de Estadística, 1943.

Mexico, Departamento de Antropología de México and Manuel Gamio. *La población del valle de Teotihuacán.* Mexico City: Dirección de Talleres Gráficos, Secretaría de Educación Pública, 1922.

Miles, Walter R. "Raymond Dodge, 1871–1942: A Biographical Memoir." Washington, D.C.: National Academy of Sciences, 1956. http://www.nasonline.org/publications/biographicalmemoirs/memoir-pdfs/dodge-raymond.pdf.

Morgan, Lewis Henry. *Ancient Society: Or, Researches in the Lines of Human Progress from Savagery through Barbarism to Civilization.* New York: Henry Holt, 1877.

National Research Council. *Fifth Annual Report of the National Research Council.* Washington, D.C.: Government Printing Office, 1921.

———. *Sixth Annual Report of the National Research Council.* Washington, D.C.: Government Printing Office, 1922.

National Research Council, Division of Behavioral Sciences. Committee on War Service of Anthropologists. "Anthropology during the War and After." Memorandum. Washington, D.C., 1943.

Pan American Scientific Congress. *Acta final del Tercer Congreso Científico Panamericano.* Lima: N.p., 1938.

———. *Proceedings of the Second Pan American Scientific Congress, Monday, December 27, 1915, to Saturday, January 8, 1916.* Vol. 1. Washington, D.C.: Government Printing Office, 1917.

Pan American Union. *Eighth International Conference of American States, Lima, Peru, December 9, 1938: Special Handbook for the Use of Delegates.* Washington, D.C.: Pan American Union, 1938.

Ramírez, Rafael. *Cómo dar a México un idioma: Resultado de una encuesta.* Mexico City: Publicaciones de la Secretaría de Educación Pública, 1928.

Redfield, Robert. *Tepoztlan, a Mexican Village: A Study of Folk Life.* Chicago: University of Chicago Press, 1930.

———. *A Village That Chose Progress: Chan Kom Revisited.* Chicago: University of Chicago Press, 1950.

Redfield, Robert, and Alfonso Villa Rojas. *Chan Kom: A Maya Village.* Washington, D.C.: Carnegie Institution, 1934.

Sáenz, Moisés. *Antología de Moisés Sáenz.* Mexico City: Oasis, 1970.

———. *Carapan.* 3rd ed. Pátzcuaro, Michoacán: OEA-CREFAL, 1992. http://www.crefal.edu.mx/crefal25/images/publicaciones/libros/carapan.pdf.

———. *México íntegro.* Lima: Imprenta Torres Aguirre, 1939.

Social Science Research Council. *Consolidated List of Council Committees, 1924–1997.* New York: Social Science Research Council, 1998.

Stanford University, Faculty Senate. "Memorial Resolution: Felix Maxwell Keesing, 1902–1961." Available online at https://exhibits.stanford.edu/stanford-senate/catalog/hj389nj2398.

Steward, Julian Haynes. *The People of Puerto Rico: A Study in Social Anthropology.* Urbana.: University of Illinois Press, 1956.

Tannenbaum, Frank. "Agrarismo, Indianismo, y Nacionalismo." *Hispanic American Historical Review* 23, no. 3 (August 1943): 394–423.

Thompson, Laura. *Beyond the Dream: A Search for Meaning.* Mangilao: University of Guam Press, 1991.

———. *Fijian Frontier.* San Francisco: American Council, Institute of Pacific Relations, 1940.

Truman, Harry S. Executive Order 9710. Terminating the Office of Inter-American Affairs and Transferring Certain of Its Functions, Apr. 10, 1946. http://trumanlibrary.org/executiveorders/index.php?pid=444.

United States, Delegation to the International American Conference. *Report of the Delegates of the United States of America to the Sixth International Conference* of American States held at Habana, Cuba, January 16 to February 20, 1928. Washington, D.C.: Government Printing Office.

Universidad Nacional Autónoma de México. *Estudios antropológicos publicados en homenaje al doctor Manuel Gamio.* Mexico City: Universidad Nacional Autónoma de México, 1956.

Universidad Nacional Autónoma de México, Instituto de Investigaciones Sociales. *Etnografía de México: Síntesis monográficas.* Mexico City: Universidad Nacional Autónoma de México, Instituto de Investigaciones Sociales, 1957.

University of California, Berkeley, Institute of International Studies, and Center for Advanced Study in the Behavioral Sciences (Stanford, Calif.). *Trends in Social Science Research in Latin American Studies: A Conference Report: Some Aspects of a Conference.* Berkeley: Institute of International Studies, University of California, 1965.

University of Chicago, Committee on Human Development. *Environment and Education: A Symposium Held in Connection with the Fiftieth Anniversary Celebration of the University of Chicago.* Chicago: University of Chicago, 1942.

Vasconcelos, José, and Manuel Gamio. *Aspects of Mexican Civilization: Lectures on the Harris Foundation, 1926.* Chicago: University of Chicago Press, 1926.

Warner, W. Lloyd, Marcia Meeker, and Kenneth Eells. *Social Class in America: A Manual of Procedure for the Measurement of Social Status.* Chicago: Science Research Associates, 1949.

Wissler, Clark. *Final Report of the Committee on the Scientific Problems of Human Migration.* Washington, D.C.: National Research Council, 1929.

Yoakum, Clarence S., and Robert M. Yerkes. *Army Mental Tests.* New York: Henry Holt, 1920.

Secondary Sources

Aguirre Beltrán, Gonzalo. *Aportación de Vicente Lombardo Toledano al indigenismo mexicano.* Mexico City: Centro de Estudios Filosóficos, Políticos y Sociales Vicente Lombardo Toledano, 2003.

Alberto, Paulina L. *Terms of Inclusion: Black Intellectuals in Twentieth-Century Brazil.* Chapel Hill: University of North Carolina Press, 2011.

American Anthropological Association. "Uncensoring Franz Boas." Resolution adopted by a vote of the AAA membership, June 15, 2005. http://www.americananthro.org/ConnectWithAAA/Content.aspx? ItemNumber=2134.

Anderson, Warwick. "From Subjugated Knowledge to Conjugated Subjects: Science and Globalisation, or Postcolonial Studies of Science?" *Postcolonial Studies* 12, no. 4 (2009): 389–400.

Andrews, George Reid. *Afro-Latin America, 1800–2000.* New York: Oxford University Press, 2004.

Appelbaum, Nancy P. *Muddied Waters: Race, Region, and Local History in Colombia, 1846–1948.* Durham, N.C.: Duke University Press, 2003.

Appelbaum, Nancy P., Anne S. Macpherson, and Karin Alejandra Rosemblatt, eds. *Race and Nation in Modern Latin America*. Chapel Hill: University of North Carolina Press, 2003.

Armus, Diego. *The Ailing City: Health, Tuberculosis, and Culture in Buenos Aires, 1870–1950*. Durham, N.C.: Duke University Press, 2011.

Baker, Lee. *Anthropology and the Racial Politics of Culture*. Durham, N.C.: Duke University Press, 2010.

———. *From Savage to Negro: Anthropology and the Construction of Race, 1896–1954*. Berkeley: University of California Press, 1998.

Balibar, Etienne, and Immanuel Wallerstein. *Race, Nation, Class: Ambiguous Identities*. London: Verso, 1994.

Barsh, Russel Lawrence. "Progressive-Era Bureaucrats and the Unity of Twentieth-Century Indian Policy." *American Indian Quarterly* 15, no. 1 (Winter 1991): 1–17.

Barkan, Elazar. *The Retreat of Scientific Racism: Changing Concepts of Race in Britain and the United States between the World Wars*. Cambridge: Cambridge University Press, 1992.

Basave Benítez, Agustín F. *México mestizo: Análisis del nacionalismo mexicano en torno a la mestizofilia de Andrés Molina Enríquez*. Mexico City: Fondo de Cultura Económica, 1992.

Bashford, Alison, and Philippa Levine, eds. *The Oxford Handbook of the History of Eugenics*. New York: Oxford University Press, 2010.

Benton-Cohen, Katherine. "Other Immigrants: Mexicans and the Dillingham Commission." *Journal of American Ethnic History* 30, no. 2 (Spring 2011): 33–57.

Berger, Mark T. *Under Northern Eyes: Latin American Studies and U.S. Hegemony in the Americas, 1898–1990*. Bloomington: Indiana University Press, 1995.

Bertely Busquets, María, ed. *Historias, saberes indígenas y nuevas etnicidades en las escuelas*. Mexico City: Centro de Investigaciones y Estudios Superiores en Antropología Social, 2006.

Birn, Anne-Emanuelle. "Child Health in Latin America: Historiographic Perspectives and Challenges." *História, Ciências, Saúde-Manguinhos* 14, no. 3 (July–September 2007): 677–708.

———. "Six Seconds per Eyelid: The Medical Inspection of Immigrants at Ellis Island, 1892–1914." *Dynamis* 17 (1997): 281–316.

Blaut, J. M. "Diffusionism: A Uniformitarian Critique." *Annals of the Association of American Geographers* 77, no. 1 (March 1987): 30–47.

Blum, Ann S. *Domestic Economies: Family, Work, and Welfare in Mexico City, 1884–1943*. Lincoln: University of Nebraska Press, 2009.

Borges, Dain. "'Puffy, Ugly, Slothful and Inert': Degeneration in Brazilian Social Thought, 1880–1940." *Journal of Latin American Studies* 25, no. 2 (May 1993): 235–56.

Bourdieu, Pierre, and Loïc Wacquant. "On the Cunning of Imperialist Reason." *Theory, Culture, and Society* 16 (1996): 41–58.

Bowler, Peter J. *The Eclipse of Darwinism: Anti-Darwinian Evolution Theories in the Decades around 1900*. Baltimore: Johns Hopkins University Press, 1983.

————. *Evolution: The History of an Idea*. 25th anniversary ed. Berkeley: University of California Press, 2009.

Boyer, Christopher R. *Becoming Campesinos: Politics, Identity, and Agrarian Struggle in Postrevolutionary Mexico, 1920–1935*. Stanford: Stanford University Press, 2003.

Brading, David. "Manuel Gamio and Official Indigenismo in Mexico." *Bulletin of Latin American Research* 7, no. 1 (1988): 75–89.

Briggs, Laura. *Reproducing Empire: Race, Sex, Science, and U.S. Imperialism in Puerto Rico*. Berkeley: University of California Press, 2002.

Britton, John A. *Educación y radicalismo en México*. Mexico City: Secretaría de Educación Pública, Dirección General de Divulgación, 1976.

————. "Moisés Sáenz: Nacionalista mexicano." *Historia Mexicana* 22, no. 1 (1972): 77–97.

Bronfman, Alejandra. *Measures of Equality: Social Science, Citizenship, and Race in Cuba, 1902–1940*. Chapel Hill: University of North Carolina Press, 2004.

Bruno-Jofré, Rosa, and Carlos Martínez Valle. "Ruralizando a Dewey: El amigo americano, la colonización interna y la escuela de la acción en el México posrevolucionario (1921–1940)." *Encuentros sobre Educación* 10 (Fall 2009): 43–64.

Bueno, Cristina. "*Forjando Patrimonio*: The Making of Archaeological Patrimony in Porfirian Mexico." *Hispanic American Historical Review* 90, no. 2 (2010): 215–45.

Calderón Mólgora, Marco A. "Historias rurales y construcción del estado social, México y Estados Unidos." Paper delivered at XI Congreso Nacional de Investigación Educativa, Guanajuato, Guanajuato, November 18–22, 2013. http://www.comie.org.mx/congreso/memoriaelectronica/v11/docs/area_12/0244.pdf.

Calhoun, Craig J., Frederick Cooper, and Kevin W. Moore, eds. *Lessons of Empire: Imperial Histories and American Power*. New York: New Press, 2006.

Camiscioli, Elisa. *Reproducing the French Race: Immigration, Intimacy, and Embodiment in the Early Twentieth Century*. Durham, N.C.: Duke University Press, 2009.

Caplan, Karen D. *Indigenous Citizens: Local Liberalism in Early National Oaxaca and Yucatán*. Stanford: Stanford University Press, 2009.

Carson, John. "Army Alpha, Army Brass, and the Search for Army Intelligence." *Isis* 84, no. 2 (June 1993): 278–309.

————. *The Measure of Merit: Talents, Intelligence, and Inequality in the French and American Republics, 1750–1940*. Princeton, N.J.: Princeton University Press, 2007.

Casini, Paolo. "Evolutionary Theory and Philosophical Darwinism." In *The Theory of Evolution and Its Impact*, edited by Aldo Fasolo, 53–68. New York: Springer, 2012.

Cassata, Francesco. *Building the New Man: Eugenics, Racial Science and Genetics in Twentieth-Century Italy*. Translated by Erin O'Loughlin. New York: Central European Press, 2011.

Castañeda, Quetzil E. *In the Museum of Maya Culture: Touring Chichén Itzá*. Minneapolis: University of Minnesota Press, 1996.

———. "Stocking's Historiography of Influence: The 'Story of Boas,' Gamio and Redfield at the Cross-'Road to Light.'" *Critique of Anthropology* 23, no. 3 (2003): 235–63.

Chakrabarty, Dipesh. "Postcoloniality and the Artifice of History: Who Speaks for 'Indian' Pasts?" *Representations* 37 (1992): 1–26.

Chang, David A. *The Color of the Land: Race, Nation, and the Politics of Landownership in Oklahoma, 1832–1929.* Chapel Hill: University of North Carolina Press, 2010.

Chang, Jason Oliver. "Toward a Hemispheric Asian American History." In *The Oxford Handbook of Asian American History*, edited by David K. Yoo and Eiichiro Azuma, 30–49. New York: Oxford University Press, 2016.

Chatterjee, Paratha. *The Nation and Its Fragments: Colonial and Postcolonial Histories.* Princeton, N.J.: Princeton University Press, 1993.

Clark, Kim A. "Race, 'Culture,' and Mestizaje: The Statistical Construction of the Ecuadorian Nation, 1930– 1950." *Journal of Historical Sociology* 11, no. 2 (June 1998): 185–211.

Cogan, Doloris Coulter. *We Fought the Navy and Won.* Honolulu: University of Hawai'i Press, 2008.

Cohen, Theodore. "In Black and Brown: Intellectuals, Blackness, and Inter-Americanism in Mexico after 1910." Ph.D. diss., University of Maryland, College Park, 2013.

Conklin, Alice L. *In the Museum of Man: Race, Anthropology, and Empire in France, 1850–1950.* Ithaca, N.Y.: Cornell University Press, 2013.

Cooper, Frederick. "Race, Ideology, and the Perils of Comparative History." *American Historical Review* 101, no. 4 (October 1996): 1122–38.

Coronil, Fernando. "Beyond Occidentalism: Toward Nonimperial Geohistorical Categories." *Cultural Anthropology* 11, no. 1 (1996): 51–87.

Costa, Emilia Viotti da. *The Brazilian Empire: Myths and Histories.* 2nd ed. Chapel Hill: University of North Carolina Press, 2000.

Cotter, Joseph. *Troubled Harvest: Agronomy and Revolution in Mexico, 1880–2002.* Westport, Conn.: Praeger, 2003.

Cravens, Hamilton. *Before Head Start: The Iowa Station and America's Children.* Chapel Hill: University of North Carolina Press, 1993.

———. "History of the Social Sciences." *Osiris* 1 (1985): 183–207.

———. *The Triumph of Evolution: American Scientists and the Heredity-Environment Controversy, 1900–1941.* Philadelphia: University of Pennsylvania Press, 1978.

Dawson, Alexander S. "Histories and Memories of the Indian Boarding Schools in Mexico, Canada, and the United States." *Latin American Perspectives* 39, no. 5 (September 2012); 80–99.

———. *Indian and Nation in Revolutionary Mexico.* Tucson: University of Arizona Press, 2004.

de la Cadena, Marisol. *Indigenous Mestizos: The Politics of Race and Culture in Cuzco, Peru (1919–1991).* Durham, N.C.: Duke University Press, 2000.

de la Peña, Guillermo. "Nacionales y extranjeros en la historia de la antropología mexicana." In *La historia de la antropología en México: Fuentes y transmisión*, edited by Mechthild Rutsch, 41–81. Mexico City: Universidad Iberoamericana, Instituto Nacional Indigenista, Plaza y Valdés Editores, 1996.

Delpar, Helen. *The Enormous Vogue of Things Mexican: Cultural Relations between the United States and Mexico, 1920–1935.* Tuscaloosa: University of Alabama Press, 1995.

Dillingham, Alan Shane. "*Indigenismo* and Its Discontents: Bilingual Teachers and the Democratic Opening in the Mixteca Alta of Oaxaca, Mexico, 1954–1982." Ph.D. diss., University of Maryland, College Park, 2012.

Dorotinsky Alperstein, Deborah. "La puesta en escena de un archivo indigenista: El archivo México Indígena del Instituto de Investigaciones Sociales de la UNAM." *Cuicuilco* 14, no. 41 (September–December 2007): 43–77.

Drake, Paul W., and Lisa Hilbink. "Latin American Studies: Theory and Practice." In *The Politics of Knowledge: Area Studies and the Disciplines*, edited by David L. Szanton, 34–73. Berkeley: University of California Press, 2004.

Earle, Rebecca. *The Return of the Native: Indians and Myth-Making in Spanish America, 1810–1930.* Durham, N.C.: Duke University Press, 2007.

Ehrick, Christine. *The Shield of the Weak: Feminism and the State in Uruguay, 1903–1933.* Albuquerque: University of New Mexico Press, 2005.

Engerman, David C. *Modernization from the Other Shore: American Intellectuals and the Romance of Russian Development.* Cambridge, Mass.: Harvard University Press, 2004.

———. "Social Science in the Cold War." *Isis* 101, no. 2 (2010): 393–400.

Engerman, David C., Nils Gilman, Mark H. Haefele, and Michael E. Latham, eds. *Staging Growth: Modernization, Development, and the Global Cold War.* Amherst: University of Massachusetts Press, 2003.

Evans, R. Tripp. *Romancing the Maya: Mexican Antiquity in the American Imagination, 1820–1915.* Austin: University of Texas Press, 2004.

Fairchild, Amy L. *Science at the Borders: Immigrant Medical Inspection and the Shaping of the Modern Industrial Labor Force.* Baltimore: Johns Hopkins University Press, 2003.

Fallace, Thomas D. *Dewey and the Dilemma of Race: An Intellectual History, 1895–1922.* New York: Teachers College Press, 2011.

Fallaw, Ben. *Cárdenas Compromised: The Failure of Reform in Postrevolutionary Yucatán.* Durham, N.C.: Duke University Press, 2001.

Farish, Matthew. "Archiving Areas: The Ethnogeographic Board and the Second World War." *Annals of the Association of American Geographers* 95, no. 3 (2005): 663–79.

Fell, Claude. *José Vasconcelos: Los años del águila, 1920–1925: Educación, cultura e iberoamericanismo en el México postrevolucionario.* Mexico City: UNAM, 1989.

Ferrer, Ada. *Insurgent Cuba: Race, Nation, and Revolution, 1868–1898.* Chapel Hill: University of North Carolina Press, 1999.

FitzGerald, David Scott, and David Cook-Martin. *Culling the Masses: The Democratic Origins of Racist Immigration Policy in the Americas*. Cambridge, Mass.: Harvard University Press, 2014.

Flores, Ruben. *Backroads Pragmatists: Mexico's Melting Pot and Civil Rights in the United States*. Philadelphia: University of Pennsylvania Press, 2014.

Foster, George McClelland, and Gabriel Ospina. *Empire's Children: The People of Tzintzuntzan*. Mexico City: Imprenta Nuevo Mundo, 1948.

Freed, Stanley A. and Ruth S. Freed. *Clark Wissler, 1870–1947: A Biographical Memoir*. Washington, D.C.: National Academy of Sciences, 1992.

French, John D. "The Missteps of Anti-Imperialist Reason: Bourdieu, Wacquant and Hanchard's *Orpheus and Power*." *Theory, Culture and Society* 17, no. 1 (2000): 107–28.

García Mora, Carlos, and Esteban Krotz, eds. *La antropología en México: Panorama histórico*. 15 vols. Mexico City: Instituto Nacional de Antropología e Historia, 1987–88.

Gershenhorn, Jerry. *Melville J. Herskovits and the Racial Politics of Knowledge*. Lincoln: University of Nebraska Press, 2004.

Gerstle, Gary. *American Crucible: Race and Nation in the Twentieth Century*. Princeton, N.J.: Princeton University Press, 2002.

———. "Liberty, Coercion, and the Making of Americans." *Journal of American History* 84, no. 2 (September 1997): 524–58.

Gieryn, Thomas F. "City as Truth-Spot: Laboratories and Field-Sites in Urban Studies." *Social Studies of Science* 36, no. 1 (February 2006): 5–38.

Gillespie, Richard. *Manufacturing Knowledge: A History of the Hawthorne Experiments*. Cambridge: Cambridge University Press, 1991.

Gillingham, Paul, and Benjamin Smith, eds. *Dictablanda: Politics, Work, and Culture in Mexico, 1938–1968*. Durham, N.C.: Duke University Press, 2014.

Giraudo, Laura. "'No hay propiamente todavía Instituto': Los inicios del Instituto Indigenista Interamericano (abril 1940–marzo 1942)." *América Indígena* 62, no. 2 (April–June 2006): 6–32.

Giraudo, Laura, and Stephen E. Lewis, eds. Special issue: "Rethinking Indigenismo on the American Continent." *Latin American Perspectives* 39, no. 5 (September 2012).

Giraudo, Laura, and Juan Martín Sánchez, eds. *La ambivalente historia del indigenismo: Campo interamericano y trayectorias nacionales, 1940–1970*. Lima: Instituto de Estudios Peruanos, 2011.

Glick, Thomas F., Miguel Angel Puig-Samper, and Rosaura Ruiz, eds. *The Reception of Darwinism in the Iberian World: Spain, Spanish America, and Brazil*. Dordrecht: Kluwer Academic, 2001.

Godoy, Ricardo. "Franz Boas and His Plans for an International School of American Archaeology and Ethnology in Mexico." *Journal of the History of the Behavioral Sciences* 13 (1977): 228–42.

Goldstein, Alyosha, ed. *Formations of United States Colonialism*. Durham, N.C.: Duke University Press, 2014.

González Gamio, Ángeles. *Manuel Gamio: Una lucha sin fin*. Mexico City: Universidad Nacional Autónoma de México, 2003.

Gordon, Linda. *Woman's Body, Woman's Right: Birth Control in America.* New York: Grossman/Viking, 1976.

Gotkowitz, Laura, ed. *Histories of Race and Racism: The Andes and Mesoamerica from Colonial Times to the Present.* Durham, N.C.: Duke University Press, 2011.

Guerrier, Elizabeth. "Applying Anthropology in the Interest of the State: John Collier, the Indian Office, and the Bureau of Sociological Research." *Histories of Anthropology Annual* 3 (2007): 199–221.

Guridy, Frank Andre. *Forging Diaspora: Afro-Cubans and African Americans in a World of Empire and Jim Crow.* Chapel Hill: University of North Carolina Press, 2010.

Guy, Donna J. "The Politics of Pan-American Cooperation: Maternalist Feminism and the Child Rights Movement, 1913–1960." *Gender and History* 10, no. 3 (1998): 449–69.

Hale, Charles. "Political and Social Ideas in Latin America, 1870–1930." In *The Cambridge History of Latin America*, vol. 4, edited by Leslie Bethell, 367–44. Cambridge: Cambridge University Press, 1986.

Hale, Piers J. *Political Descent: Malthus, Mutualism, and the Politics of Evolution in Victorian England.* Chicago: University of Chicago Press, 2014.

Hanchard, Michael George, ed. *Racial Politics in Contemporary Brazil.* Durham, N.C.: Duke University Press, 1999.

Haraway, Donna Jeanne. *Primate Visions: Gender, Race, and Nature in the World of Modern Science.* New York: Routledge, 1989.

Harding, Sandra. *Sciences from Below: Feminisms, Postcolonialities, and Modernities.* Durham, N.C.: Duke University Press, 2008.

Hauptman, Laurence. "Africa View: John Collier, the British Colonial Service and American Indian Policy, 1933–1945." *Historian* 48, no. 3 (May 1986): 359–74.

Hayashi, Brian Masaru. *Democratizing the Enemy: The Japanese American Internment.* Princeton, N.J.: Princeton University Press, 2004.

Hernández Luna, Juan. "Polémica de Caso contra Lombardo sobre la Universidad." *Historia Mexicana* 19, no. 1 (July–September 1969): 87–104.

Hewitt de Alcántara, Cynthia. *Anthropological Perspectives on Rural Mexico.* London: Routledge, 1984.

Holt, Thomas C. *The Problem of Race in the Twenty-First Century.* Cambridge, Mass.: Harvard University Press, 2002.

Hsueh, Yeh. "The Hawthorne Experiments and the Introduction of Jean Piaget in American Industrial Psychology, 1929–1932." *History of Psychology* 5, no. 2 (May 2002): 163–89.

Igo, Sarah E. *The Averaged American: Surveys, Citizens, and the Making of a Mass Public.* Cambridge, Mass.: Harvard University Press, 2008.

Isaac, Joel. "The Human Sciences in Cold War America." *Historical Journal* 50, no. 3 (2007): 725–46.

———. *Working Knowledge: Making the Human Sciences from Parsons to Kuhn.* Cambridge, Mass.: Harvard University Press, 2012.

Jacobson, Matthew Frye. *Whiteness of a Different Color: European Immigrants and the Alchemy of Race.* Cambridge, Mass.: Harvard University Press, 1998.

Joseph, Alice, and Rosamond B. Spicer. *The Desert People: A Study of the Papago Indians.* Chicago: University of Chicago Press, 1949.

Joseph, Gilbert M. *Revolution from Without: Yucatán, Mexico, and the United States, 1880–1924.* Durham, N.C.: Duke University Press, 1987.

Joseph, Gilbert M., and Jürgen Buchenau. *Mexico's Once and Future Revolution: Social Upheaval and the Challenge of Rule since the Late Nineteenth Century.* Durham, N.C.: Duke University Press, 2013.

Joseph, Gilbert M., Catherine C. Legrand, and Ricardo D. Salvatore, eds. *Close Encounters of Empire: Writing the Cultural History of U.S.-Latin American Relations.* Durham, N.C.: Duke University Press, 1998.

Joseph, Gilbert M., and Daniel Nugent, eds. *Everyday Forms of State Formation: Revolution and the Negotiation of Rule in Modern Mexico.* Durham, N.C.: Duke University Press, 1994.

Kaplan, Amy, and Donald E. Pease, eds. *Cultures of United States Imperialism.* Durham, N.C.: Duke University Press, 1993.

Kelly, Lawrence C. "Anthropology and Anthropologists in the Indian New Deal." *Journal of the History of the Behavioral Sciences* 16, no. 1 (January 1980): 6–24.

———. *The Assault on Assimilation: John Collier and the Origins of Indian Policy Reform.* Albuquerque: University of New Mexico Press, 1983.

Kevles, Daniel. *In the Name of Eugenics: Genetics and the Uses of Human Heredity.* New York: Alfred A. Knopf, 1985.

Kline, Wendy. *Building a Better Race: Gender, Sexuality, and Eugenics from the Turn of the Century to the Baby Boom.* Berkeley: University of California Press, 2001.

Knight, Alan. "Cardenismo: Juggernaut or Jalopy?" *Journal of Latin American Studies* 26, no. 1 (February 1994): 73–107.

———. "Racism, Revolution, and Indigenismo: Mexico, 1910–1940." In *The Idea of Race in Latin America, 1870–1940*, edited by Richard Graham, 71–113. Austin: University of Texas Press, 1990.

Kourí, Emilio. "Interpreting the Expropriation of Indian Pueblo Lands in Porfirian Mexico: The Unexamined Legacies of Andrés Molina Enríquez." *Hispanic American Historical Review* 82, no. 1 (February 2002): 69–117.

———. "La invención del ejido." *Nexos* (January 1, 2015): http://www.nexos.com.mx/?p=23778.

Kramer, Paul A. "Power and Connection: Imperial Histories of the United States in the World." *American Historical Review* 116 (December 2011): 1348–91.

Krotz, Esteban. "Anthropologies of the South: Their Rise, Their Silencing, Their Characteristics." *Critique of Anthropology* 17, no. 3 (1997): 237–51.

Kuklick, Henrika. "Personal Equations: Reflections on the History of Fieldwork, with Special Reference to Sociocultural Anthropology." *Isis* 102, no. 1 (March 2011): 1–33.

———. "The Theory of Evolution and Cultural Anthropology." In *The Theory of Evolution and Its Impact*, edited by Aldo Fasolo, 83–102. New York: Springer, 2012.

Kunitz, Stephen J. "The Social Philosophy of John Collier." *Ethnohistory* 18, no. 3 (Summer 1971): 213–29.

Kuper, Adam. "Anthropology." In *The Cambridge History of Science*, vol. 7, edited by Theodore M. Porter and Dorothy Ross, 354–78. Cambridge: Cambridge University Press, 2003.

Larson, Brooke. *Trials of Nation Making: Liberalism, Race, and Ethnicity in the Andes, 1810–1910*. New York: Cambridge University Press, 2004.

Latour, Bruno. *We Have Never Been Modern*. Translated by Catherine Porter. Cambridge, Mass.: Harvard University Press, 1993.

Lavrin, Asunción. *Women, Feminism, and Social Change in Argentina, Chile, and Uruguay, 1890–1940*. Lincoln: University of Nebraska Press, 1995.

Lawson, Bill E., and Donald F. Koch. *Pragmatism and the Problem of Race*. Bloomington: Indiana University Press, 2004.

Lee, Raymond M. "'The Most Important Technique . . . ': Carl Rogers, Hawthorne, and the Rise and Fall of Nondirective Interviewing in Sociology." *Journal of the History of the Behavioral Sciences* 47, no. 2 (Spring 2011): 123–46.

Lemov, Rebecca M. *World as Laboratory: Experiments with Mice, Mazes, and Men*. New York: Hill and Wang, 2005.

Leonard, Thomas C. *Illiberal Reformers: Race, Eugenics, and American Economics in the Progressive Era*. Princeton, N.J.: Princeton University Press, 2016.

L'Estoile, Benoît de, Federico Neiburg, and Lygia Maria Sigaud, eds. *Empires, Nations, and Natives: Anthropology and State-Making*. Durham, N.C.: Duke University Press, 2005.

Lewis, Herbert S. "Boas, Darwin, Science, and Anthropology." *Current Anthropology* 42, no. 3 (June 2001): 381–406.

Lewis, Stephen E. *The Ambivalent Revolution: Forging State and Nation in Chiapas, 1910–1945*. Albuquerque: University of New Mexico Press, 2005.

Linstrum, Erik. "The Politics of Psychology in the British Empire, 1898–1960." *Past and Present* 215 (May 2012): 195–233.

Lomnitz-Adler, Claudio. *Deep México, Silent México: An Anthropology of Nationalism*. Minneapolis: University of Minnesota Press, 2001.

———. *Exits from the Labyrinth: Culture and Ideology in the Mexican National Space*. Berkeley: University of California Press, 1992.

López, Rick A. *Crafting Mexico: Intellectuals, Artisans, and the State after the Revolution*. Durham, N.C.: Duke University Press, 2010.

Loveman, Mara. *National Colors: Racial Classification and the State in Latin America*. Oxford: Oxford University Press, 2014.

Lomawaima, K. Tsianina. "Federalism: Native, Federal, and State Sovereignty." In *Why You Can't Teach United States History without American Indians*, edited by Susan Sleeper-Smith, Juliana Barr, Jean M. O'Brien, Nancy Shoemaker, and Scott Manning Stevens, 273–86. Chapel Hill: University of North Carolina Press, 2015.

Loyo Bravo, Engracia. "¿Escuelas o empresas? Las centrales agrícolas y las regionales campesinas (1926–1934)." *Mexican Studies/Estudios Mexicanos* 20, no. 1 (Winter 2004): 69–98.

———. *Gobiernos revolucionarios y educación popular en México, 1911–1928*. Mexico City: El Colegio de México, Centro de Estudios Históricos, 1999.

Mallon, Florencia E. *Peasant and Nation: The Making of Postcolonial Mexico and Peru*. Berkeley: University of California Press, 1995.

———, ed. *Decolonizing Native Histories: Collaboration, Knowledge, and Language in the Americas*. Durham, N.C.: Duke University Press, 2012.

Matchett, Karin. "At Odds over Inbreeding: An Abandoned Attempt at Mexico/United States Collaboration to 'Improve' Mexican Corn, 1940–1950." *Journal of the History of Biology* 39, no. 2 (Summer 2006): 345–72.

McCormick, Gladys I. *The Logic of Compromise in Rural Mexico: How the Countryside Was Key to the Emergence of Authoritarianism*. Chapel Hill: University of North Carolina Press, 2016.

McCoy, Alfred, and Francisco A. Scarano, eds. *Colonial Crucible: Empire in the Making of the Modern American State*. Madison: University of Wisconsin Press, 2009.

McNamara, Patrick. *Sons of the Sierra: Juárez, Díaz, and the People of Ixtlán, Oaxaca, 1855–1920*. Chapel Hill: University of North Carolina Press, 2012.

Medina, Andrés. *Recuentos y figuraciones: Ensayos de antropología mexicana*. Mexico City: Universidad Nacional Autónoma de México, Instituto de Investigaciones Antropológicas, 1996.

Mehta, Uday S. "Liberal Strategies of Exclusion." *Politics and Society* 18, no. 4 (December 1990): 427–54.

Mejía Zúñiga, Raúl. *Moisés Sáenz, educador de México*. 2nd ed. México: Federación Editorial Mexicana, 1976.

Merkx, Gilbert. "Editor's Foreword." *Latin American Research Review* 29, no. 1 (1994): 4–5.

———. "Editor's Foreword." *Latin American Research Review* 30, no. 1 (1995): 1–4.

Miranda, Marisa, and Gustavo Vallejo, eds. *Derivas de Darwin: Cultura y política en clave biológica*. Buenos Aires: Siglo XXI, 2010.

———. "Sociodarwinismo y psicología de la inferioridad de los pueblos hispanoamericanos: Notas sobre el pensamiento de Carlos Bunge." *Frenia* 6, no. 1 (2006): 57–77.

Molina, Natalia. *Fit to Be Citizens? Public Health and Race in Los Angeles, 1879–1939*. Berkeley: University of California Press, 2006.

———. *How Race Is Made in America: Immigration, Citizenship, and the Historical Power of Racial Scripts*. Berkeley: University of California Press, 2014.

Moreton-Robinson, Aileen, ed. *Critical Indigenous Studies: Engagements in First World Locations*. Tucson: University of Arizona Press, 2016.

Morgan, Mindy J. "'Working' from the Margins: Documenting American Indian Participation in the New Deal Era." In *Why You Can't Teach United States History without American Indians*, edited by Susan Sleeper-Smith, Juliana Barr, Jean M. O'Brien, Nancy Shoemaker, and Scott Manning Stevens, 181–96. Chapel Hill: University of North Carolina Press, 2015.

Nahmad Sitton, Salomón, and Thomas Weaver. "Manuel Gamio, el primer antropólogo aplicado y su relación con la antropología norteamericana." *América Indígena* 50, no. 4 (1992): 291–321.

Neiburg, Federico G., and Mariano Ben Plotkin, eds. *Intelectuales y expertos: La constitución del conocimiento social en la Argentina*. Buenos Aires: Paidós, 2004.

Ngai, Mae M. *Impossible Subjects: Illegal Aliens and the Making of Modern America.* Princeton, N.J.: Princeton University Press, 2004.

Nobles, Melissa. *Shades of Citizenship: Race and the Census in Modern Politics.* Stanford: Stanford University Press, 2000.

Numbers, Ronald L., and John Stenhouse, eds. *Disseminating Darwinism: The Role of Place, Race, Religion, and Gender.* Cambridge: Cambridge University Press, 1991.

Nunes, Eduardo Silveira Netto. "La infancia latinoamericana y el Instituto Internacional Americano de Protección a la Infancia (1916–1940)." In *Nuevas miradas a la historia de la infancia en América Latina: Entre prácticas y representaciones,* edited by Elena Jackson and Susana Sosenski, 273–302. Mexico City: Rústicas, 2012. Available online at http://www.historicas.unam.mx/publicaciones/publicadigital/libros/miradas/miradas.html.

Nye, Robert A. "The Rise and Fall of the Eugenics Empire: Recent Perspectives on the Impact of Biomedical Thought in Modern Society." *Historical Journal* 36, no. 3 (September 1993): 687–700.

O'Connor, Alice. *Poverty Knowledge: Social Science, Social Policy, and the Poor in Twentieth-Century U.S. History.* Princeton, N.J.: Princeton University Press, 2001.

Olivé Negrete, Julio César. *La antropología mexicana.* [Mexico City]: Colegio Mexicano de Antropólogos, 1981.

Olvera Serrano, Margarita. *Economía y sociología en México: Revistas especializadas, liderazgos y procesos de institucionalización, 1928–1959.* Mexico City: Universidad Autónoma Metropolitana-Azcapotzalco, 2013.

———. "La institucionalización de la economía y de la sociología como disciplinas científicas modernas en México: Una reconstrucción historiográfica a través de sus revistas especializadas (1928–1958)." Ph.D. diss., Universidad Autónoma Metropolitana, Azcapotzalco, 2011.

———. "La primera socialización intelectual de Lucio Mendieta y Núñez." *Sociológica* 14 (1999): 91–122.

Omura, Kanae. "Manuel Gamio y Japón." *Revista de la Universidad de México* no. 19 (2005): 89–94.

Orosco, Jose-Antonio. "José Vasconcelos, White Supremacy and the Silence of American Pragmatism." *Inter-American Journal of Philosophy* 2, no. 2 (December 2011): 1–13.

Palacios, Guillermo. "Postrevolutionary Intellectuals, Rural Readings and the Shaping of the 'Peasant Problem' in Mexico: *El Maestro Rural,* 1932–34." *Journal of Latin American Studies* 30, no. 2 (May 1998): 309–39.

———. *La pluma y el arado: Los intelectuales pedagogos y la construcción sociocultural del "problema campesino" en México, 1932–1934.* Mexico City: Centro de Estudios Históricos, Colegio de México, 1999.

Parman, Donald Lee. *The Navajos and the New Deal.* New Haven, Conn.: Yale University Press, 1976.

Pateman, Carol. *The Sexual Contract.* Stanford: Stanford University Press, 1988.

Paul, Diane. *Controlling Human Heredity: 1865 to the Present.* Atlantic Highlands, N.J.: Humanities Press, 1995.

———. "Eugenics and the Left." *Journal of the History of Ideas* 45, no. 4 (October–December 1984): 567–90.

———. "'In the Interests of Civilization': Marxist Views of Race and Culture in the Nineteenth Century." *Journal of the History of Ideas* 42, no. 1 (January–March 1981): 115–38.

———. "The Selection of the 'Survival of the Fittest.'" *Journal of the History of Biology* 21, no. 3 (Autumn 1988): 411–24.

Philp, Kenneth R. *John Collier's Crusade for Indian Reform, 1920–54.* Tucson: University of Arizona Press, 1977.

Pick, Daniel. *Faces of Degeneration: A European Disorder, c. 1848–c. 1918.* New York: Cambridge University Press, 1989.

Pinet, Alexandro. "Conmemoración del 60 aniversario de la ENAH." In *60 años de la ENAH,* edited by Eyra Cárdenas Barahona, 15–30. Mexico City: La Escuela, [c. 1999].

Porter, Theodore M., and Dorothy Ross, eds. *The Cambridge History of Science.* Vol. 7, *The Modern Social Sciences.* Cambridge: Cambridge University Press, 2003.

Price, David. "'The Shameful Business': Leslie Spier on the Censure of Franz Boas." *History of Anthropology Newsletter* 28, no. 2 (December 2001): 9–12.

Prakash, Gyan. "Writing Post-Orientalist Histories of the Third World: Perspectives from Indian Historiography." *Comparative Studies in Society and History* 32, no. 2 (April 1990): 383–408.

Purcell, Edward A., Jr. *The Crisis of Democratic Theory: Scientific Naturalism and the Problem of Value.* Lexington: University Press of Kentucky, 1973.

Purnell, Jennie. *Popular Movements and State Formation in Revolutionary Mexico: The Agraristas and Cristeros of Michoacán.* Durham, N.C.: Duke University Press, 1999.

Putnam, Lara. *Radical Moves: Caribbean Migrants and the Politics of Race in the Jazz Age.* Chapel Hill: University of North Carolina Press, 2013.

Ramsden, Edmund. "Carving Up Population Science: Eugenics, Demography and the Controversy over the 'Biological Law' of Population Growth." *Social Studies of Science* 32, no. 5–6 (October–December 2002): 857–99.

———. "Eugenics from the New Deal to the Great Society: Genetics, Demography and Population Quality." *Studies in History and Philosophy of Science, Part C* 39 (2008): 391–406.

———. "Social Demography and Eugenics in the Interwar United States." *Population and Development Review* 29, no. 4 (December 2003): 547–93.

Reinhardt, Akim D. "A Crude Replacement: The Indian New Deal, Indirect Colonialism, and Pine Ridge Reservation." *Journal of Colonialism and Colonial History* 6, no. 1 (Spring 2005). DOI 10.1353/cch.2005.0019.

Romero Contreras, A. Tonatiuh. *Historia de la ciencia en México: La antropología.* [Mexico City]: Universidad Autónoma del Estado de México, 2001.

Rodriguez, Julia. "Beyond Prejudice and Pride: The Human Sciences in Nineteenth- and Twentieth-Century Latin America." *Isis* 104, no. 4 (2013): 807–17.

———. *Civilizing Argentina: Science, Medicine, and the Modern State*. Chapel Hill: University of North Carolina Press, 2006.

Romo, Anadelia A. *Brazil's Living Museum: Race, Reform, and Tradition in Bahia*. Chapel Hill: University of North Carolina Press, 2010.

Rosemblatt, Karin Alejandra. "Modernization, Dependency, and the Global in Mexican Critiques of Anthropology." *Journal of Global History* 9, no. 1 (March 2014): 94–121.

———. "Other Americas: Transnationalism, Scholarship, and the Culture of Poverty in Mexico and the United States." *Hispanic American Historical Review* 89, no. 4 (2009): 603–41.

———. "Sexuality and Biopower in Chile and Latin America." *Political Power and Social Theory* 15 (2001): 315–72.

Rosier, Paul C. "'The Old System Is No Success': The Blackfeet Nation's Decision to Adopt the Indian Reorganization Act of 1934." *American Indian Culture and Research Journal* 23, no. 1 (1999): 1–37.

———. "'The Real Indians, Who Constitute the Real Tribe': Class, Ethnicity, and IRA Politics on the Blackfeet Reservation." *Journal of American Ethnic History* 18, no. 4 (Summer 1999): 3–39.

Ross, Dorothy. *The Origins of American Social Science*. New York: Cambridge University Press, 1991.

Rowe, John Carlos, ed. *Post-Nationalist American Studies*. Berkeley: University of California Press, 2000.

Rusco, Elmer R. *A Fateful Time: The Background and Legislative History of the Indian Reorganization Act*. Reno: University of Nevada Press, 2000.

Rutsch, Mechthild. *Entre el campo y el gabinete: Nacionales y extranjeros en la profesionalización de la antropología mexicana (1877–1920)*. Mexico City: Instituto Nacional de Antropología e Historia, 2007.

———, ed. *La historia de la antropología en México: Fuentes y transmisión*. Mexico City: Universidad Iberoamericana, Instituto Nacional Indigenista, Plaza y Valdés, 1996.

Rutsch, Mechthild, and Mette Marie Wacher, eds. *Alarifes, amanuenses y evangelistas: Tradiciones, personajes, comunidades y narrativas de la ciencia en México*. Mexico City: Instituto Nacional de Antropología e Historia/ Universidad Iberoamericana, 2004.

Safford, Frank. "Race, Integration, and Progress: Elite Attitudes and the Indian in Colombia, 1750–1870." *Hispanic American Historical Review* 71, no. 1 (February 1991): 1–33.

Saldaña-Portillo, María Josefina. *Indian Given: Racial Geographies across Mexico and the United States*. Durham, N.C.: Duke University Press, 2016.

Saldívar, Emiko. "Everyday Practices of Indigenismo: An Ethnography of Anthropology and the State in Mexico." *Journal of Latin American and Caribbean Anthropology* 16, no. 1 (April 2011): 67–89.

———. "'It's Not Race, It's Culture': Untangling Racial Politics in Mexico." *Latin American and Caribbean Ethnic Studies* 9, no. 1 (January 2014): 89–108.

Saldívar, Emiko, and Casey Walsh. "Racial and Ethnic Identities in Mexican Statistics." *Journal of Iberian and Latin American Research* 20, no. 3 (2014): 455–75.

Sandeen, Eric J. *Picturing an Exhibition: The Family of Man and 1950s America.* Albuquerque: University of New Mexico Press, 1995.

Scarzanella, Eugenia. "Criminología, eugenesia y medicina social en el debate entre científicos argentinos e italianos, 1912–1941." In *Ideas, cultura e historia en la creación intelectual latinoamericana: Siglos XIX y XX,* edited by Hugo Troncoso and Carmen Sierra, 217–34. Quito: Ediciones Abya-Yala, 1997.

Schiavone Camacho, Julia María. *Chinese Mexicans: Transpacific Migration and the Search for a Homeland, 1910–1960.* Chapel Hill: University of North Carolina Press, 2012.

Schwartz, E. A. "Red Atlantis Revisited: Community and Culture in the Writings of John Collier." *American Indian Quarterly* 18, no. 4 (1994): 507–31.

Seigel, Micol. "Beyond Compare: Comparative Method after the Transnational Turn." *Radical History Review* 91 (2005): 62–90.

———. *Uneven Encounters: Making Race and Nation in Brazil and the United States.* Durham, N.C.: Duke University Press, 2009.

Selcer, Perrin. "The View from Everywhere: Disciplining Diversity in Post–World War II International Social Science." *Journal of the History of the Behavioral Sciences* 45, no. 4 (Fall 2009): 309–29.

Shapin, Steven. "Placing the View from Nowhere: Historical and Sociological Problems in the Location of Science." *Transactions of the Institute of British Geographers* 23, no. 1 (1998): 5–12.

Shukla, Sandhya, and Heidi Tinsman, eds. *Imagining Our Americas: Toward a Transnational Frame.* Durham, N.C.: Duke University Press, 2007.

Shumsky, Neil Larry. "Zangwill's 'The Melting Pot': Ethnic Tensions on Stage." *American Quarterly* 27, no. 1 (March 1975): 29–41.

Silber, Norman. "Chase, Stuart." *American National Biography Online* (2000): http://www.anb.org/articles/14/14-00950.html.

Simpson, Audra, and Andrea Smith, eds. *Theorizing Native Studies.* Durham, N.C.: Duke University Press, 2014.

Simpson, Eyler Newton. *The Ejido: Mexico's Way Out.* Chapel Hill: University of North Carolina Press, 1937.

Sleeper-Smith, Susan, Juliana Barr, Jean M. O'Brien, Nancy Shoemaker, and Scott Manning Stevens, eds. *Why You Can't Teach United States History without American Indians.* Chapel Hill: University of North Carolina Press, 2015.

Sommer, Doris. *Foundational Fictions: The National Romances of Latin America.* Berkeley: University of California Press, 1991.

Spenser, Daniela. "El viaje de Vicente Lombardo Toledano al mundo del porvenir." *Desacatos* (September–December 2010): 77–96.

Spicer, Edward H. "Early Applications of Anthropology in North America." In *Perspectives on Anthropology, 1976,* edited by Anthony F. C. Wallace, Laurence Angel, Richard Fox, Nancy McLendon, Rachel Sady, and Robert Sharer, 116–41. Washington, D.C.: American Anthropological Association, 1997.

Stavans, Ilan. *José Vasconcelos: The Prophet of Race*. New Brunswick, N.J.: Rutgers University Press, 2011.

Stehn, Alexander V. "From Positivism to 'Anti-Positivism' in Mexico: Some Notable Continuities." In *Latin American Positivism: New Historical and Philosophic Essays*, edited by Gregory Gilson and Irving Levinson, 49–81. Lanham, Md.: Lexington Books, 2012.

Steinmetz, George, ed. *Sociology and Empire: The Imperial Entanglements of a Discipline*. Durham, N.C.: Duke University Press, 2013.

Stepan, Nancy Leys. *"The Hour of Eugenics": Race, Gender, and Nation in Latin America*. Ithaca, N.Y.: Cornell University Press, 1991.

Stern, Alexandra Minna. "Buildings, Boundaries, and Blood: Medicalization and Nation-Building on the. U.S.-Mexico Border, 1910–1930." *Hispanic American Historical Review* 79, no. 1 (February 1999): 41–81.

———. "An Empire of Tests: Psychometrics and the Paradoxes of Nationalism in the Americas." In *Haunted by Empire: Geographies of Intimacy in North American History*, edited by Ann Laura Stoler, 325–43. Durham, N.C.: Duke University Press, 2006.

———. *Eugenic Nation: Faults and Frontiers of Better Breeding in Modern America*. Chapel Hill: University of North Carolina Press, 2015.

———. "'The Hour of Eugenics' in Veracruz, Mexico: Radical Politics, Public Health, and Latin America's Only Sterilization Law." *Hispanic American Historical Review* 91, no. 3 (2011): 431–43.

———. "Responsible Mothers and Normal Children: Eugenics, Nationalism, and Welfare in Post-Revolutionary Mexico, 1920–1940." *Journal of Historical Sociology* 12, no. 4 (1999): 369–97.

Stocking, George F., Jr. *After Tylor: British Social Anthropology, 1888–1951*. Madison: University of Wisconsin Press, 1995.

———, ed. *The Ethnographer's Magic and Other Essays in the History of Anthropology*. Madison: University of Wisconsin Press, 1992.

———. *Race, Culture and Evolution: Essays in the History of Anthropology*. New York: Free Press, 1968.

———. *Romantic Motives: Essays on Anthropological Sensibility*. Madison: University of Wisconsin Press, 1989.

Stoler, Ann Laura. *Carnal Knowledge and Imperial Power: Race and the Intimate in Colonial Rule*. Berkeley: University of California Press, 2002.

———. "Imperial Formations and the Opacities of Rule." In *Lessons of Empire: Imperial Histories and American Power*, edited by Craig J. Calhoun, Frederick Cooper, and Kevin W. Moore, 48–60. New York: New Press, 2006.

———. *Race and the Education of Desire: Foucault's "History of Sexuality" and the Colonial Order of Things*. Durham, N.C.: Duke University Press, 1995.

———. "Tense and Tender Ties: The Politics of Comparison in North American History and (Post)Colonial Studies." *Journal of American History* 88, no. 3 (December 2001): 829–65.

Suárez y López Guazo, Laura. *Eugenesia y racismo en México*. Mexico City: Universidad Nacional Autónoma de México, 2005.

———. "Evolucionismo, mejoramiento racial y medicina legal." In *La ética y los avances recientes de la ciencia y la técnica*. Mexico City: Universidad Autónoma de Metropolitana-Xochimilco, CSH, Departamento de Educación y Comunicación, 2005.

Szanton, David, ed. *The Politics of Knowledge: Area Studies and the Disciplines*. Berkeley: University of California Press, 2004.

Telles, Edward, and the Project on Ethnicity and Race in Latin America (PERLA). *Pigmentocracies: Ethnicity, Race, and Color in Latin America*. Chapel Hill: University of North Carolina Press, 2014.

Tenorio Trillo, Mauricio. "Stereophonic Scientific Modernisms: Social Science between Mexico and the United States, 1880s–1930s." *Journal of American History* 86, no. 3 (1999): 1156–87.

Tilley, Helen. *Africa as a Living Laboratory: Empire, Development, and the Problem of Scientific Knowledge, 1870–1950*. Chicago: University of Chicago Press, 2011.

Turda, Marius, and Aaron Gillette. *Latin Eugenics in Comparative Perspective*. London: Bloomsbury Academic, 2014.

Urías Horcasitas, Beatriz. *Historias secretas del racismo en México (1920–1950)*. Mexico City: Tusquets Editores, 2007.

Vargas Lozano, Gabriel. "La polémica Caso-Lombardo (revisitada)." In *El esbozo histórico de la filosofía en México (siglo XX) y otros ensayos*, 1–10. Mexico City: Facultad de Filosofía y Letras de la Universidad Autónoma de Nueva León, Consejo para la Cultura y las Artes, Nuevo León, 2005. Available online at http://csh.izt.uam.mx/cen_doc/cefilibe/demo/Esbozo_libro/esbozo.html.

Vaughan, Mary Kay. *Cultural Politics in Revolution: Teachers, Peasants, and Schools in Mexico, 1930–1940*. Tucson: University of Arizona Press, 1997.

Vaughan, Mary Kay, and Stephen E. Lewis, eds. *The Eagle and the Virgin: Nation and Cultural Revolution in Mexico, 1920–1940*. Durham, N.C.: Duke University Press, 2006.

Verran, Helen. "A Postcolonial Moment in Science Studies: Alternative Firing Regimes of Environmental Scientists and Aboriginal Landowners." *Social Studies of Science* 32, no. 5–6 (December 2002): 729–62.

———. *Science and an African Logic*. Chicago: University of Chicago Press, 2001.

Villoro, Luis. *Los grandes momentos del indigenismo en México*. Mexico City: Colegio de México, 1950.

Wade, Peter. *Race, Nature, Culture: An Anthropological Perspective*. London: Pluto Press, 2002.

———. *Race and Ethnicity in Latin America*. 2nd ed. London: Pluto Press, 2010.

———. "Rethinking *Mestizaje*: Ideology and Lived Experience." *Journal of Latin American Studies* 37 (May 2005): 239–57.

Walch, Michael C. "Terminating the Indian Termination Policy." *Stanford Law Review* 35, no. 6 (July 1983): 1181–215.

Walsh, Casey. "Eugenic Acculturation: Manuel Gamio, Migration Studies, and the Anthropology of Development in Mexico, 1910–1940." *Latin American Perspectives* 31, no. 5 (2004): 118–45.

Walsh, Sarah Irene. "Reason and Faith: A Study of Interwar Chilean Eugenic Discourse, 1900–1950." Ph.D. diss., University of Maryland, College Park, 2013.

Weinstein, Barbara. *The Color of Modernity: São Paulo and the Making of Race and Nation in Brazil*. Durham, N.C.: Duke University Press, 2015.

———. "Erecting and Erasing Boundaries: Can We Combine the 'Indo' and the 'Afro' in Latin American Studies?" *Estudios Interdisciplinarios de América Latina y el Caribe* 19, no. 1 (2008): 129–44.

Wilcox, Clifford. *Robert Redfield and the Development of American Anthropology*. Lanham, Md.: Lexington Books, 2004.

Willey, Gordon R. *Alfred Vincent Kidder, 1885–1963: A Biographical Memoir*. Washington, D.C.: National Academy of Sciences, 1967. Available online at http://www.nasonline.org/publications/biographical-memoirs/memoir-pdfs/kidder-alfred.pdf.

Wilkie, James Wallace, and Edna Monzón de Wilkie. *Frente a la Revolución Mexicana: 17 protagonistas de la etapa constructiva: Entrevistas de historia oral*. Mexico City: Universidad Autónoma Metropolitana, 1995.

Wolfe, Patrick. *Settler Colonialism and the Transformation of Anthropology: The Politics and Poetics of an Ethnographic Event*. London: Cassell, 1999.

Young, Elliot. *Alien Nation: Chinese Migration in the Americas from the Coolie Era through World War II*. Chapel Hill: University of North Carolina Press, 2014.

Young, Robert J. C. *Colonial Desire: Hybridity in Theory, Culture and Race*. London: Routledge, 1995.

Yurchenco, Henrietta. *Around the World in 80 Years: A Memoir, a Musical Odyssey*. Point Richmond, Va.: MRI, 2002.

Zimmerman, Andrew. *Alabama in Africa: Booker T. Washington, the German Empire, and the Globalization of the New South*. Princeton, N.J.: Princeton University Press, 2010.

Zimmerman, Eduardo A. "Racial Ideas and Social Reform: Argentina, 1890–1916." *Hispanic American Historical Review* 72, no. 1 (February 1992): 23–46.

Index

AAA (American Anthropological Association), 19, 63
AAU (Applied Anthropology Unit of U.S. Indian Service), 112, 113, 204n25
Academic disciplines, 3, 4, 24. *See also names of individual disciplines*
Acculturation, 24, 85, 171, 204n25; Collier and, 102, 103–4, 110–11, 113; in Latin America, 84–86; of Native peoples, 91, 95; race and, 50, 104; science of, 101–34, 127, 199n67. *See also* Assimilation; Culture, cultures
Acoma Pueblo, 112
Actopan, 61, 143
Adaptation, evolution and, 22, 23, 44, 144–45
Administration: colonialism and postwar governance and, 125–32, 180; of Native peoples, 173–74
Advisory Committee on Interracial Relations (SSRC), 78
Africa, Africans, 25, 32, 35, 80, 81–84, 131
African Americans, 2, 4, 25, 61–62, 76, 78–80, 176, 184n3
Afro-descendant populations, 6, 24, 79, 82, 84, 156
Aggregation, 15, 138
Agrarian laws and reform, 41, 93, 135. *See also* Lands and landholding, Native
Agraristas, 97
Agriculture, 19, 141, 146, 167; livestock, 112, 113; Native, 25, 94, 96, 137, 140; reform and, 18, 23
Agronomists, 3, 57, 97, 142
Alanís Patiño, Emilio, 57, 164–66, 172, 209n33

Alaska, 130, 180
Alemán, Miguel, 131
Alexander, Will, 79
Allotment system, 19, 20, 89, 97, 172, 201n15
Amalgamation, 48, 62, 66
América Indígena (IAII journal), 126, 169; debate in, 175, 177, 182
American Indian Defense Association, 98, 105
Americanists' Congresses, 33, 98, 195n7
Americanization, 14, 18, 25, 67, 77, 103, 104, 118
American Museum of Natural History (New York), 32
American Psychological Association, 63
Americas, 32, 48, 87, 98, 106, 119–20, 131–32, 174. *See also* Central America; Latin America; North America; South America
Anarchism, anarchists, 103, 104, 179
Anglo-Americans, 4, 8, 20, 27, 28, 31, 76, 84, 113; eugenics of, 27, 48, 49
Anglo-Europeans, 6
Anglo-Saxons, 56, 177
Anthropologists, 3, 12, 19, 21, 24, 90, 97, 102, 112, 170, 173, 179, 182; colonialism and, 117, 118; IS and, 14, 116. *See also* Intellectuals and scholars; Intellectuals and scholars, Mexican; Intellectuals and scholars, U.S.
Anthropology, 75, 80, 94, 115, 143, 182, 185n24, 204–5n44; applied, 30, 107, 112, 118; Boas and, 3, 83; colonialism and, 122, 185n20, 204–5n44;

England, English, 2, 36, 37, 43, 48.
  See also Great Britain; Language,
  languages: English
Environment, 23, 28, 34, 57, 68, 72, 79,
  145; heredity and, 58, 81; in neo-
  Lamarckianism, 22, 53
Epistemology, evolution and, 156–59
Equality, 7, 36, 59, 135, 147; liberalism
  and, 5, 18
Escuela Nacional Preparatoria
  (National Preparatory School), 142
Escuelas Normales Rurales (Normal
  Rural Schools), 142
Escuelas Vocacionales Agrícolas
  (Agricultural Vocational Schools),
  141, 143
Eskimos, 129
Estrada Discua, Raúl, 157
Ethnicity, 9, 15, 25, 38, 50, 100, 129, 134,
  144, 168; biological markers of, 6, 7
  ethnic groups and, 93, 156
Ethnographic relativism, evolution
  and, 33–37
Ethnography, ethnographers, 3, 15, 35,
  47, 91, 141, 152, 157; Collier and, 90,
  179; in Mexico, 90, 157
Ethnohistorians, 139
Ethnology, 32
Ethnos (journal), 56
Eugenics, eugenicists, 68, 79, 80, 106,
  187n12, 194n86; Anglo-American,
  27, 49, 51; biological determinism
  and, 54, 62; child welfare and,
  51–58; hardline, 28, 31; immigration
  and, 51–58, 63–68; international
  conferences on, 51, 54–56, 65; Latin,
  27, 31, 55, 176; movement of, 25,
  67; Nordic, 56–57; population and,
  51–58; schism of, 27–28; selective,
  26, 27, 57; theories of, 17, 54
Eugenics Record Office, 71
Europe, Europeans, 2, 4, 9, 25, 38, 49,
  165; immigration from, 19, 64, 65,
  73, 103. *See also* Colonialism; *and
  names of European nations*

Evolution, 4, 6, 15, 20, 39, 87, 139, 149,
  152, 167, 178, 182, 187n16, 207nn4, 5;
  adaptation and, 23, 144–45; culture
  and, 24, 58, 59, 168; epistemology
  of compilation and, 156–59;
  ethnographic relativism and, 33–37;
  Gamio and, 37–40, 169; immigrants
  and, 60–61; Mexico and, 44, 168;
  paradigms of, 2, 17, 22, 138, 146, 179;
  science and, 21, 42–45, 191n40
Evolutionism, evolutionists, 24, 103;
  cultural, 24, 59, 135–68, 170–71, 181
Exceptionalism: Mexican, 7, 28; U.S.,
  28, 97, 185n14
Exclusion, 47, 48
Expertise, Native agency and, 107–14
Exploitation: colonialism and, 174, 175;
  of Native Mexicans, 40
Extermination of Native peoples, 174

Fábila, Alfonso, 144–46
Fascism, fascists, 116, 120–21, 125, 128;
  Nazis, 26, 167
Federal Bureau of Investigation, 124
Feminism, feminists, 26, 51, 71, 187n12
Fieldwork, fieldworkers, 10–13, 74,
  101, 115, 132, 159, 185n24. *See also*
  Anthropologists; Anthropology;
  Ethnography, ethnographers
Fiji, 114, 116
First Conference of Philologists and
  Linguists (1939), 148
First Congress of Mexican Universities
  (1933), 143
First International Eugenics
  Conference (London, 1912), 51, 56,
  192n68
First Pan-American Child Congress
  (Buenos Aires, 1916), 51, 54
First Pan-American Conference
  on Eugenics and Homiculture
  (Havana, 1927), 51, 54–55
First Universal Races Congress
  (London, 1911), 56
Folk culture and folklore, 2, 33, 60, 87

IS (U.S. Indian Service), 14, 20, 91, 95, 97, 99, 108, 111–12, 117–19, 173, 176, 180; acculturation and, 101, 204n25; Commissioner of, 20, 134; experimentation of, 126–27; Native Americans and, 113, 181; personnel of, 116, 120, 122, 131; Poston Japanese American internment camp and, 99, 123–25. *See also* AAU; Collier, John

Isolationism, 128, 132

Italians, 56, 57, 65

IUSIPP (International Union for the Scientific Investigation of Population Problems), 27, 28, 51

Ixmiquilpan, 164

James, William, 105

Japan, 38, 39, 154; U.S. occupation of, 99, 124, 126, 133, 181

Japanese, 99, 116, 129, 202n22; Gamio and, 39, 101, 154, 209n41; as immigrants, 65, 75

Japanese Americans, 66; World War II internment of, 14, 99, 101, 122–25, 129, 132. *See also* Poston, Arizona, Japanese American internment camp

Jenks, Albert, 72, 202n23

Jesuits, 106

Jews, 68, 74

Jim Crow, 6–7, 131, 171. *See also* Segregation

Jiménez, Dr. Carlos, 54

Johnson, Charles, 79

Johnson-Reed Act (1924), 19

Jones, Harold E., 83

Kaw, 108

Keesing, Felix, 106, 128; Collier and, 114–19; *The South Seas in the Modern World* (1941), 114, 115, 118

Kidder, Alfred, 30

Kluckhohn, Clyde, 128

Knowledge: geopolitics of, 10; Pan-American project of, 98–99; practices of, 97; production of, 11

Kroeber, Alfred, 83

Kropotkin, Peter, 103

Ku Klux Klan, 19

Labor, 67, 73, 74, 75, 76

Ladinos, 171, 172

Laissez-faire capitalism, 22, 39, 177–78; Social Darwinism and, 38, 57

Landázuri, Elena, 61

Lands and landholding, Native, 18–20, 25, 36, 40, 97; distribution and redistribution of, 95, 116, 145–46, 175; ownership and tenure of, 35, 137, 144, 145; reform and, 34–35, 92, 94, 140, 173. *See also* Allotment system

Language, languages, 39, 172, 209n33; bilingualism and, 50, 137, 166; education and, 93, 148; English, 12, 18–20, 52–53, 86, 94, 104, 147, 164; linguistics, 32, 33; Nahuatl, 32, 86; national, 20, 45; of Native peoples, 25, 47, 50, 64, 94, 135, 146–49, 177. *See also* Spanish (language)

Latin America, Latin Americans, 26, 32, 58, 76, 105, 127–28, 173, 176, 195n7, 202n12; democracy and citizenship in, 36, 62; as forge or lab for racial mixing, 38, 84, 87; independence movements in, 38, 174; *mestizaje* in, 82, 84–86; Pan-American Child Congresses in, 51, 54; studies of, 7, 14, 61–62, 64, 185n15; United States and, 8, 25, 63, 172; in World War II, 119, 167

Latin Eugenics Federation, 28

Latin eugenics movement, 56–59, 176

Laughlin, Henry, 71

Laura Spelman Rockefeller Memorial, 67, 73, 198n40

Laws of the Indies, 35, 105, 107, 174

Mesa Andraca, Manuel, 142, 144

Mestizaje (racial mixing), 18, 20, 110, 147, 165; in Latin America, 57, 84–86

Mestizo, mestizos, 2, 18, 40, 50, 57, 75, 92, 169, 200n10; Native Mexicans and, 40–41, 49

Mestizo nation, 46, 48

Mexican American (magazine), 30

Mexican Americans, 52–53, 62, 78, 101, 131, 195n2; as immigrants, 30, 60–61, 65, 74–78, 144, 175. *See also* Spanish Americans

Mexican Communist Party, 148. *See also* Marxism, Marxists

Mexican Constitution of 1917, 18, 141

Mexican Independence, 7, 39

Mexicanization, 176

Mexican Revolution, 3, 14, 17, 18, 86, 93, 108, 174; character of, 30, 59, 168; Gamio and, 35, 38

Mexicans, 48, 66, 191n36, 203n21; migration of, 73–78. *See also* Intellectuals and scholars, Mexican; Native Mexicans

Mexico, 1, 3, 28, 58, 74–75, 84, 100, 167–68, 171, 193n80; anthropology in, 31–33, 43, 131; censuses of, 50, 57, 164–65; Collier and, 101, 105–8; eugenics in, 26, 51, 82; evolution and, 24, 37–38; forging of, 37–42; middle classes of, 36, 44; as nation, 7, 17, 31, 39, 49, 76; national government of, 15, 31–32, 45, 46; Native peoples and, 7, 60, 102, 108, 136, 201n10, 205n44; child congresses in, 51, 52, 54; race and ethnicity in, 6, 48, 61, 87, 156; reform in, 20, 92; socialism in, 92, 139–43; United States and, 3, 7, 14, 29, 48–49, 61, 63, 113, 115, 175, 177. *See also* New Spain

Mexico City, 2, 18, 50, 54, 60, 86, 136, 143; conferences in, 28, 33, 98; schools in, 46, 53; U.S. scholars in, 32, 61, 106

México indígena exhibit (1946), 156–57, 159–61

Mezquital Valley, 61, 90; Gamio's research in, 144–45, 151, 155, 162, 164; poverty of, 155–56; research on, 143–46. *See also* El Mexe

Michoacán, 86, 98

Middle class: in Mexico, 36, 44; in United States, 2

Migration, migrants, 24–25, 32, 52, 58, 60, 65, 70, 139; African Americans and, 62, 67, 74, 76; international, 76, 103; Mexican, 74–78. *See also* immigrants and immigration entries

Ministry of Agriculture and Development, 140–41, 151, 207n6

Minorities, 4, 124, 127, 129; in United States, 14, 49, 51, 131–32

Misiones Culturales y Enseñanza Normal (Cultural Missions and Normal Schools), 142

Missions, cultural, of SEP, 46, 48, 93, 143, 145

MIT (Massachusetts Institute of Technology), 1

Mixing and mixed peoples, 14, 27, 39, 59; cultures and, 39, 50, 58; race and, 79, 84, 85

Modernism, 15, 43, 185n22, 191n36

Modernity, 2, 4, 11, 24, 45, 100, 119, 159, 173; capitalism and, 59, 179; Collier and U.S. scholars and, 13, 104–5, 134, 176; Gamio and, 14, 56; Mexico and, 9, 15, 21, 23, 168; Native peoples and, 9, 25, 101, 110, 114; universal, 9–10; West and, 10, 15, 16, 31, 43

Modernization, 86, 91, 94, 100, 116, 155, 170, 181; age of, 89–100; economic, 137, 167, 168; evolution and, 147; in Mexico, 93, 95, 149, 168; science and, 99, 127, 134

Molina, Natalia, 101

Molina Enríquez, Andrés, 34–35

Montevideo, 98

Morelos, 39

of, 25–28. *See also* Eugenics, eugenicists

Populism, antiracist, 89–100

Populist culturalism, 146

Porifiriato, 18, 31–35, 52, 201n15; indigenistas and, 22, 97; positivism of, 22–23, 142. *See also* Díaz, Porfirio

Positivism, 10, 22–23, 142

Postcolonialism, 9, 11

Poston, Arizona, Japanese American internment camp, 123, 132, 181, 202n22; Bureau of Social Research of, 124–25, 133, 180, 206n59; Collier and, 14, 99, 176; IS and, 99, 126

Pragmatism, 10, 169; Collier and, 102, 124

Primitivism, 104–5, 135

Private property, 19, 25, 35, 36, 59

PRM (Partido de la Revolución Mexicana; Party of the Mexican Revolution), 92

Productivism, 146, 148

Progress, 15, 167

Progressives, 177; immigrants and, 18–19, 103

Proletariat, 165; *indios* as, 135, 136

Propaganda, 73, 127, 128

Psychodrama, 121, 122

Psychology, psychologists, 102, 104, 121–22, 133, 180, 198n40

Public health, 142; Native Mexicans and, 23, 26

Public opinion, shaped by government, 128, 129

Pueblo Indians, 101, 104–5, 113, 120, 202n8

Puericulture, 26

Puerto Rico, Puerto Ricans, 129, 130

Puig Casauranc, José Manuel, 46

Pukui, Mary Kawen, 115

Quantification, 152. *See also* Data; Numbers and numerical aggregation; Statistics

Quintana Roo, 40

Race, races, 25, 47, 50, 57, 59, 60, 76, 91; biology and, 6, 78–84, 169, 171; Boas and, 33, 81; categorizing, 49, 84, 100, 135–68, 169, 185n13; class and, 100, 181–82; concepts of, 4, 5, 61; conflict and violence over, 19, 60, 79, 129; culture and, 6, 48, 66, 75, 78, 103–4, 118, 172, 174, 210n56; culture and class and, 169–82; degeneration and, 26, 27; democracy and, 102, 177; differences of, 3, 21, 27, 74, 79, 102, 118, 171–72, 175–77, 182; eugenics and, 26, 49; heredity and, 105, 118; immigration and, 54, 62; Mexico and, 14, 54, 57, 61, 76, 135–68, 207n4; mixing of, 27, 57, 61, 66–67, 70, 79, 84–85, 174; purity of, 2, 26, 48–49, 82, 176; relations of, 60, 74, 106, 199n67; taxonomies of, 168; theories and science of, 5, 8, 14, 31, 72, 83, 207n4; United States and, 48–49, 61, 99

Racial discrimination and prejudice, 129, 171; in United States, 19, 52, 62, 76–77, 101, 123, 172

Racism, 8, 40, 55, 78, 121, 147, 173, 203n14; antiracism, 18, 26, 89–100, 119, 125; in Mexico, 15, 172; modernization and, 4, 138; Nazi, 6, 167; as term, 4–6, 80, 87, 210n56; in United States, 19, 52, 56, 62, 76–77, 101, 123, 172

Radcliffe-Brown, A. R., 179, 181

Radcliffe College, 115

Ramírez, Rafael, 46

Rationality, 5, 9

Redfield, Greta Park, 60

Redfield, Robert, 2, 3, 12, 77–78, 85, 172, 195n2; Collier and, 102, 204n25; research of, 60–61, 74; Tax and, 171, 182; Tepoztlán and, 21, 60, 76, 86, 87, 175; *A Village That Chose Progress* (1950), 60

Reed-Johnson Act (1924), 65

Reform, 51, 105, 149, 166, 175; agrarian, 93, 135; in Mexico, 18, 26, 92, 94,

135, 146; of Native landholding, 18, 34–35, 92–94, 140, 173; Progressives and, 18–19; rural, 18, 51, 93–94; social, 4, 26, 141, 142

Reinhardt, Akim, 112

Relativism, 34

Reproduction, human, 26, 55, 104, 187n12

Reservations, 6, 36, 107; land policy and, 19–20; politics and self-government on, 96, 180; as segregation, 31, 47, 49; in Southwest United States, 61, 99

Revista Mexicana de Sociologia, 158

Rights, 36, 62, 97; human, 173, 182

Ripley, William, 56

Ritual, rituals, 20, 104–5, 111, 140, 157, 171

Rockefeller, Nelson, 119, 131

Rockefeller Foundation, 112, 155

Romanticism, 94, 170, 182

Rome, 45

Roosevelt, Franklin D., 2, 14, 20, 84, 119; Good Neighbor Policy of, 91, 97

Rosier, Paul, 96

Russell Sage Foundation, 73

Sacco, Nicola, 19

Sady, Emil, 128, 173, 174, 182

Sáenz, Moisés, 12, 40, 46–49, 112, 146–47, 159, 164, 170–72, 191n36, 207n12, 210n55; Collier and, 106, 109, 110; on culture, 40–42; death of, 12, 98, 109; intelligence tests and, 52–53; in United States, 48, 61

Salz, Beate, 173

Samoa, 64, 114

Sánchez, Graciano, 93

San Cristóbal de las Casas, 61

San Diego, 53

Santa Fe Railway, 74

Santa María Tepeji, 90–91, 92

Santamarina, Rafael, 52, 55, 58, 72

Schools, 45, 53–54, 92, 108; boarding, 20, 46, 93, 94, 192n50, 200n8; DAI and, 93, 200n8; Native Americans and, 94, 111; Native Mexicans and, 106, 110, 137, 140, 141, 210n55; reform of, 18, 26. *See also* Education; Schoolteachers

Schoolteachers, 92, 97, 145; Indian Personality Project and, 113, 114

Schopenhauer, Arthur, 142

Science, scientists, 28, 30, 72, 127, 139–42, 167; evolution and, 42–45, 59, 191n40; Gamio and, 42, 171, 176; history of, 10, 11, 185n24; *indigenistas* and, 15, 58; modernity and, 5, 119, 134; nation and, 44, 89–100, 156, 159; technology and, 4, 94, 100, 111–12, 135, 141, 145, 148, 170–71; unity and, 29, 42–43; universal laws and, 133, 179. *See also* Social sciences, social scientists; *and names of individual disciplines*

Scientific management (Taylorism), 154

Second International Eugenics Conference (New York, 1921), 51, 56, 63–64

Second Pan-American Conference on Eugenics and Homiculture (Buenos Aires, 1934), 28, 42–43, 51

Second Pan-American Scientific Conference (Washington, D.C.), 35, 42–43

Secretaría de Economía (Ministry of the Economy), 145

Segregation, 41, 46, 58, 61, 70, 77, 174; reservations as, 6, 31, 47; in United States, 48, 131, 171

Selcer, Perrin, 10–11

Seler, Edward, 32, 33

Self-government: of Native peoples, 117, 120, 180; local democratic, 181; in United States, 95, 103, 120, 180–81; after World War II, 127–30

Senior, Clarence, 128

SEP (Secretaría de Educación Pública; Department of Education), 12,

CPSIA information can be obtained
at www.ICGtesting.com
Printed in the USA
LVHW03s0100130918
589927LV00004B/270/P